God, Evil, and Ethics

God, Evil, and Ethics

A Primer in the Philosophy of Religion

Eric v.d. Luft

➤➤ North Syracuse, New York ◄◄
◄◄ Gegensatz Press ➤➤
➤➤ 2004 ◄◄

iv

Cataloging-in-Publication:

Luft, Eric v.d. (Eric von der), 1952-
    God, evil, and ethics : a primer in the philosophy of religion / Eric v.d. Luft.
        p. ; cm.
        "... presents the basic elements of the philosophy of religion tradition in a new and provocative way. ... The history and concepts of philosophy of religion emerge more clearly through ... integration and interrelation of classical texts with modern summary and interpretation."
        Includes bibliographical references and index.
        ISBN 0-9655179-1-8
1. Religion — Philosophy. 2. God — Proof. 3. God — Attributes. 4. God — Knowableness. 5. Knowledge, Theory of (Religion). 6. Philosophical theology. 7. Natural theology. 8. Revelation. 9. Experience (Religion). 10. Theism. 11. Holy, The. 12. Miracles. 13. Theodicy. 14. Good and evil. I. Title.
BL 51 L83g 2004
210—dc22   AACR2
Library of Congress Control Number 2004094823

First edition, first printing. Printed in the United States of America by United Book Press, Inc., Baltimore.

The guillemets, or two pairs of opposing chevrons, dark on the lower cusps and light on the upper, are a trademark of Gegensatz Press.

Distributed to the trade worldwide by:
Gegensatz Press
108 Deborah Lane
North Syracuse, NY 13212-1931

Designed by the author. Printed on acid-free paper. ∞

Contents

Preface

This book originated in microeconomics. The textbook that I prefer to use to teach introductory philosophy of religion, Louis P. Pojman's *Philosophy of Religion: An Anthology*, became too expensive for most of my students to afford. Rather than allow that prohibitive influence to lower the enrollment in my courses, I decided to find an adequate and cheaper substitute. My first thought was just to compile an anthology of readings and — as so many professors have done when faced with similar economic realities — have it reproduced and assembled by a commercial or academic photocopy center. But those products look shoddy and soon fall apart. So I decided to write and publish my own textbook with a sturdy and attractive binding. Aesthetics matters too.

An edited anthology might be 95 per cent quoted texts and five per cent editorial additions; an authored book might be 95 per cent original and five per cent quoted passages. This is an authored book with anthologistic tendencies. It is a bit less than half original and a bit more than half quoted. The reason for doing it this way is to present the full range of issues, classical texts, and important theories without descending into either the uniformity of a monograph or the episodic irregularity of an anthology. By straddling that line, this book exemplifies both continuity and variety.

In order to keep the retail cost to a minimum, all long passages quoted herein are from the public domain. Some shorter passages not in the public domain are quoted, but not at sufficient length either to violate copyright or to require securing permission to reproduce. Rather than quote long passages that are still under copyright protection, I have resorted to summary and exegesis, trusting this strategy not to undermine the book's usefulness.

Unless specifically noted, all translations are my own.

In order to keep the difference between new material and long quoted texts conspicuous, the latter are printed in the Abadi Condensed Light font instead of the usual Times New Roman.

This book would have been better but more expensive with large selections from several post-1923 texts, such as Alfred North

Whitehead's *Religion in the Making*, which, under current American copyright law, will not come into public domain until January 1, 2022. But if a new edition of *God, Evil, and Ethics* appears after that date, it will contain at least some part of this important work.

Presentation of material is as objective as possible. Interpretation is expository rather than speculative. The purpose of the book is to familiarize students with basic concepts, not to argue a point of view.

Some passages in this book are reworked versions of portions of the following:

In Chapter 1: Luft, Eric von der, "Toward a Definition of Religion as Philosophy." *Process Studies* 16, 1 (Spring 1987): 37-40; online at <www.religion-online.org/cgi-bin/relsearchd.dll/showarticle?item_id=2575>.

In Chapter 2: Luft, Eric von der, "The Empirical Version of the Ontological Argument and the A Priori Version of the Cosmological Argument," in: *Existence of God: Essays from the Basic Issues Forum*, edited by John R. Jacobson and Robert Lloyd Mitchell (Problems in Contemporary Philosophy, vol. 9), (Lewiston, New York: Edwin Mellen, 1988), pp. 149-161. Luft, Eric von der, "[Review of] Donald Wayne Viney, *Charles Hartshorne and the Existence of God.*" *Process Studies* 15, 3 (Fall 1986): 207-212.

In Chapter 3: Luft, Eric v.d., "The Cartesian Circle: Hegelian Logic to the Rescue." *The Heythrop Journal* 30, 4 (October 1989): 403-418.

In Chapter 4: *Hegel, Hinrichs, and Schleiermacher on Feeling and Reason in Religion: The Texts of Their 1821-22 Debate*, edited, translated, and with introductions by Eric von der Luft, also including a new critical edition of the German text of Hegel's "Hinrichs Foreword" (Studies in German Thought and History, vol. 3). Lewiston, New York: Edwin Mellen, 1987.

In Chapters 8 and 15: Luft, Eric von der, "Sources of Nietzsche's 'God is Dead!' and its Meaning for Heidegger." *Journal of the History of Ideas* 45, 2 (April-June 1984): 263-276.

In Chapter 12: Luft, Eric v.d., "Would Hegel Have Liked to Burn Down All the Churches and Replace Them with Philosophical Academies?" *The Modern Schoolman* 68, 1 (November 1990): 41-56.

I appreciate the kind and learned help of Sandra Barrett, J. Brad Benson, Fred Crysler, G. Scott Davis, Lewis Ford, William D. Geoghegan, Jennifer Hamlin-Navias, George L. Kline, Diane Davis Luft, Mary Grace Luft, Sarah Luft, Edward Pols, Heidi M. Ravven, David White, the late Robert L. DeWitt, the late José Ferrater Mora, the late C. Douglas McGee, the late Jean A. Potter, the late Isabel S. Stearns, and my students, past and present, in bringing this book into being. Some of this assistance may have been inadvertent.

I lovingly dedicate this book to my wife, Diane.

1

Why is the Philosophy of
Religion Important?

Religion — whether we are theists, deists, atheists, gnostics, agnostics, Jews, Christians, Muslims, Hindus, Buddhists, Taoists, Confucians, Shintoists, Zoroastrians, animists, polytheists, pagans, Wiccans, secular humanists, Marxists, or cult devotees — is a matter of ultimate concern. Everything we are and do finally depends upon such questions as whether there is a God, whether we continue to exist after death, whether any God is active in human history, and whether human ethical relations have spiritual or supernatural dimensions. If God is real, then this is a different world than it would be if God were not real.

The basic human need that probably exists for some sort of salvation, deliverance, release, liberation, pacification, or whatever it may be called, seems to be among the main foundations of all religion. There may also be a basic human need for mystery, wonder, fear of the sacred, romantic worship of the inexplicable, awe in the presence of the completely different, or emotional response to the "numinous," which is the topic of *The Idea of the Holy* by German theologian Rudolf Otto (1869-1937) and *The Sacred and the Profane* by Romanian philosopher and anthropologist of religion Mircea Eliade (1907-1986). This need also may be a foundation of religion. Yet doubt exists that humans feel any general need *for* mystery. On the contrary, the human need to *solve* mysteries seems to be more basic than any need to *have* mysteries. For example, mythology in all known cultures has arisen from either the need or the desire to provide explanations for certain types of occurrences, either natural or interpersonal, and thus to attempt to do away with those mysteries. Moreover, if any basic human need exists for deliverance, salvation, etc., then it may be manifest in part as a need for deliverance from mystery, salvation from ignorance, etc.

Even in the post-Enlightenment era, the primeval feeling of

a need for mystery continues. Those who still feel this need seem to be seduced both by tradition itself and their own uncritical approach to tradition. Immanuel Kant (1724-1804), the founder of German critical philosophy, wrote *Sapere aude!* ("Dare to know!") in *What is Enlightenment?* — but they will not take this dare. Many remain sincere and unabashed about feeling a deep need for mystery in their lives. Such people are generally members of some kind of religious group.

Many intelligent, well educated people still say such things as: "Whatever the controversy, and however strong the scholarly arguments against it, I choose to believe in the supernatural aspects of my faith, simply because it is very important for me in the life of my faith to be radically aware of sacred mysteries." If one chooses to make the supernatural element a central aspect of one's religion, scripture and tradition will certainly support such a set of beliefs. However — and this is well worth noting — the various scriptures, without adding more internal contradiction than is already present in their pages, will also support commonsensical, naturalistic, non-supernatural, metaphorical, allegorical, or symbolic interpretations of their texts and theologies. Such a plurality of defensible interpretations is possible, not because the texts are vague, for indeed they are usually not, but because the content of these texts is typically universal in its domain of application and ambivalent rather than ambiguous in its language. Thus it is a strength, not a weakness, of most scriptures that they speak to otherworldly as well as thisworldly interests, for in that way they assure that they will continue to speak to every era, nation, and successive *Zeitgeist* in world history.

German-British philologist Max Müller (1823-1900), one of the founders of the modern scholarly study of comparative religion, asserted in 1873 that whoever knows only one religion knows none. Against this claim, German theologian Adolf von Harnack (1851-1930) responded in 1901 that whoever knows one religion knows them all. These assertions are not contradictory. Both are correct. They equivocate on two kinds of knowledge. The distinction remains ambiguous in English, but is clear enough for French and German speakers, who have at their service the respective juxtapositions of *savoir / connaître* and *wissen / kennen*. Müller means the scientific or objective knowledge (*savoir* or *wissen*) of a religion, which naturally entails scrupulous comparisons with the data of other religions; while Harnack, on the other hand, means the subjective acquaintance or familiarity (*connaître* or *kennen*) that only an insider, i.e., a devout believer, can achieve. Moreover, Harnack refers specifically to Christianity, claiming that it is the only religion worth knowing, and that to know it intimately, i.e., to believe it, is in effect to know and believe the true essence and meaning of all religions, since they all aim at the same spiritual goal, though all except Christianity fall short. In short, Müller speaks as a philosopher; Harnack as a theologian.

Religion must make sense to the believer, not necessarily common sense, but some sort of sense; i.e., believers ought to be able at some level to justify their beliefs. At the lowest level, such defense is accomplished by appeal to authority or tradition; at the highest level, it is done either through philosophy or through philosophical or systematic theology. The preeminent German idealist philosopher, Georg Wilhelm Friedrich Hegel (1770-1831), believed that religion in its highest form is philosophy, that philosophy in its true form is religion, and that the true content of each is the same, even though their respective expressions may differ. In their development they move toward each other, since in the historical development of culture, the concept of God moves toward the philosophical, i.e., away from the anthropomorphic and toward the ever more comprehensively spiritual.

A few definitions of key terms are necessary at the outset:

Theism, from the Greek word for "God," *theos* (θεός), is belief in a God who is active in human affairs. Deism, from the Latin word for "God," *deus*, is belief in a God who created the world and then left it alone. Atheism, from the Greek meaning "no God," is belief in just that. Atheism, theism, and deism are each claims to knowledge. Agnosticism, from the Greek meaning "not knowing," *agnôstos* (ἄγνωστος), is a refusal to decide.

Monotheism, from the Greek for "alone, "single," or "unique," *monos* (μόνος), and henotheism, from the Greek for "one," *hen* (ἕν), each denote belief in one God, but monotheism means one God in and for the entire universe, while henotheism means one God for us, e.g., for our tribe, not denying the possibility that other tribes might have their own equally valid Gods.

Pantheism is the belief that everything is God. Animism is the belief that everything is spiritual, or that even apparently inanimate objects have souls. Panentheism is the belief that God completely permeates everything, like water in a saturated sponge.

Polytheism is the belief in many irreducible Gods, perhaps two, perhaps three, usually more. The Christian trinity is monotheistic, not polytheistic, because Yahweh the Father, Jesus Christ the Son, and the Holy Spirit are each recognized as aspects of one God, not as three separate Gods, just as ice, liquid water, and water vapor are each recognized as aspects of a single substance, H_2O, not as three separate substances. The Hindu trinity of Brahma, Vishnu, and Shiva, on the other hand, is part of a gigantic polytheistic order.

As for a definition of religion itself, that is very controversial. The word comes from the Latin *religare* ("to tie" or "to bind") and *religio* ("conscientiousness," "respect," "awe," or "sanctity"). The idea is that the soul is bound to God. Religion has been defined as everything from the immediate awareness of identity with the absolute, to the passionate striving (*eros*) for the transcendent, to the psychological projection of the idealized human self onto the infinite, to the consciousness of the highest social values. For German theologian Friedrich Daniel Ernst Schleiermacher (1768-1834), religion is the feeling of utter dependence; for Danish philosopher Harald Höffding (1843-1931), the individual's desire to conserve value; for Kant, the recognition of moral duties as divine commands; for Dutch-American anthropologist Annemarie de Waal Malefijt (b. 1914), any system of actions and interactions based on culturally shared beliefs in sacred supernatural powers; for Müller, the intuitive faculty of apprehending the infinite; for British historian Arthur Darby Nock (1902-1963), the human refusal to accept helplessness; for ancient Greek philosopher Plato (427-347 B.C.E.), the science of begging and getting gifts from the Gods; and for German socialist philosopher Karl Marx (1818-1883), the opiate of the people.

In essence, religion is an attitude, or a sum of attitudes, constituting a way of life. Religion may thus be the total of an individual's sincere attitudes and predispositions toward that which serves as the final expression of his or her particular primary interest or goal. The various institutions of religion would arise only after a group shares certain attitudes that were first felt by an individual, and as a result of this sharing.

Perhaps the most accurate definition combines the ideas of two German-Americans, liberal theologian Paul Tillich (1886-1965) and psychologist Erich Fromm (1900-1980): any system of thought, feeling, and action, typically shared by a group, which gives the individual a frame of orientation, a meaning of life, and an object of devotion, which is regarded as a matter of ultimate concern.

British-American philosopher Alfred North Whitehead

(1861-1947) wrote in *Religion in the Making*: "Religion is what the individual does with his [or her] own solitariness." But what the individual actually does with true solitariness, that curious amalgam of loneliness and reflectivity, is philosophize. In the same book Whitehead wrote, "Religion is force of belief cleansing the inward parts. For this reason the primary religious virtue is sincerity, a penetrating sincerity." But similarly, philosophy is force of thought cleansing the inward parts. Thus the primary philosophical virtue is precisely the same penetrating sincerity.

Algerian-French novelist and philosopher Albert Camus (1913-1960) wrote in *The Myth of Sisyphus* that there is only one truly philosophical question: suicide. His focus was perhaps too narrow, but he was on the right track. The same question, more broadly stated, is whether life is worth living. Philosophers have asked this broader version at least since Socrates in the fifth century B.C.E. If life turns out not to be worth living, then that in itself is not sufficient reason to commit suicide. We may prefer just to endure life. Conversely, if we judge that life is worth living, then that alone is not sufficient reason to avoid suicide. Socrates himself, who believed quite firmly that life, especially a philosophically examined life such as his own, was worth living, fell afoul of a moral dilemma and had to commit suicide to preserve his moral integrity.

So the central question is life. What, beyond the obvious physical and biomedical aspects, is life? What does it mean? Why live? Why persist? Why surrender? Why bother? Why care? Why strive? Why have children? Why laugh? Why cry? Reason seems sometimes at a loss. The devout churchgoers who deliberately reject any scholarly conclusions about the content of the Christian faith because of the great comfort and sense of importance they gain by believing that Jesus is the Son of God cannot risk anything, even reason, shaking that belief.

The historical development of religion proceeds in stages which can be analyzed in terms of dialectical progress or unfolding. Such is the case both with individual religions and with religion in general. Anthropologists, psychologists, and sociologists, especially those who study folklore and oral traditions, have done much good work in classifying such stages, all the way from the most primitive animism to the most sophisticated philosophical monotheism. But their classification is in general only formal. What they have largely failed to do is to discover and define precisely the reasons why a given stage passes over into another. They have failed in general to see the progressive development of religion and religions as a unified and deliberate series of God's revelations of reason designed specifically to lead us gradually toward the most adequate and profound understanding and appreciation of God which is humanly possible. This is a task which only a philosopher can achieve. Hegel conceived and attempted such a project — to learn the ultimate, divinely sanctioned reasons why one religious stage passes over into another — but that movement, plagued from the start by bad anthropological data, died out in the mid-nineteenth century, and was only revived in the late twentieth century.

The narrative of Elijah (fl. 860 B.C.E.) overcoming the prophets of Baal on Mount Carmel in I Kings 18 tells of the supersession of the God(s) of fertility by the God of historical intervention. Likewise, the whole New Testament can be seen as the tale of the supersession of the God of historical intervention by the God of supernatural salvation. The Roman Catholic Church gradually came to see this God as the God of supernatural salvation by priestly intermediation. The Protestant Reformation was in the main a movement to replace this Catholic God with the God of supernatural salvation by direct faith. All of these were rational transitions, demanded by and right for their times, and each unable to have happened at any other time. Each successive stage must make more sense in its time than each supplanted stage. For example, Augustinian Christianity survived its Pelagian, Manichaean, and Donatist rivals chiefly because, in its time, it made more philosophical sense than they did.

Progress in religion is not characterized by mere iconoclasm. Rather, as human civilization gains through history a more adequate self-awareness, the concepts of God which were once adequate for individual cultures are successively replaced by more adequate concepts of God. The ancient Hebrew transition from henotheism to monotheism is an excellent example of such development. The God of Israel was adequate for the confrontation between Israel and Egypt, but the God who could intervene in the long struggle among Israel, Assyria, and Babylon had to be the God of the whole world. Such a transition from a particular God to a universal God is a mark of genuine progress in culture, religion, and world-view (*Weltanschauung*). The development of more adequate concepts of God is a mirror of the development of civilization itself.

The historical evolution, on the scale relative to culture, of more adequate concepts of God must also be seen as the evolution on the absolute scale, or *sub specie aeternitatis*, of ever more nearly true concepts of God. That of Deutero-Isaiah (fl. 540 B.C.E.) more nearly approached the true nature of God than did that of Moses (fl. ca. 1300 B.C.E.). Similarly, that of Augustine (354-430) was more highly developed and thus more accurate than Isaiah's. This means, not that Isaiah was either more intelligent or more devout than Moses, or Augustine more than Isaiah, but that their respective theologies are to a significant degree products of the total of learned culture in their respective times, and thus that these theologies themselves reflect these several levels of cultural development and philosophical refinement.

As the early twenty-first century has scientific, epistemological, and even metaphysical reasons to abandon former beliefs in the supernatural, the time may have come for another rationally ordained supersession of an old God. The God of supernatural salvation, in whatever form, may be ripe for replacement by the God of what might be called in English "earthly peace," "cohesive social order," "social coherence," "ethical solidarity," "the order of ethical life," or, in Tillich's vocabulary, "theonomy," the law of God written in human hearts. But this social ideal of philosophical religion is better expressed by untranslatable terms such as *Sittlichkeit* in Hegel's nineteenth-century German, *koinônia* (κοινωνία) in New Testament Greek, or *chesed* (חֶסֶד) in ancient Hebrew. It is a goal toward which philosophy, religion, and politics must all cooperate.

The difference — or bifurcation — between the many subjective worlds that involve God and those conceived without God drives immediately to the root of human existence. The various doctrines and traditions of established religions — particularly because they are so often uncompromisingly at odds with one another — are not adequate to answer the most serious and basic questions of human existence, life, and meaning. Theology does a better job of answering them than doctrines or traditions do, but to address them in a fully satisfying way we need philosophy. Either French Prince Charles Maurice de Talleyrand or French prime minister Georges Clemenceau is supposed to have said that war is too important to leave to the generals. Similarly, religion is too important to leave to the priests. A more detached, objective, bird's-eye view is needed.

Philosophy is the science that sits in judgment of all matters of concern. "Science" is any rigorous discipline that uses impartial powers of reason and logic. The tribunal of reason weighs topics of inquiry on their own merits, according to their own logic, and in relation to other topics, then completes its analysis without prejudice on the basis of wherever reason leads, according to its own logic.

The goal of philosophical scrutiny is clarity, accuracy, and truth.

Given this mission of philosophy, its highest duty is to sit in judgment of the most important matters, with a view toward improving human life, ethical relations, and the world in general by injecting reason into our judgments and by identifying, describing, and communicating what makes sense and what does not. Philosophy thus promotes intelligence, clear understanding, and civilization but condemns stupidity, ignorance, and barbarity. This is the normative or prescriptive aspect of philosophy, which is most effective when done implicitly. Philosophy aims to become the architecture of ethical, meaningful life, not by preaching or by being dogmatic, but just by discovering the facts and displaying them in clear light to intelligent minds who will then make their own decisions.

The philosophy of religion is not the same as theology. While theologians examine a particular religion from within and interpret it for its own community of believers, philosophers of religion analyze religion in general, from external or non-sectarian points of view, and evaluate it systematically. Theology is part of the data for philosophy of religion.

The philosophy of religion was originally subsumed under metaphysics, the philosophical science of first principles. Its central issue, the reality and nature of God, was considered a metaphysical question. But in the late seventeenth and early eighteenth centuries philosophers began to consider questions about God separately from other metaphysical questions and to ask about ethics in religious contexts. As a result of these new lines of inquiry, especially in Britain and Germany, the philosophy of religion had become an independent discipline within philosophy probably by the end of the eighteenth century and surely by the beginning of the nineteenth.

The philosophy of religion, like most philosophy, is not a linear discipline. That is, its concepts cannot be learned sequentially, but must be gradually fitted together like the pieces of a jigsaw puzzle. In whatever order they are presented, some concepts presented earlier will remain obscure until other concepts are presented later. This is unavoidable. Readers should therefore be patient and try to avoid frustration as they wade through difficult material in the first few chapters, confident that as they subsequently approach equally difficult material in later chapters, their understanding of the whole will suddenly and dramatically increase as they begin to grasp the interrelationships among these concepts. The reward is at the end.

2

Is God Real?

The carefully established and rigorously precise technical vocabulary of philosophy is key to grasping clearly the subtle concepts that these words represent. Traditionally we speak of the "existence" of God, ask whether God "exists," and offer several standard arguments for or against God's "existence." But such terminology is misleading. To speak of God's "reality" is clearer and more accurate.

In §§ 3-4 of *Being and Time*, German existentialist philosopher Martin Heidegger (1889-1976) described the "ontological difference" between beings and being. On one hand, there are "beings," the multitude of finite, circumscribable "things" that exist. On the other hand, there is simply "being," the bare fact that there is something rather than nothing. Being does not "exist." The split is clearer in German, because, while English must say "being" in each case, Heidegger can use the infinitival noun *Sein* to mean "being in general" and the present participial noun *Seiendes* to mean "a being."

For Heidegger, the adjective "ontic" refers to particular beings while the adjective "ontological" refers to being in general. The difference between being in general and particular beings is ontological rather than ontic, because they exhibit different types of being. An ontic investigation is an inquiry into the things of this world, i.e., things that "exist." Examples would be natural science, social science, or most everyday conversation. An ontological investigation, on the other hand, is an inquiry into the nature of being in general, i.e., what does not "exist," but simply "is." Examples are traditional metaphysics, Heidegger's project, and various arguments for theism.

The English word "existence" derives from the Latin *exsistere* and the Greek *existêmi* (ἐξίστημι), both of which mean "to stand out." Particular beings exist because they are differentiated from, or "stand out" against, other beings. That is, beings that merely "exist" are circumscribable. But being itself is "real," not "existent." It does not exist in itself, but only through particular "beings."

That is, being would not be being unless there were particular beings in which being would be manifest or determinate.

It is useful to define a clear distinction between the existence of God and the reality of God. If God only "existed," then God would be just a being among other beings, even if the greatest being. But if God is regarded as "real" rather than "existent," then God transcends being as just a being, or can be the source of both being in general and all particular beings alike. A valid God cannot be conceived as circumscribable. Hence it makes more sense to speak of God's "reality" than of God's "existence," because the "ground of being," as Tillich calls it, could not "exist" alongside finite beings, yet it must be "real."

God is not ontic, i.e, God is not an entity of the same ontological type as other entities, even if God is taken to be the greatest of all entities. Nor is God equivalent to being itself, unless we accept pantheism. God, if there is a God, can never just exist as a being among other beings, even a being that is different from all other beings, because no being can ever be infinite, inasmuch as it is necessarily bounded by other beings. God, being infinite, cannot be a being, but must be beyond being, underlying being, as the ground of being. God cannot be "the old man in the sky" or any circumscribable "thing." Anthropomorphism is completely undermined by the most elementary application of philosophy to theology.

The philosophical problem, accordingly, is to determine whether the ultimate "ground of being" is a reality or a fantasy. Since most religions, with the notable exception of the original version of Buddhism (which was really a philosophical teaching), center upon God, the most logical starting point for a philosophical investigation of religion is to ascertain whether or not God is real. Faith, like emotion, is capable of generating any response, so it is an unreliable evaluator of the evidence. But reason, because it is less wild than faith and must submit to rigorous rules of inference, is much more dependable on this and most other matters.

Dominican monk Thomas Aquinas (1225?-1274) offered five related proofs of the reality of God from the evidence of the natural world, i.e., through natural theology. The Five Ways are so important that, in order to study them precisely, they are presented here in the original Latin from *Summa theologiae Thomae Aquinatis, pars prima*, 2. *De Deo an sit*, 3. *Utrum Deum sit*, interspersed with the slightly modified 1920 English translation by the Fathers of the English Dominican Province:

I q. 2 a. 3 arg. 1. ... Videtur quod Deus non sit. Quia si unum contrariorum fuerit infinitum, totaliter destruetur aliud. Sed hoc intelligitur in hoc nomine Deus, scilicet quod sit quoddam bonum infinitum. Si ergo Deus esset, nullum malum inveniretur. Invenitur autem malum in mundo. Ergo Deus non est.

Objection 1. It seems that God is not; because if one of two contraries be infinite, the other would be altogether destroyed. But the word "God" means that He is infinite goodness. If, therefore, God were, there would be no evil discoverable; but there is evil in the world. Therefore God is not.

I q. 2 a. 3 arg. 2. Praeterea, quod potest compleri per pauciora principia, non fit per plura. Sed videtur quod omnia quae apparent in mundo, possunt compleri per alia principia, supposito quod Deus non sit, quia ea quae sunt naturalia, reducuntur in principium quod est natura; ea vero quae sunt a proposito, reducuntur in principium quod est ratio humana vel voluntas. Nulla igitur necessitas est ponere Deum esse.

Objection 2. Further, it is superfluous to suppose that what can be accounted for by a few principles has been produced by many. But it seems that everything we see in the world can be accounted for by other principles, supposing God is not. For all natural things can be reduced to one principle which is nature; and all voluntary things can be reduced to one principle which is human reason, or will. Therefore there is no need to suppose God's being.

I q. 2 a. 3 s. c. Sed contra est quod dicitur Exodi III, ex persona Dei, "ego sum qui sum."

On the contrary, It is said in the person of God: I am who am" (Exodus 3:14).

I q. 2 a. 3 co. Respondeo dicendum quod Deum esse quinque viis probari potest.

I answer that, The being of God can be proved in five ways.

Prima autem et manifestior via est, quae sumitur ex parte motus. Certum est enim, et sensu constat, aliqua moveri in hoc mundo. Omne autem quod movetur, ab alio movetur. Nihil enim movetur, nisi secundum quod est in potentia ad illud ad quod movetur, movet autem aliquid secundum quod est actu. Movere enim nihil aliud est quam educere aliquid de potentia in actum, de potentia autem non potest aliquid reduci in actum, nisi per aliquod ens in actu, sicut calidum in actu, ut ignis, facit lignum, quod est calidum in potentia, esse actu calidum, et per hoc movet et alterat ipsum. Non autem est possibile ut idem sit simul in actu et potentia secundum idem, sed solum secundum diversa, quod enim est calidum in actu, non potest simul esse calidum in potentia, sed est simul frigidum in potentia. Impossibile est ergo quod, secundum idem et eodem modo, aliquid sit movens et motum, vel quod moveat seipsum. Omne ergo quod movetur, oportet ab alio moveri. Si ergo id a quo movetur, moveatur, oportet et ipsum ab alio moveri et illud ab alio. Hic autem non est procedere in infinitum, quia sic non esset aliquod primum movens; et per consequens nec aliquod aliud movens, quia moventia secunda non movent nisi per hoc quod sunt mota a primo movente, sicut baculus non movet nisi per hoc quod est motus a manu. Ergo necesse est devenire ad aliquod primum movens, quod a nullo movetur, et hoc omnes intelligunt Deum.

The first and more manifest way is the argument from motion. It is certain, and evident to our senses, that in the world some things are in motion. Now whatever is in motion is put in motion by another, for nothing can be in motion except it is in potentiality to that towards which it is in motion; whereas a thing moves inasmuch as it is in act. For motion is nothing else than the reduction of something from potentiality to actuality. But nothing can be reduced from potentiality to actuality, except by something in a state of actuality. Thus that which is actually hot, as fire, makes wood, which is potentially hot, to be actually hot, and thereby moves and changes it. Now it is not possible that the same thing should be at once in actuality and potentiality in the same respect, but only in different respects. For what is actually hot cannot simultaneously be potentially hot; but it is simultaneously potentially cold. It is therefore impossible that in the same respect and in the same way a thing should be both mover and moved, i.e., that it should move itself. Therefore, whatever is in motion must be put in motion by another. If that by which it is put in motion be itself put in motion, then this also must needs be put in motion by another, and that by another again. But this cannot go on to infinity, because then there would be no first mover, and, consequently, no other mover; seeing that subsequent movers move only inasmuch as they are put in motion by the first mover; as the staff moves only because it is put in motion by the hand. Therefore it is necessary to arrive at a first mover, put in motion by no other; and this everyone understands to be God.

Secunda via est ex ratione causae efficientis. Invenimus enim in istis sensibilibus esse ordinem causarum efficientium, nec tamen invenitur, nec est possibile, quod aliquid sit causa efficiens sui ipsius; quia sic esset prius seipso, quod est impossibile. Non autem est possibile quod in causis efficientibus procedatur in infinitum. Quia in omnibus causis efficientibus ordinatis, primum est causa medii, et medium est causa ultimi, sive media sint plura sive unum tantum, remota autem causa, removetur effectus, ergo, si non fuerit primum in causis efficientibus, non erit ultimum nec medium. Sed si procedatur in infinitum in causis efficientibus, non erit prima causa efficiens, et sic non erit nec effectus ultimus, nec causae efficientes mediae, quod patet esse falsum. Ergo est necesse ponere aliquam causam efficientem primam, quam omnes Deum nominant.

The second way is from the nature of the efficient cause. In the world of sense we find there is an order of efficient causes. There is no case known (neither is it, indeed, possible) in which a thing is found to be the efficient cause of itself; for so it would be prior to itself, which is impossible. Now in efficient causes it is not possible to go on to infinity, because in all efficient causes following in order, the first is the cause of the intermediate cause, and the intermediate is the cause of the ultimate cause, whether the intermediate cause be several, or only one. Now to take away the cause is to take away the effect. Therefore, if there be no first cause among efficient causes, there will be no ultimate, nor any intermediate cause. But if in efficient causes it is possible to go on to infinity, there will be no first efficient cause, neither will there be an ultimate effect, nor any intermediate efficient causes; all of which is plainly false. Therefore it is necessary to admit a first efficient cause, to which everyone gives the name of God.

Tertia via est sumpta ex possibili et necessario, quae talis est. Invenimus enim in rebus quaedam quae sunt possibilia esse et non esse, cum quaedam inveniantur generari et corrumpi, et per consequens possibilia esse et non esse. Impossibile est autem omnia quae sunt, talia esse, quia quod possibile est non esse, quandoque non est. Si igitur omnia sunt possibilia non esse, aliquando nihil fuit in rebus. Sed si hoc est verum, etiam nunc nihil esset, quia quod non est, non incipit esse nisi per aliquid quod est; si igitur nihil fuit ens, impossibile fuit quod aliquid inciperet esse, et sic modo nihil esset, quod patet esse falsum. Non ergo omnia entia sunt possibilia, sed oportet aliquid esse necessarium in rebus. Omne autem necessarium vel habet causam suae necessitatis aliunde, vel non habet. Non est autem possibile quod procedatur in infinitum in necessariis quae habent causam suae necessitatis, sicut nec in causis efficientibus, ut probatum est. Ergo necesse est ponere aliquid quod sit per se necessarium, non habens causam necessitatis aliunde, sed quod est causa necessitatis aliis, quod omnes dicunt Deum.

The third way is taken from possibility and necessity, and runs thus. We find in nature things that are possible to be and not to be, since they are found to be generated, and to corrupt, and consequently, they are possible to be and not to be. But it is impossible for these always to exist, for that which is possible not to be at some time is not. Therefore, if everything is possible not to be, then at one time there could have been nothing in existence. Now if this were true, even now there would be nothing in existence, because that which does not exist only begins to exist by something already existing. Therefore, if at one time nothing was in existence, it would have been impossible for anything to have begun to exist; and thus even now nothing would be in existence, which is absurd. Therefore, not all beings are merely possible, but there must be something the being of which is necessary. But every necessary thing either has its necessity caused by another, or not. Now it is impossible to go on to infinity in necessary things which have their necessity caused by another, as has been already proved in regard to efficient causes. Therefore we cannot but postulate the reality of some being having of itself its own necessity, and not receiving it from another, but rather causing in others their necessity. This all men speak of as God.

Quarta via sumitur ex gradibus qui in rebus inveniuntur. Invenitur enim in rebus aliquid magis et minus bonum, et verum, et nobile, et sic de aliis huiusmodi. Sed magis et minus dicuntur de diversis secundum quod appropinquant diversimode ad aliquid quod maxime est, sicut magis calidum est, quod magis appropinquat maxime calido. Est igitur aliquid quod est verissimum, et optimum, et nobilissi-mum, et per consequens maxime ens, nam quae sunt maxime vera, sunt maxime entia, ut dicitur II Metaphys. Quod autem dicitur maxime tale in aliquo genere, est causa omnium quae sunt illius generis, sicut ignis, qui est maxime calidus, est causa omnium calidorum, ut in eodem libro dicitur. Ergo est aliquid quod omnibus entibus est causa esse, et bonitatis, et cuiuslibet perfectionis, et hoc dicimus Deum.

The fourth way is taken from the gradation to be found in things. Among beings there are some more and some less good, true, noble and the like. But "more" and "less" are predicated of different things, according as they resemble in their different ways something which is the maximum, as a thing is said to be hotter according as it more nearly resembles that which is hottest; so that there is something which is truest, something best, something noblest and, conse-quently, something which is uttermost being; for those things that are greatest in truth are greatest in being, as it is written in [Aristotle's] Metaphysics II. Now the maximum in any genus is the cause of all in that genus; as fire, which is the maximum heat, is the cause of all hot things. Therefore there must also be something which is to all beings the cause of their being, goodness, and every other perfection; and this we call God.

Quinta via sumitur ex gubernatione rerum. Videmus enim quod aliqua quae cogni-tione carent, scilicet corpora naturalia, operantur propter finem, quod apparet ex hoc quod semper aut frequentius eodem modo operantur, ut consequantur id quod est optimum; unde patet quod non a casu, sed ex intentione perveniunt ad finem. Ea autem quae non habent cognitionem, non tendunt in finem nisi directa ab aliquo cognoscente et intelligente, sicut sagitta a sagittante. Ergo est aliquid intelligens, a quo omnes res naturales ordinantur ad finem, et hoc dicimus Deum.

The fifth way is taken from the governance of the world. We see that things which lack intelligence, such as natural bodies, act for an end, and this is evident from their acting always, or nearly always, in the same way, so as to obtain the best result. Hence it is plain that not fortuitously, but designedly, they achieve their end. Now whatever lacks intelligence cannot move towards an end, unless it be directed by some being endowed with knowledge and intelligence; as the arrow is shot to its mark by the archer. Therefore there is some intelligent being by whom all natural things are directed to their end; and this being we call God.

I q. 2 a. 3 ad 1. Ad primum ergo dicendum quod, sicut dicit Augustinus in Enchiridio, "Deus, cum sit summe bonus, nullo modo sineret aliquid mali esse in operibus suis, nisi esset adeo omnipotens et bonus, ut bene faceret etiam de malo." Hoc ergo ad infinitam Dei bonitatem pertinet, ut esse permittat mala, et ex eis eliciat bona.

Reply to Objection 1. As Augustine says in Enchiridion [xi]: "Since God is the highest good, He would not allow any evil to exist in His works, unless His omnipotence and goodness were such as to bring good even out of evil." This is part of the infinite goodness of God, that He should allow evil to exist, and out of it produce good.

I q. 2 a. 3 ad 2. Ad secundum dicendum quod, cum natura propter determinatum finem operetur ex directione alicuius superioris agentis, necesse est ea quae a natura fiunt, etiam in Deum reducere, sicut in primam causam. Similiter etiam quae ex proposito fiunt, oportet reducere in aliquam altiorem causam, quae non sit ratio et voluntas humana, quia haec mutabilia sunt et defectibilia; oportet autem omnia mobilia et deficere possibilia reduci in aliquod primum principium immobile et per se necessarium, sicut ostensum est.

Reply to Objection 2. Since nature works for a determinate end under the direction of a higher agent, whatever is done by nature must needs be traced back to God, as to its first cause. So also whatever is done voluntarily must also be traced back to some higher cause other than human reason or will, since these can change or fail; for all things that are changeable and capable of defect must be traced back to an immovable and self-necessary first principle, as was shown in the body of the article.

Sometimes all the Five Ways taken together are called the cosmological argument. Sometimes only the Third Way is called cosmological. Sometimes the first four are called cosmological while the Fifth Way is called the teleological argument, from the Greek *telos* (τέλος), "purpose," "goal," "aim," or "end." Each of the five is known by a standard brief description: First Way, *argumentum ex motu*, the argument from motion; Second Way, *argumentum ex causa efficiens*, the argument from efficient cause; Third Way, *argumentum ex contingentia mundi*, the argument from the contingency of the world; Fourth Way, *argumentum ex gradu*, the argument from the degrees of being; Fifth Way, *argumentum ex guber-*

natione mundi, the argument from the governance of the world. All five are empirical or *a posteriori*, or at least were intended by their author to be so.

To some extent they each depend upon rejecting the possibility of "infinite regress," i.e., the possibility that causes and reasons can be multiplied infinitely backward in either time or logic. Starting with any earthly fact and inquiring after its cause or reason-for-being will lead to an illustration of the "no-infinite-regress" principle, since that cause or reason must itself have a cause or reason, and so on. At some point, there must be a first cause or first reason for the existence of these ordinary phenomena.

Benedictine monk and Archbishop of Canterbury Anselm (1033-1109) presented in the *Proslogium* an *a priori* analysis of the special being of God as the famous "ontological argument." While Thomas Aquinas derived his basic philosophical outlook, including all Five Ways, from Aristotle, Anselm took his from neo-Platonic philosophy. The *Proslogium* is a single long prayer in the form of a non-vicious circle, the kind of neo-Platonic circle that Hegel would later use so effectively to describe the progressive development and mediation of phenomena in history through the logic of their interaction. The circle begins with an inadequately defined or poorly understood phenomenon, proceeds through a logically connected series of dialectical phases, and returns to its original phenomenon, which is now adequately defined and better understood because of the mind's journey through these phases. The movement away from the point of origin is the *proödos* (πρόοδος) and the movement that returns to this point and clarifies or redefines it is the *epistrophê* (ἐπιστροφή). The "inaccessible light" which Anselm emphasizes in the *Proslogium* is the standard neo-Platonic representation of the milieu of God, as well as, for both Anselm and Plato, God *per se*.

Anselm first intended to entitle the following work *Faith in Search of Understanding* (*Fides quaerens intellectum*), but finally called it just *Proslogium*, which means "A Discourse." Nevertheless, *Fides quaerens intellectum* has become a convenient slogan for Anselm's approach to philosophy. His argument for the reality of God is called "ontological" because it examines *a priori* the nature of being, without reference to phenomena or conditions in the natural or "ontic" world. It is given in the slightly revised 1903 translation of Sidney Norton Deane, and, because Chapters II, III, IV, and XV are crucial to understand the ontological argument, they are given also, for reference, in Latin:

Chapter I: ... Up now, slight man! Flee your occupations for a moment; hide yourself from your disturbing thoughts for a moment. Cast aside, now, your burdensome cares, and put away your toilsome business. Yield room for some little time to God; and rest for a little time in Him. Enter your mind's inner chamber; shut out all thoughts save that of God, and such as can aid you in seeking Him; close your door and seek Him. Speak now, my whole heart! Speak now to God, saying, I seek Your face; Your face, Lord, I seek. Come, O Lord my God, teach my heart now where and how it may seek You, where and how it may find You.

Lord, if You are not here, where shall I seek You, being absent? But if You are everywhere, why do I not see You present? Truly you dwell in inaccessible light. But where is inaccessible light, or how shall I come to it? Or who shall lead me to that light and into it, that I may see You in it? Again, by what marks, under what form, shall I seek You? I have never seen You, O Lord, my God; I do not know Your form. What, O most high Lord, shall this man do, an exile far from You? What shall Your servant do, anxious in his love of You, and cast out afar from Your face? He pants to see You, and Your face is too far from him. He longs to come to You, and Your dwelling place is inaccessible. He is eager to find You, and knows not Your place. He desires to seek You, and does not know Your face. Lord, You are my God, and You are my Lord, and never have I seen You. It is You that has made me, and has made me anew, and has bestowed upon me all the blessing I enjoy; and not yet do I know You. Finally, I was created to see You, and not yet have I done that for which I was made.

O wretched lot of man, when he has lost that for which he was made! O hard and terrible fate! Alas, what has he lost, and what has he found? What has departed, and what remains? He has lost the blessedness for which he was made, and has found the misery for which he was not made. That has departed without which nothing is happy, and that remains which, in itself, is only miserable. Man once did eat the bread of angels, for which he hungers now; he eats now the bread of sorrows, of which he knew not then. Alas! For the mourning of all mankind, for the universal lamentation of the sons of Adam! He choked with satiety, we sigh with hunger. He abounded, we beg. He possessed in happiness, and miserably forsook his possession; we suffer want in unhappiness, and feel a miserable longing. And alas! We remain empty.

Why did he not keep for us, when he could so easily, that whose lack we should feel so heavily? Why did he shut us away from the light, and cover us over with darkness? With what purpose did he rob us of life, and inflict death on us? Wretches that we are, from where have we been driven out; to where are we driven? From where hurled? To where consigned to ruin? From a native country into exile, from the vision of God into our present blindness, from the joy of immortality into the bitterness and horror of death. Miserable exchange of how great a good, for how great an evil! Heavy loss, heavy grief, heavy all our fate!

But alas! Wretched that I am, one of the sons of Eve, far removed from God! What have I undertaken? What have I accomplished? To where was I striving? How far have I come? To what did I aspire? Amid what thoughts am I sighing? I sought blessings, and lo, confusion! I strived toward God, and I stumbled on myself. I sought calm in privacy, and I found tribulation and grief, in my inmost thoughts. I wished to smile in the joy of my mind, and I am compelled to frown by the sorrow of my heart. Gladness I hoped for, and lo, a source of frequent sighs!

And You too, O Lord, how long? How long, O Lord, do You forget us; how long do You turn Your face from us? When will You look upon us, and hear us? When will You enlighten our eyes, and show us Your face? When will You restore Yourself to us? Look upon us, Lord; hear us, enlighten us, reveal Yourself to us. Restore Yourself to us, that it may be well with us — Yourself, without whom it is so ill with us. Pity our toilings and strivings toward You since we can do nothing without You. You do invite us; do You help us. I beseech You, O Lord, that I may not lose hope in sighs, but may breathe anew in hope. Lord, my heart is made bitter by its desolation. Sweeten it, I beseech You, with Your consolation. Lord, in hunger I began to seek You. I beseech You that I may not cease to hunger for You. In hunger I have come to You. Let me not go unfed. I have come in poverty to the Rich, in misery to the Compassionate. Let me not return empty and despised. And if, before I eat, I sigh, grant, even after sighs, that which I may eat. Lord, I am bowed down and can only look downward. Raise me up that I may look upward. My iniquities have gone over my head; they overwhelm me; and, like a heavy load, they weigh me down. Free me from them; unburden me, that the pit of iniquities may not close over me.

Be it mine to look up to Your light, even from afar, even from the depths. Teach me to seek You, and reveal Yourself to me, when I seek You, for I cannot seek You, except You teach me, nor find You, except You reveal Yourself. Let me seek You in longing, let me long for You in seeking. Let me find You in love, and love You in finding. Lord, I acknowledge and I thank You that You have created me in Your image, in order that I may be mindful of You, may conceive of You, and love You; but that image has been so consumed and wasted away by vices, and obscured by the smoke of wrongdoing, that it cannot achieve that for which it was made, unless You renew it, and create it anew. I do not endeavor, O Lord, to penetrate Your sublimity, for in no way do I match my understanding with it; but I long to understand in some degree Your truth, which my heart believes and loves. For I do not seek to understand that I may believe, but I believe in order to understand. For this also I believe — that unless I believe, I will not understand.

Capitulum II: Quod vere sit deus.

Ergo, domine, qui das fidei intellectum, da mihi, ut quantum scis expedire intelligam, quia es sicut credimus, et hoc es quod credimus. Et quidem credimus te esse aliquid quo nihil maius cogitari possit. An ergo non est aliqua talis natura, quia "dixit insipiens in corde suo: non est deus"? Sed certe ipse idem insipiens, cum audit hoc ipsum quod dico: "aliquid quo maius nihil cogitari potest," intelligit quod audit; et quod intelligit in intellectu eius est, etiam si non intelligat illud esse. Aliud enim est rem esse in intellectu, aliud intelligere rem esse. Nam cum pictor praecogitat quae facturus est, habet quidem in intellectu, sed nondum intelligit esse quod nondum fecit. Cum vero iam pinxit, et habet in intellectu et intelligit esse quod iam fecit. Convincitur ergo etiam insipiens esse vel in intellectu aliquid quo nihil maius cogitari potest, quia hoc cum audit intelligit, et quidquid intelligitur in intellectu est. Et certe id quo maius cogitari nequit, non potest esse in solo intellectu. Si enim vel in solo intellectu est, potest cogitari esse et in re, quod maius est. Si ergo id quo maius cogitari non potest, est in solo intellectu: id ipsum quo maius cogitari non potest, est quo maius cogitari potest. Sed certe hoc esse non potest. Existit ergo procul dubio aliquid quo maius cogitari non valet, et in intellectu et in re.

Chapter II: *Truly there is a God.*

And so, Lord, You, who give understanding to faith, give me, so far as You know it to be profitable, to understand that You are as we believe; and that You are that which we believe. And indeed, we believe that You are a being than which nothing greater can be conceived. Or is there no such nature, since "the fool has said in his heart, there is no God" [Psalms 14:1]? But, at any rate, this very fool, when he hears of this being of which I speak — a being than which nothing greater can be conceived — understands what he hears, and what he understands is in his understanding, although he does not understand it to be. For it is one thing for an object to be in the understanding, and another to understand that the object is. When a painter first conceives of what he will afterwards perform, he has it in his understanding, but he does not yet understand it to be, because he has not yet executed it. But after he has done the painting, he both has it in his understanding, and he understands that it is, because he has made it. Hence, even the fool is convinced that something is in the understanding, at least, than which nothing greater can be conceived. For, when he hears of this, he understands it. And whatever is understood, is in the understanding. And assuredly that, than which nothing greater can be conceived, cannot be in the understanding alone. For, suppose it is in the understanding alone. Then it can be conceived to be in reality; which is greater. Therefore, if that than which nothing greater can be conceived is in the understanding alone, then that very being than which nothing greater can be conceived is that than which a greater can be conceived. But obviously this is impossible. Hence, there is no doubt that there is a being than which nothing greater can be conceived, and it is both in the understanding and in reality.

Capitulum III: Quod non posit cogitari non esse.

Quod utique sic vere est, ut nec cogitari possit non esse. Nam potest cogitari esse aliquid, quod non posit cogitari non esse; quod maius est quam quod non esse cogitari potest. Quare si id quo maius nequit cogitari, potest cogitari non esse: id ipsum quo maius cogitari nequit, non est id quo maius cogitari nequit; quod convenire non potest. Sic ergo vere est aliquid quo maius cogitari non potest, ut nec cogitari possit non esse.

Et hoc es tu, domine deus noster. Sic ergo vere es, domine deus meus, ut nec cogitari possis non esse. Et merito. Si enim aliqua mens posset cogitare aliquid melius te, ascenderet creatura super creatorem, et iudicaret de creatore; quod valde est absurdum. Et quidem quidquid est aliud praeter te solum, potest cogitari non esse. Solus igitur verissime omnium, et ideo maxime omnium habes esse: quia quidquid aliud est non sic vere, et idcirco minus habet esse. Cur itaque "dixit insipiens in cordo suo: non est deus," cum tam in promptu sit rationali menti te maxime omnium esse? Cur, nisi quia stultus et insipiens?

Chapter III: *God cannot be conceived not to be.*

And this assuredly is so truly, that it cannot be conceived not to be. For it is possible to conceive of a being which cannot be conceived not to be; and this is greater than one which can be conceived not to be. Hence, if that than which nothing greater can be conceived can be conceived not to be, it is not that than which nothing greater can be conceived. But this is an irreconcilable contradiction. There is, then, so truly a being than which nothing greater can be conceived to be, that it cannot even be conceived not to be.

And this being You are, O Lord, our God. So truly, therefore, You are, O Lord, my God, that You cannot be conceived not to be; and rightly. For, if a mind could conceive of a being better than You, the creature would rise above the Creator; and this is most absurd. And indeed, whatever else there is, except You alone, can be conceived not to be. To You alone, therefore, it belongs to be more truly than all other beings, and hence in a higher degree than all others. For whatever else is, is not so truly real, and hence in a less degree it belongs to it to be. Why then has the fool said in his heart, there is no God, since it is so evident to a rational mind that You are real in the highest degree of all? Why, except that he is dull and a fool?

Capitulum IV: Quomodo insipiens dixit in corde, quod cogitari non potest.

Verum quomodo dixit in corde quod cogitare non potuit; aut quomodo cogitare non potuit quod dixit in corde, cum idem sit dicere in corde et cogitare? Quod si vere, immo quia vere et cogitavit quia dixit in corde, et non dixit in corde quia cogitare non potuit: non uno tantum modo dicitur aliquid in corde vel cogitatur. Aliter enim cogitatur res cum vox eam significans cogitatur, aliter cum id ipsum quod res est intelligitur. Illo itaque modo potest cogitari deus non esse, isto vero minime. Nullus quippe intelligens id quod deus est, potest cogitare quia deus non est, licet haec verba dicat in corde, aut sine ulla aut cum aliqua extranea significatione. Deus enim est id quo maius cogitari non potest. Quod qui bene intelligit, utique intelligit id ipsum sic esse, ut nec cogitatione queat non esse. Qui ergo intelligit sic esse deum, nequit eum non esse cogitare.

Gratias tibi, bone domine, gratias tibi, quia quod prius credidi te donante, iam sic intelligo te illuminante, ut si te esse nolim credere, non possim non intelligere.

Chapter IV: *How the fool has said in his heart what cannot be conceived.*

But how has the fool said in his heart what he could not conceive; or how is it that he could not conceive what he said in his heart, since it is the same to say in the heart, and to conceive? But, if he really — or since he really — both conceived, because he said in his heart; and did not say in his heart, because he could not conceive; there is more than one way in which a thing is said in the heart or conceived. For, in one sense, an object is conceived when the word signifying it is conceived; and in another sense, when the very entity, which the object is, is understood. In the former sense, then, God can be conceived not to be; but in the latter, not at all. For no one who understands what fire and water are can conceive fire to be water, in accordance with the nature of the facts themselves, although this is possible according to the words. So, then, no one who understands what God is can conceive that God is not, even though he says these words in his heart, either without any or with some foreign signification. For God is that than which a greater cannot be conceived. And he who thoroughly understands this, assuredly understands that this being so truly is, that not even in concept can it be non-existent. Therefore, he who understands that God is so, cannot conceive that God does not exist.

I thank You, gracious Lord, I thank You; because what I formerly believed by Your bounty, I now so understand by Your illumination, that if I were unwilling to believe that You do exist, I should not be able not to understand this to be true.

Chapter V: *God is whatever it is better to be than not to be; and He, as the only self-existent being, creates all things from nothing.*

What are You, then, Lord God, than whom nothing greater can be conceived? But what are You, except that which, as the highest of all beings, alone is through itself, and creates all other things from nothing? For, whatever is not this is less than a thing which can be conceived of. But this cannot be conceived of You. What good, therefore, does the supreme Good lack, through which every good is? Therefore, You are just, truthful, blessed, and whatever it is better to be than not to be. For it is better to be just than not just; better to be blessed than not blessed.

Chapter VI: *How God is sensitive although He is not a body.*

But, although it is better for You to be sensitive, omnipotent, compassionate, passionless, than not to be these things; how are You sensitive, if You are not a body; or omnipotent, if You have not all powers; or at once compassionate and passionless? For, if only corporeal things are sensitive, since the senses encompass a body and are in a body, how are You sensitive, although You are not a body, but a supreme Spirit, who is superior to body? But, if feeling is only cognition, or for the sake of cognition — for he who feels obtains knowledge in accordance with the proper functions of his senses; as through sight, of colors; through taste, of flavors — whatever in any way cognizes is not inappropriately said, in some sort, to feel. Therefore, O Lord, although You are not a body yet You are truly sensitive in the highest degree in respect of this, that You do cognize all things in the highest degree; and not as an animal cognizes, through a corporeal sense.

Chapter VII: *How He is omnipotent, although there are many things which He cannot do.*

But how are You omnipotent, if You are not capable of all things? Or, if You cannot be corrupted, and cannot lie, nor make what is true false — as, for example, if You should make what has been done not to have been done, and the like — how are You capable of all things? Or else to be capable of these things is not power, but impotence. For he who is capable of these things is capable of what is not for his good, and of what he ought not to do; and the more capable of them he is, the more power have adversity and perversity against him; and the less has he himself against these. He, then, who is thus capable is so not by power, but by impotence. For, he is not said to be able because he is able of himself, but because his impotence gives something else power over him. Or, by a figure of speech, just as many words are improperly applied, as when we use "to be" for "not to be," and "to do" for what is really "not to do," or "to do nothing." For often we say to a man who denies the existence of something, "It is as you say it is," though it might seem more proper to say, "It is not, as you say it is not." In the same way, we say, "This man sits just as that man does," or, "This man rests just as that man does"; although to sit is not to do anything, and to rest is to do nothing. So, then, when one is said to have the power of doing or experiencing what is not for his good, or what he ought not to do, impotence is understood in the word power. For, the more he possesses this power, the more powerful are adversity and perversity against him, and the more powerless is he against them. Therefore, O Lord, our God, the more truly are You omnipotent, since You are capable of nothing through impotence, and nothing has power against You.

Chapter VIII: *How He is both compassionate and passionless.*

But how are You compassionate, and, at the same time, passionless?

For, if You are passionless, You do not feel sympathy; and if You do not feel sympathy, Your heart is not wretched from sympathy for the wretched ; but this it is to be compassionate. But if You are not compassionate, from where comes such great consolation for the wretched?

How, then, are You compassionate and not compassionate, O Lord, unless because You are compassionate in terms of our experience, and not compassionate in terms of Your being. Truly, You are so in terms of our experience, but You are not so in terms of Your own. For, when You behold us in our wretchedness, we experience the effect of compassion, but You do not experience the feeling. Therefore, You are both compassionate, because You save the wretched, and spare those who sin against You; and not compassionate because You are not affected by sympathy for wretchedness.

Chapter IX: *How the all-just and supremely just God spares the wicked, and justly pities the wicked.*

But how do You spare the wicked, if You are all-just and supremely just? For how, being all-just and supremely just, do You anything that is not just? Or, what justice is that to give him who merits eternal death everlasting life? How, then, gracious Lord, good to the righteous and the wicked, can You save the wicked, if this is not just, and You do not anything that is not just? Or, since Your goodness is incomprehensible, is this hidden in the inaccessible light wherein You dwell? Truly, in the deepest and most secret parts of Your goodness is hidden the fountain from which the stream of Your compassion flows. For You are all-just and supremely just, yet You are kind even to the wicked, simply because You are supremely good. For You would be less good if You were not kind to every wicked being. For, he who is good, both to the righteous and the wicked, is better than he who is good to the wicked alone; and he who is good to the wicked, both by punishing and sparing them, is better than he who is good by punishing them alone. Therefore, You are compassionate, because You are supremely good. And, although it appears that You should reward the good with goods and the evil with evils; yet this, at least, is most wonderful, that You, the all-just and supremely just, who lacks nothing, bestows goods on the wicked and on those who are guilty toward You.

How deep is Your goodness, O God! The source of Your compassion appears, and yet is not clearly seen! We see from where the river flows, but the spring from where it arises is not seen. For it is from the abundance of Your goodness that You are good to those who sin against You; and in the depth of Your goodness is hidden the reason for this kindness. For, although You reward the good with goods and the evil with evils, out of goodness, yet this is what the concept of justice seems to demand. But, when You bestow goods on the evil, and it is known that the Supremely Good One has willed to do this, we wonder why the Supremely Just One has been able to will this.

O compassion, from what abundant sweetness and what sweet abundance do You well forth to us! O boundless goodness of God, how passionately should sinners love You! For You save the just, because justice goes with them; but You free sinners by the authority of justice: the former by the help of their deserts; the latter, although their deserts oppose; the former by acknowledging the goods You have granted; the latter by pardoning the evils You hate. O boundless goodness, which so exceeds all understanding, let that compassion come upon me, which proceeds from Your so great abundance! Let it flow upon me, for it wells forth from You. Spare, in mercy; avenge not, in justice. For, though it is hard to understand how Your compassion is not inconsistent with Your justice; yet we must believe that it does not oppose justice at all, because it flows from goodness, which is no goodness without justice; indeed, it is in true harmony with justice. For, if You are compassionate only because You are supremely good, and supremely good only because You are supremely just, truly You are compassionate even because You are supremely just. Help me, just and compassionate God, whose light I seek; help me to understand what I say. Truly, then, You are compassionate even because You are just.

Is, then, Your compassion born of Your justice? And do You spare the wicked, therefore, out of justice? If this is true, my Lord, if this is true, teach me how it is. Is it because it is just, that You should be so good that You cannot be conceived better; and that You should work so powerfully that You cannot be conceived more powerful? For what can be more just than this? Assuredly it could not be that You should be good only by retaliating and not by sparing, and that You should make good only those who are not good, and not the wicked also. In this way, therefore, it is just that You should spare the wicked, and make good souls of evil. Finally, what is not done justly ought not to be done; and what ought not to be done is done unjustly. If, then, You do not justly pity the wicked, You ought not to pity them. And, if You ought not to pity them, You pity them unjustly. And if It is impious to suppose this, it is right to believe that You justly pity the wicked.

Chapter X: *How He justly punishes and justly spares the wicked.*

But it is also just that You should punish the wicked. For what is more just than that the good should receive goods, and the evil, evils? How, then, is it just that You should punish the wicked, and, at the same time, spare the wicked?

Or, in one way, do You justly punish, and, in another, justly spare them? For, when You punish the wicked, it is just, because it is consistent with their deserts; and when, on the other hand, You spare the wicked, it is just, not because it is compatible with their deserts, but because it is compatible with Your goodness. For, in sparing the wicked, You are as just, according to Your nature, but not according to ours, as You are compassionate, according to our nature, and not according to Yours. Seeing that, by saving us, whom it would be just for You to destroy, You are compassionate, not because You feel an affection, but because we feel the effect, so also You are just, not because You punish us as we deserve, but because You do that which becomes You as the supremely good Being. In this way, therefore, without contradiction You justly punish and justly spare.

Chapter XI: *How all the ways of God are compassion and truth; and yet God is just in all His ways.*

But, is there any reason why it is not also just, according to Your nature, O Lord, that You should punish the wicked? Surely it is just that You should be so just that You cannot be conceived more just; and this You would in no way be if You did only render goods to the good, and not evils to the evil. For, he who requites both good and evil according to their deserts is more just than he who so requites the good alone. It is, therefore, just, according to Your nature, O just and gracious God, both when You punish and when You spare. Truly, then, "all the paths of the Lord are steadfast love [*chesed* (חֶסֶד)] and faithfulness" [Psalms 25: 10]; and yet "the Lord is just in all his ways" [Psalms 145:17]. And this is assuredly so without inconsistency, for it is not just that those whom You will to punish should be saved, and that those whom You will to spare should be condemned. For that alone is just which You will; and that alone unjust which You do not will. So, then, Your compassion is born of Your justice. For it is just that You should be so good that You are good in sparing also; and this may be the reason why the supremely Just can will goods for the evil. But if it can be comprehended in any way why You can will to save the wicked, yet by no consideration can we comprehend why, of those who are alike wicked, You save some rather than others, through supreme goodness; and why You condemn the latter rather than the former, through supreme justice.

So, then, You are truly sensitive, omnipotent, compassionate, and passionless, as You are living, wise, good, blessed, eternal: and whatever it is better to be than not to be.

Chapter XII: *God is the very life whereby He lives; and so of other like attributes.*

But undoubtedly, whatever You are, You are that through nothing else than through Yourself. Therefore, You are the very life whereby You live; and the wisdom with which You are wise; and the very goodness whereby You are good to the righteous and the wicked; and so of other like attributes.

Chapter XIII: *How He alone is uncircumscribed and eternal, although other spirits are uncircumscribed and eternal.*

But everything that is in any way bounded by place or time is less than that which no law of place or time can limit. Since, then, nothing is greater than You, no place or time contains You; but You are everywhere and always. And since this can be said of You alone, You alone are uncircumscribed and eternal. How is it, then, that other spirits also are said to be uncircumscribed and eternal?

Assuredly You are alone eternal; for You alone among all beings not only do not cease to be but also do not begin to be. But how are You alone uncircumscribed? Is it that a created spirit, when compared with You is circumscribed, but when compared with matter, uncircumscribed? For altogether circumscribed is that which, when it is wholly in one place, cannot at the same time be in another. And this is seen to be true of corporeal things alone. But uncircumscribed is that which is, as a whole, at the same time everywhere. And this is understood to be true of You alone. But circumscribed, and, at the same time, uncircumscribed is that which, when it is anywhere as a whole, can at the same time be somewhere else as a whole, and yet not everywhere. And this is recognized as true of created spirits. For, if the soul were not as a whole in the separate members of the body, it would not feel as a whole in the separate members. Therefore, You, Lord, are peculiarly uncircumscribed and eternal; and yet other spirits also are uncircumscribed and eternal.

Chapter XIV: *How and why God is seen and yet not seen by those who seek Him.*
Have you found what you sought, my soul? You sought God. You have found him to be a being which is the highest of all beings, a being than which nothing better can be conceived; that this being is life itself, light, wisdom, goodness, eternal blessedness and blessed eternity; and that it is everywhere and always. For, if You have not found Your God, how is He this being which you have found, and which you have conceived Him to be, with such certain truth and such true certainty? But, if you have found Him, why is it that you do not feel that you have found Him? Why, O Lord, our God, does not my soul feel You, if it has found You?

Or, has it not found Him whom it found to be light and truth? For how did it understand this, except by seeing light and truth? Or, could it understand anything at all of You, except through Your light and Your truth? Hence, if it has seen light and truth, it has seen You; if it has not seen You, it has not seen light and truth. Or, has it seen both light and truth, but still has not yet seen You, because it has seen You only in part, but has not seen You as You are?

Lord my God, my creator and renewer, speak to the desire of my soul, tell it what You are besides what it has seen, that it may clearly see what it desires. It strains to see You more, and sees nothing beyond this which it has seen, except darkness. It does not see darkness, of which there is none in You; but it sees that it cannot see farther, because of its own darkness. Why is this, Lord, why is this? Is the eye of the soul darkened by its infirmity, or dazzled by Your glory? Surely it is both darkened in itself, and dazzled by You. Doubtless it is both obscured by its own insignificance, and overwhelmed by Your infinity. Truly, it is both contracted by its own narrowness and overcome by Your greatness. For how great is that light from which shines every truth that gives light to the rational mind? How great is that truth in which is everything that is true, and outside which is only nothingness and the false? How boundless is the truth which sees at one glance whatsoever has been made, and by whom, and through whom, and how it has been made from nothing? What purity, what simplicity, what certainty, what splendor is there! It is assuredly more than a creature can conceive.

Capitulum XV: Quod maior sit quam cogitari possit.

   Ergo domine, non solum es quo maius cogitari nequit, sed es quiddam maius quam cogitari possit. Quoniam namque valet cogitari esse aliquid huius-modi: si tu non es hoc ipsum, potest cogitari aliquid maius te; quod fieri nequit.

Chapter XV: *He is greater than can be conceived.*

   Therefore, O Lord, You are not only that than which a greater cannot be conceived, but You are greater than can be conceived. For, since it can be conceived that there is such a thing, if You are not this very one, a greater than You could be conceived. But this is impossible.

Chapter XVI: *This is the inaccessible light wherein He dwells.*

   Truly, O Lord, this is the inaccessible light in which You dwell; for truly there is nothing else which can penetrate this light, that it may see You there. Truly, I see it not, because it is too bright for me. And yet, whatever I see, I see through it, as the weak eye sees what it sees through the light of the sun, which in the sun itself it cannot look upon. My understanding cannot reach that light, for it shines too brightly. It does not comprehend it, nor does my soul's eye endure to gaze upon it long. It is dazzled by the brightness, it is overcome by the greatness, it is overwhelmed by the infinity, it is dazed by the immensity of the light. O supreme and inaccessible light! O whole and blessed truth, how far are You from me, who am so near to You! How far removed are You from my vision, though I am so near to Yours! Everywhere You are wholly present, and I see You not. In You I move, and in You I have my being; and I cannot come to You. You are within me, and about me, and I feel You not.

Chapter XVII: *In God is harmony, fragrance, sweetness, pleasantness to the touch, beauty, after His ineffable manner.*

   Still You are hidden, O Lord, from my soul in Your light and Your blessedness; and therefore my soul still walks in its darkness and wretchedness. For it looks, and does not see Your beauty. It hearkens, and does not hear Your harmony. It smells, and does not perceive Your fragrance. It tastes, and does not recognize Your sweetness. It touches, and does not feel Your pleasantness. For You have these attributes in Yourself, Lord God, after Your ineffable manner. You have given them to the objects You created, after their sensible manner; but the sinful senses of my soul have grown rigid and dull, and have been obstructed by their long listlessness.

Chapter XVIII: *Neither God nor His eternity are divisible into parts.*

Lo, again confusion, again grief and mourning meet him who seeks for joy and gladness. My soul now hoped for satisfaction; and lo, again it is over-whelmed with need. I desired now to feast, and lo, I hunger more. I tried to rise to the light of God, and I have fallen back into my darkness. Not only have I fallen into it, but I feel that I am enveloped in it. I fell before my mother conceived me. Truly, in darkness I was conceived, and in the cover of darkness I was born. Truly, in him we all fell, in whom we all sinned. In him we all lost, who kept easily and wickedly lost to himself and to us that which, when we wish to seek it, we do not know; when we seek it, we do not find; when we find, it is not that which we seek. Help me for Your goodness' sake! Lord, I sought Your face; Your face, Lord, will I seek; hide not Your face far from me. Raise me from myself toward You. Cleanse, heal, sharpen, enlighten the eye of my mind, that it may behold You. Let my soul recover its strength, and with all its understanding let it strive toward You, O Lord.

What are You, Lord, what are You? What shall my heart conceive You to be? Assuredly You are life, You are wisdom, You are truth, You are goodness, You are blessedness, You are eternity, and You are every true good. Many are these attributes. My limited understanding cannot see so many at one view, that it may be gladdened by all at once. How, then, O Lord, are You all these things? Are they parts of You, or is each one of these rather the whole, which You are? For, whatever is composed of parts is not altogether one, but is in some sort plural, and diverse from itself; and either in fact or in concept is capable of dissolution. But these things are alien to You, than whom nothing better can be conceived. Hence, there are no parts in You, Lord, nor are You more than one. But You are so truly a unitary being, and so identical with Yourself, that in no respect are You unlike Yourself; rather You are unity itself, indivisible by any conception. There-fore, life and wisdom and the rest are not parts of You, but all are one; and each of these is the whole, which You are, and which all the rest are. In this way, then, it appears that You have no parts, and that Your eternity, which You are, is nowhere and never a part of You or of Your eternity. But everywhere You are as a whole, and Your eternity is as a whole forever.

Chapter XIX: *He does not exist in place or time, but all things exist in Him.*

But if through Your eternity You have been, and are, and will be; and to have been is not to be destined to be; and to be is not to have been or to be destined to be; how does Your eternity exist as a whole forever?

Or is it true that nothing of Your eternity passes away, so that it is not now; and that nothing of it is destined to be, as if it were not yet? You were not, then, yesterday, nor will You be tomorrow; but yesterday and today and tomorrow You are; or, rather, neither yesterday nor today nor tomorrow You are; but simply, You are, outside all time. For yesterday and today and tomorrow have no exis-tence, except in time; but You, although nothing is without You, nevertheless do not exist in space or time, but all things exist in You. For nothing contains You, but You contain all.

Chapter XX: *He is before all things and transcends all things, even eternal things.*

Hence, You do permeate and embrace all things. You are before all, and do transcend all. And surely You are before all; for before they were made, You were and are. But how do You transcend all? In what way do You transcend those beings which will have no end? Is it because they cannot exist at all without You; while You are in no way less, if they should return to nothingness? For so, in a certain sense, You do transcend them. Or, is it also because they can be conceived to have an end; but You, by no means? For so they actually have an end, in a certain sense; but You, in no sense. And certainly, what in no sense has an end transcends what is ended in any sense. Or, in this way also do You transcend all things, even the eternal, because Your eternity and theirs is present as a whole with You; while they have not yet that part of their eternity which is to come, just as they no longer have that part which is past? For so You do ever transcend them, since You are ever present with Yourself, and since that to which they have not yet come is ever present with You.

Chapter XXI: *Whether this the age of the age, or the ages of ages.*

Is this, then, the age of the age, or the ages of ages? For, as an age of time contains all temporal things, so Your eternity contains even the ages of time themselves. And these are indeed an age, because of their indivisible unity; but ages, because of their endless immeasurability. And, although You are so great, O Lord, that all things are full of You, and exist in You; yet You are so without all space, that neither middle, nor half, nor any part, is in You.

Chapter XXII: *He alone is what He is and who He is.*

Therefore, You alone, O Lord, are what You are; and You are He who You are. For, what is one thing in the whole and another in the parts, and in which there is any mutable element, is not altogether what it is. And what begins from non-existence, and can be conceived not to exist, and unless it subsists through something else, returns to non-existence; and what has a past existence, which is no longer, or a future existence, which is not yet, this does not properly and absolutely exist. But You are what You are, because, whatever You are at any time, or in any way, You are as a whole and forever.

And You are He who You are, properly and simply; for You have neither a past existence nor a future, but only a present existence; nor can You be conceived as at any time non-existent. But You are life, and light, and wisdom, and blessedness, and many goods of this nature. Yet You are only one supreme good; You are all-sufficient to Yourself, and need none; and You are He whom all things need for their existence and well being. ...

Chapter XXIV: *Conjecture as to the character and the magnitude of this good.*

Now, my soul, arouse and lift up all Your understanding, and conceive, so far as You can, of what character and how great is that good! For, if individual goods are delectable, conceive in earnestness how delectable is that good which contains the pleasantness of all goods; and not such as we have experienced in created objects, but as different as the Creator from the creature. For, if the created life is good, how good is the creative life! If the salvation given is delightful, how delightful is the salvation which has given all salvation! If wisdom in the knowledge of the created world is lovely, how lovely is the wisdom which has created all things from nothing! Finally, if there are many great delights in delectable things, what and how great is the delight in Him who has made these delectable things. ...

Chapter XXVI: *Is this the fullness of joy which the Lord promises?*

... Show me, O Lord, show Your servant in his heart whether this is the joy into which Your servants shall enter, who shall enter into the joy of their Lord. But that joy, surely, with which Your chosen ones shall rejoice, no eye has seen nor ear heard, neither has it entered into the human heart. Not yet, then, have I told or conceived, O Lord, how greatly those blessed ones of Yours shall rejoice. Doubtless they shall rejoice according as they shall love; and they shall love according as they shall know. How far they will know You, Lord, then, and how much they will love You! Truly, no eye has seen, nor ear heard, neither has it entered into the human heart in this life, how far they shall know You, and how much they shall love You in that life.

I pray, O God, to know You, to love You, that I may rejoice in You. And if I cannot attain to full joy in this life may I at least advance from day to day, until that joy shall come to the full. Let the knowledge of You advance in me here, and there be made full. Let the love of You increase, and there let it be full, that here my joy may be great in hope, and there full in truth. Lord, through Your Son You command, indeed, You counsel us to ask; and You promise that we shall receive, that our joy may be full. I ask, O Lord, as You counsel through our wonderful Counsellor. I will receive what You promise by virtue of Your truth, that my joy may be full. Faithful God, I ask. I will receive, that my joy may be full. Meanwhile, let my mind meditate upon it; let my tongue speak of it. Let my heart love it; let my mouth talk of it. Let my soul hunger for it; let my flesh thirst for it; let my whole being desire it, until I enter into Your joy, O Lord, who are the Three and the One God, blessed for ever and ever. Amen.

The two strongest arguments for the reality of God are Thomas Aquinas's Third Way, the cosmological, and the *ratio Anselmi*, the ontological. Yet they can both be made stronger.

One important and long recognized problem with the ontological argument, even in formulations based on *Proslogium* XV, is inherent in the very nature of Anselm's *credo ut intelligam* ("I believe so that I may understand") or *fides quaerens intellectum* project, namely, unless we already believe in God, we are not likely to be convinced by this argument. That is because the argument deals *a priori* with the nature of being and seems to have no clear connection to the real world. It needs to have an empirical premise added. This can be done.

Philosophers and theologians make a standard distinction between God as God really is (*Deus in re*) and God as God is conceived in the mind (*Deus in intellectu*). According to formulations of the ontological argument based only on *Proslogium* II-IV, *Deus in re* should be equivalent to *Deus in intellectu* if *Deus in intellectu* is the superlative conception. But such a conclusion violates the spirit of Anselm, for if *Deus in re* were really the equivalent of any *Deus in intellectu*, then there would be no "inaccessible light." If, on the other hand, following *Proslogium* XV, *Deus in re* is taken to be necessarily greater than any possible *Deus in intellectu*, then this not only upholds Anselm's project, but also provides a means to introduce the required empirical premise to bolster the argument, namely, the simple assertion that there exists a conception of God. Thus the ontological argument may be expressed deductively as follows, using the ordinary notation of symbolic logic:

Let C = is God according to the greatest possible conception of God.
Let G = is in fact God.
Let I = is at most the greatest possible *Deus in intellectu*.
Let R = is at least the least possible *Deus in re*.

Given that, according to Anselm's final definition of God in *Proslogium* XV, God must be greater than any possible conception of God, therefore:

$$\forall xy \ [(Cx \ \& \ Gy) \equiv (y > x)] \text{ and } \forall xy \ [(Ix \ \& \ Ry) \equiv (y > x)]$$

Hence, to show that God is real: $?\exists y \ (Gy)$

Premise 1. $\forall x \ [Cx \equiv (Ix \ \& \ \Box{\sim}Rx)]$
Premise 2. $\forall y \ [\Box Gy \equiv (Iy \ \& \ Ry)]$
Premise 3. $\forall xy \ (Ix \supset Ry)$
Premise 4. $\forall y \ (Ry \supset Iy)$

Premise 5 (the empirical premise). $\exists x\ (Cx)$

6. Cg	5 Existential Instantiation
7. Cg $\equiv$ (Ig & $\square\sim$Rg)	1 Universal Instantiation, Material Equivalence, Simplification
8. (Iz & Rz) $\supset \square$Gz	2 Universal Instantiation, Material Equivalence, Commutation, Simplification
9. Ig $\supset$ Rz	3 Universal Instantiation
10. Rz $\supset$ Iz	4 Universal Instantiation
11. Ig & $\square\sim$Rg	6,7 Modus Ponens
12. Ig	11 Simplification
13. Rz	9,12 Modus Ponens
14. Iz	10,13 Modus Ponens
15. Iz & Rz	13,14 Conjunction
16. $\square$Gz	8,15 Modus Ponens
17. Gz	16 Necesse ad Esse
18. $\exists y\ (Gy)$	17 Existential Generalization
QED	

Without the empirical premise, the existential generalization that concludes the argument could not be made. Some logicians might balk at deriving line 18 from line 17 because Gz in line 8 was instantiated universally. It is on precisely that point that the empirical premise in line 5 strengthens the argument, because using the existentially instantiated term in line 6 as the basis of the series of modus ponens deductions culminating in line 17 eliminates concerns about the status of "z" in the relationship between the universal and the existential.

Complementing this empirical version of the ontological argument is an *a priori* version of the Third Way. A significant advantage of the argument from the contingency of the world is that it can easily be stripped of its theological underpinnings and handled in terms of ontology alone. The world is contingent; that is a philosophical fact. The argument analyzes the concept of being, specifically, the relation between the contingent and necessary aspects of being, without depending upon any empirical observation or *a posteriori* reasoning. Moreso than any of the other four, it can be considered apart from Thomistic theology and even Aristotelian metaphysics. Contrary to its author's own categorization of it, it is not really an empirical argument, but *a priori*, and is better designated as the argument from the nature of existence itself.

Particular worldly entities are contingent, but existence itself is not. Even though the basic knowledge of existence arises empirically, with daily observations of finite entities, such knowledge itself is not empirical, because to deny existence *per se* would be self-contradictory. Even though it is always possible to deny the past or future existence, or the eternity or permanent duration, of specific entities which exist in the present, or to deny the present existence of specific entities which either existed in the past or are expected to exist in the future, existence itself cannot be denied. To say, "Nothing exists," is always self-contradictory. Thus the sentence, "Something exists," is necessarily true every time, i.e., at any given present moment, that we pronounce or conceive it.

If something, anything, exists — and it does — then it is not possible that nothing exists. In other words, while it is not necessary that any particular entity exist, it is necessary that some entity exist. Thomas Aquinas proceeds this far, but then makes a controversial leap in his logic to assert that if it is necessary that some entity exist, then there must exist an entity which necessarily exists. He wants to call this necessary entity God. This claim is illegitimate because there is no justification to conclude from the bare fact of existence that there exists an entity of permanent duration.

If finite beings had sequential access to every possible present moment in the entire past, present, and future, then they could have a cumulative knowledge of the permanent duration of the totality of existence. But even that could not prove the existence of any single specific entity which would exist of necessity. Only provable would be the fact of the collectively permanent existence of any number of entities, either contingent or necessary. Such sequential access would provide *a priori* knowledge only of each present moment which the finite being actually experienced, not of the entire series. Knowledge of the fact of existence in past and future moments would remain at best *a posteriori* and at worst imaginative. Genuine *a priori* knowledge of the fact of existence over its entire span would require simultaneous, not sequential, access to every possible present moment.

The impasse is that a necessary being is apparently not deducible from the necessary fact of existence in general. Finite beings cannot assert anything definite about either the past, the future, or eternity because they live only in the present. The argument at this stage, insofar as its main point seems to be that existence itself is not contingent, seems more supportive of either pantheism or the

Aristotelian doctrine of the eternity of the world than of the idea of a theistic God.

This impasse is surmountable only if a valid logical move can be made from the concept of present necessary existence per se to the concept of the reality of God as the source or ground of that existence. Why is present existence necessary? Why, as Heidegger would ask, is there something rather than nothing? What is the nature of existence itself, or rather, the nature of the necessity of existence itself?

The ultimate ground of existence is neither itself an existent nor a cause in any of the usual Aristotelian senses of material, efficient, formal, or final causality. It is not ontic. It is simply the condition under which existence is possible. This is known *a priori*. There must be such a condition, or else there would be nothing in existence at present, which is absurd. This condition must be real because its concept follows analytically from the natural *a priori* awareness of the necessity of present existence. More than that cannot be either known or said. This condition must be real, but its nature cannot be known, or at least cannot be inferred from this argument. We know that it is, not what it is. It can be called the "ground of being," or God.

That this argument is *a priori* is the key to its cogency. Only because of some of Thomas Aquinas's *a posteriori* assertions, e.g., that if everything were contingent, then at some past time nothing would have existed, has it ever been suspect. The problem of defining God as the "necessary being" referred to at the conclusion of his empirical formulation of the Third Way is now avoided, since God is understood not as a being, not even as a transcendental being in a separate category from all other beings, but only as the condition under which there are beings.

Another cogent attestation of the reality of God is the design argument, sometimes called the teleological argument. Its *locus classicus* is the first chapter of William Paley's *Natural Theology: or, Evidences of the Existence and Attributes of the Deity, Collected from the Appearances of Nature*, published in 1802:

In crossing a heath, suppose I pitched my foot against a *stone*, and were asked how the stone came to be there; I might possibly answer, that, for any thing I knew to the contrary, it had lain there for ever: nor would it perhaps be very easy to show the absurdity of this answer. But suppose I had found a *watch* upon the ground, and it should be inquired how the watch happened to be in that place; I should hardly think of the answer which I had before given, that, for any thing I knew, the watch might have always been there. Yet why should not this answer serve for the watch as well as for the stone? why is it not as admissible in the second case, as in the first? For this reason, and for no other, viz. that, when we come to inspect the watch, we perceive (what we could not discover in the stone) that its several parts are framed and put together for a purpose, *e.g.* that they are so formed and adjusted as to produce motion, and that motion so regulated as to point out the hour of the day; that, if the different parts had been differently shaped from what they are, of a different size from what they are, or placed after any other manner, or in any other order, than that in which they are placed, either no motion at all would have been carried on in the machine, or none which would have answered the use that is now served by it. To reckon up a few of the plainest of these parts, and of their offices, all tending to one result: — We see a cylindrical box containing a coiled elastic spring, which, by its endeavour to relax itself, turns round the box. We next observe a flexible chain (artificially wrought for the sake of flexure), communicating the action of the spring from the box to the fusee. We then find a series of wheels, the teeth of which catch in, and apply to, each other, conducting the motion from the fusee to the balance, and from the balance to the pointer; and at the same time, by the size and shape of those wheels, so regulating that motion, as to terminate in causing an index, by an equable and measured progression, to pass over a given space in a given time. We take notice that the wheels are made of brass in order to keep them from rust; the springs of steel, no other metal being so elastic; that over the face of the watch there is placed a glass, a material employed in no other part of the work, but in the room of which, if there had been any other than a transparent substance, the hour could not be seen without opening the case. This mechanism being observed (it requires indeed an examination of the instrument, and perhaps some previous knowledge of the subject, to perceive and understand it; but being once, as we have said, observed and understood), the inference, we think, is inevitable, that the watch must have had a maker: that there must have existed, at some time, and at some place or other, an artificer or artificers who formed it for the purpose which we find it actually to answer; who comprehended its construction, and designed its use.

I. Nor would it, I apprehend, weaken the conclusion, that we had never seen a watch made; that we had never known an artist capable of making one; that we were altogether incapable of executing such a piece of workmanship ourselves, or of understanding in what manner it was performed; all this being no more than what is true of some exquisite remains of ancient art, of some lost arts, and, to the generality of mankind, of the more curious productions of modern manufacture. Does one man in a million know how oval frames are turned?

Ignorance of this kind exalts our opinion of the unseen and unknown artist's skill, if he be unseen and unknown, but raises no doubt in our minds of the existence and agency of such an artist, at some former time, and in some place or other. Nor can I perceive that it varies at all the inference, whether the question arise concerning a human agent, or concerning an agent of a different species, or an agent possessing, in some respects, a different nature.

II. Neither, secondly, would it invalidate our conclusion, that the watch sometimes went wrong, or that it seldom went exactly right. The purpose of the machinery, the design, and the designer, might be evident, and in the case supposed would be evident, in whatever way we accounted for the irregularity of the movement, or whether we could account for it or not. It is not necessary that a machine be perfect, in order to show with what design it was made: still less necessary, where the only question is, whether it were made with any design at all.

III. Nor, thirdly, would it bring any uncertainty into the argument, if there were a few parts of the watch, concerning which we could not discover, or had not yet discovered, in what manner they conduced to the general effect; or even some parts, concerning which we could not ascertain, whether they conduced to that effect in any manner whatever. For, as to the first branch of the case; if by the loss, or disorder, or decay of the parts in question, the movement of the watch were found in fact to be stopped, or disturbed, or retarded, no doubt would remain in our minds as to the utility or intention of these parts, although we should be unable to investigate the manner according to which, or the connexion by which, the ultimate effect depended upon their action or assistance; and the more complex is the machine, the more likely is this obscurity to arise. Then, as to the second thing supposed, namely, that there were parts which might be spared, without prejudice to the movement of the watch, and that we had proved this by experiment, — these superfluous parts, even if we were completely assured that they were such, would not vacate the reasoning which we had instituted concerning other parts. The indication of contrivance remained, with respect to them, nearly as it was before.

IV. Nor, fourthly, would any man in his senses think the existence of the watch, with its various machinery, accounted for, by being told that it was one out of possible combinations of material forms; that whatever he had found in the place where he found the watch, must have contained some internal configuration or other; and that this configuration might be the structure now exhibited, viz. of the works of a watch, as well as a different structure.

V. Nor, fifthly, would it yield his inquiry more satisfaction to be answered, that there existed in things a principle of order, which had disposed the parts of the watch into their present form and situation. He never knew a watch made by the principle of order; nor can he even form to himself an idea of what is meant by a principle of order, distinct from the intelligence of the watch-maker.

VI. Sixthly, he would be surprised to hear that the mechanism of the watch was no proof of contrivance, only a motive to induce the mind to think so:

VII. And not less surprised to be informed, that the watch in his hand was nothing more than the result of the laws of *metallic* nature. It is a perversion of language to assign any law, as the efficient, operative cause of any thing. A law presupposes an agent; for it is only the mode, according to which an agent proceeds: it implies a power; for it is the order, according to which that power acts. Without this agent, without this power, which are both distinct from itself, the *law* does nothing; is nothing. The expression, "the law of metallic nature," may sound strange and harsh to a philosophic ear; but it seems quite as justifiable as some others which are more familiar to him, such as "the law of vegetable nature," "the law of animal nature," or indeed as "the law of nature" in general, when assigned as the cause of phenomena, in exclusion of agency and power; or when it is substituted into the place of these.

VIII. Neither, lastly, would our observer be driven out of his conclusion, or from his confidence in its truth, by being told that he knew nothing at all about the matter. He knows enough for his argument: he knows the utility of the end: he knows the subserviency and adaptation of the means to the end. These points being known, his ignorance of other points, his doubts concerning other points, affect not the certainty of his reasoning. The consciousness of knowing little, need not beget a distrust of that which he does know.

Kant offered a moral argument for the reality of God in *Groundwork of the Metaphysics of Morals* and *Religion Within the Limits of Reason Alone*. He claimed that every rational being knows *a priori* that God is real because that being has a conscience. In other words, since all rational beings know intuitively their moral duty (even though they might freely choose not to perform that duty, or even recognize it), there must be a source of that duty, and that source must be innate and universal. Kant saw God as the author of the ultimate moral law, the categorical imperative: "Act always so that you would will the maxim of your actions to be a universal law" or "Act always so that you treat persons as ends in themselves, never as means."

The "Principle of Sufficient Reason" (PSR) articulated by German philosopher and mathematician Gottfried Wilhelm Freiherr von Leibniz (1646-1716) can be seen as a version of the cosmological argument. PSR says that if anything exists, then it must have a sufficient reason why it exists. Applying the no-infinite-regress principle, God emerges as the ultimate sufficient reason for everything's existence.

There are many other arguments for the reality of God, most of them neither as strong nor as famous as the nine given above.

American process philosopher Charles Hartshorne (1897-2000) presented a sixfold "cumulative case" or "global argument" for the reality of God in his article, "Six Theistic Proofs" (*The Monist*, 54, 2 [April 1970]: 159-180). The six arguments are: (1) one of his eight formulations of the ontological argument, employing the modal logic of necessity and possibility; (2) his version of the cosmological argument; (3) his version of the design argument; (4) the epistemic argument, which claims that reality would be unintelligible without a divine knower; (5) his version of the moral argument, which is quite different from Kant's, claiming instead that God's goal is to promote the good life for God and creatures alike; and (6) the aesthetic argument, which claims that the world as a whole is beautiful, but would not be so without a God to enjoy it. Hartshorne believed that each of these six was *a priori*, but this claim is especially difficult to maintain, since each except the first and second refer to earthly conditions, and since, in Hartshorne's own estimation, they are intended to be persuasive, not deductive, for theism. Hartshorne expressed them in deductive form as multilateral exclusive disjunctions, but admitted that their conclusions were only probable, evidential, or inductive, strengthening but not establishing the idea of theism. The cumulative case is that whatever weak points exist in any particular argument are negated by corresponding strong points in one or more of the other five, so that the six together are stronger than the sum of their parts. Hartshorne's critics, on the other hand, would assert that six leaky buckets all nested within one another will still eventually fail to carry water, even if their holes do not coincide. Hartshorne's cumulative case does less to show the reality of God and more to promote his own theory of "neoclassical theism," which, in the last analysis, is a kind of panentheism.

Philosophical theism is accepting one or more of the proofs for the reality of God without accepting any of the doctrines of any particular religion. Philosophical theists believe in God but do not believe in organized religion. Hegel, Whitehead, Hartshorne, and many more reflective intellectuals are among this number. Philosophical theism is compatible with, but not the same as, secular humanism, since a secular humanist, i.e., one for whom the welfare of humanity is the top ethical priority, could just as well be an atheist, deist, or agnostic as a theist. Tolerance is the watchword.

3

How Can God Be Known?

We know from the theistic proofs "that-God-is" (God's being), but they tell us nothing of "what-God-is" (God's essence). If God is the "ground of being" or the Godhead beyond being, ontologically different from all finite beings, including rational animals (humans), then questions immediately arise of how finite beings can know the divine essence. Or can God's essence never be known, but only felt, experienced, posited, or believed? We know from the ontological argument that God's essence is simply to be, and from *Proslogium* XV that it is to be beyond being and beyond finite comprehension — but what does this mean?

Some claim that God is best known — or rather "felt" — as the ultimate irrational, arbitrary, or unfathomable will. The voluntarism of German philosopher Arthur Schopenhauer (1788-1860) articulates such a view. Allah is such a God. The counterclaim is that God is supremely rational, and best known as the epitome of reason. This is the intellectualism often associated with Dutch Jewish philosopher Baruch Spinoza (1632-1677), for whom emotions had little status in religion and whose ideal of serenity was the "intellectual love of God" (*amor intellectualis Dei*).

To ask, not so much what God is, but how knowing anything about God's essence is possible for finite beings in the first place, implies three basic categories of answers to that question: (1) The evidentialism of English mathematician and philosopher William Kingdon Clifford (1845-1879) holds that no conclusion may ever be justified without solid evidence. (2) On the opposite extreme, presuppositionalism, which has existed for thousands of years but was named and codified by American conservative theologian Cornelius Van Til (1895-1987), holds that God must be presupposed to be real before God's essence can be known and that the unspiritual, the degenerate, or the "unsaved" are incapable of knowing God, however smart and preceptive they may be. (3) Between these two are varying degrees of a moderate position, probabilism, which arose in the sixteenth century and holds that to accept religious doctrine is better than to reject it, as long as that doctrine is not improbable. Hence, if we believe in God, it is probable that God is as described in scripture, therefore we believe these sacred texts.

There are two general species of theology. Natural theology investigates God from the standpoint of the natural evidence of earthly life, reasoning backward, as it were, *a posteriori* from created phenomena to God, their creator. Revealed theology studies God from the standpoint of God's special revelations, such as the Bible, the Koran, the incarnation of Christ, the avatars of Vishnu, the Zen experience of *satori* (enlightenment), and Moses's vision of the burning bush. Natural theology might use theological doctrine as data, but its focus and method are philosophical. Conversely, revealed theology might use philosophical speculation as a tool, but its goal is the elucidation of theological doctrine. Revealed theology and natural theology may be seen — controversially — as one and the same thing if revelation is seen as part of the ordinary data of human experience and thus as part of the data of natural theology. In other words, if everything that happens or exists is a revelation of God, then there is no difference between revealed and natural theology. But if revelation is taken to be always exceptional, supernatural, miraculous, or a violation of the natural order, then there can be no identity of the two kinds of theology.

Pseudo-Dionysius the Areopagite (so called because he or she was not Paul's first-century companion, but an unidentified early sixth-century neo-Platonic philosopher from Asia Minor writing as Dionysius) invented a useful variant of natural theology that provides a method to learn precisely the limit of our possible knowledge of God's essence and attributes. In two books, *The Divine Names* and *The Mystical Theology*, Pseudo-Dionysius presented "negative theology," often known as the *via negativa* ("the negative way").

Negative or mystical theology begins by assigning superlative attributes to God or by giving names to God. This is the "cataphatic" or affirmative phase, an activity purely within the limit of reason. Subsequent meditation on each attribute or name shows that whatever is thinkable or pronounceable of God is inadequate to describe any aspect of God. Finite human reason simply is not capable of the task. The culminating "apophatic" or negative phase concludes that God is "superessential," beyond reason, and ineffable. God cannot be named or described, even with superlatives. Reason itself, stretched to its logical limit, reveals that reason is not able to understand God and that neither thought nor speech is able to express God's essence. Thus, at the end of this rational process, neo-Platonism finds that mysticism is the only next step that makes sense.

Mysticism is what proceeds beyond reason once rationalism has reached its limit. The trick is to become sure when precisely rationalism has reached its limit, because to invoke reason in the service of mystical awareness prior to reaching this limit is to indulge in fanciful, sterile, and intellectually counterproductive speculation, often involving the occult, astrology, fortune-telling, and so on. But true mysticism will have none of that. It is a reasonable endeavor, grounded in verifiable reality and coherent philosophical concepts.

Neo-Platonic logic naturally generates mysticism. Learning about God begins by learning what we finite beings cannot know about God. We discover God by discovering our ignorance, and discovering our ignorance is a purely rational process. As Socrates taught in Plato's *Apology*, only the wise know that they are ignorant, and many among the truly ignorant believe that they are wise.

Neo-Platonism is a rational/mystical way of thinking derived especially from one of Plato's later dialogues, the *Timaeus*. The focus of neo-Platonism, in many guises, is on the relation between the one and the many. It typically identifies the one with God, the good, perfect, infinite, and eternal; while identifying the many with the plethora of variegated, imperfect, finite things in this world. The many may either emanate from or be created by the one, but in either case the many are subordinate to and dependent on the one. In theistic neo-Platonism, the one creates the many so that they may choose freely to return to the one. For Augustine, as created beings move away from God, their condition is aversion (*aversio*: literally "turning away"), which is tantamount to sin; but as they choose to return to God, they experience conversion (*conversio*: literally "turning toward") and eventually redemption and salvation through God's grace. The farther they flee from God, the more cursed they are; but the closer they reverently return to God, the more blessed.

The first thinker to synthesize Plato's philosophy with religious doctrine was Philo Judaeus (ca. 20 B.C.E. - ca. 50), a Hellenistic Jewish theologian in Alexandria, Egypt, who is thus regarded as the founder of neo-Platonism. In his wake came pagan thinkers such as Hellenistic Roman philosopher Plotinus (ca. 204 - ca. 270) and Greek philosopher Proclus (ca. 410-485) and Christians such as Hellenistic Egyptians Clement of Alexandria (ca. 150 - ca. 215) and Origen (ca. 185 - ca. 252), Augustine, Pseudo-Dionysius, Irish mystic John Scotus Erigena (ca. 810 - ca. 877), Anselm, and Italian Franciscan theologian Bonaventura (1221?-1274).

Neo-Platonism is called a philosophical system or school, but it is really a method. Whatever philosophical criticism may be brought against it, it has stood the test of time and remains influential in Western thought at the beginning of the twenty-first century. All neo-Platonic reasoning is circular. Asking any question is a cause of investigation or analysis, and as such, eventually leads toward God. Using the language of *proödos* and *epistrophê*, Proposition 35 of Proclus's *Elements of Theology* asserts that every effect stays in its cause, proceeds from its cause, and returns to its cause.

The writings of Pseudo-Dionysius derive their categories and method directly from Proclus and apply them to monotheism. Negative theology is the main operative through most of the *Proslogium*, whose conclusion is Anselm's mystical, epistrophic, and newly deeper awareness of the utter unknowability of God. Anselm's neo-Platonic exploration of the divine attributes in the *Proslogium* is indispensable toward understanding the ontological argument the way he intended it to be understood, not as an abstract logical *tour de force* out of context, as many commentators have taken it, but as a step on the soul's road of return to God. Anselm's goal is to discover, insofar as humanly possible, what it means to be "greater than can be conceived." The philosophical questioning in the *Proslogium* mirrors the quest of the penitent but non-philosophical soul for divine forgiveness and blessing.

For John Scotus Erigena, knowledge in general and especially what the Germans call *Heilsgeschichte* ("salvation history"), the knowledge of God's universal plan, mirrors the entire dynamic scope of creation itself. In the first of the four universal divisions of nature, God, the superessential (not created but creating), creates the second division, the divine ideas (created and creating). These ideas, analogous to Platonic forms, Stoic seminal reasons, or even Jungian archetypes, create the third division, the finite world (created and not creating). This world, our everyday world, fundamentally sterile in itself, must discover its need to return to God for its very life and for any amelioration that it may reasonably hope to expect. At last, after many trials, it returns piecemeal to the fourth division, the superessential God (not created and not creating), who now no longer needs to create because creatures have voluntarily returned to God and thus have successfully completed God's original plan. The *proödos* is moving away from God metaphysically, epistemologically, spiritually, and ethically; and likewise, the *epistrophê* is returning to God and becoming whole in all these ways.

Similarly for Bonaventura, perceptible traces of God's influence on the world provide points of meditation that become rungs on the finite spirit's ladder to the absolute. Ultimately God's presence in the human mind is innate, but is discovered by these external "clues."

In his *Third Meditation*, "Of God: That He Exists," which follows in the 1911 translation of Elizabeth Haldane and G.R.T. Ross, French mathematician, scientist, and philosopher René Descartes (1596-1650) presents an argument that his detractors call the "Cartesian circle." If, as seems to be the case, he asserts that (1) he has an innate idea of God, (2) he knows this idea is true because God must have put it in his mind, (3) therefore God is real, then he would indeed be committing the informal logical fallacy known as circular reasoning, begging the question, or *petitio principii*. This is a genuine difficulty for those who wish to accept Descartes's argument. However, interpreting the circle as neo-Platonic, wherein a pre-reflective, inadequate concept of God proceeds through analysis and returns to itself to become an articulate, more nearly adequate concept of God, shows the circle as non-vicious and non-fallacious:

I shall now close my eyes, I shall stop my ears, I shall call away all my senses, I shall efface even from my thoughts all the images of corporeal things, or at least (for that is hardly possible) I shall esteem them as vain and false; and thus holding converse only with myself and considering my own nature, I shall try little by little to reach a better knowledge of and a more familiar acquaintanceship with myself. I am a thing that thinks, that is to say, that doubts, affirms, denies, that knows a few things, that is ignorant of many, that wills, that desires, that also imagines and perceives; for as I remarked before, although the things which I perceive and imagine are perhaps nothing at all apart from me and in themselves, I am nevertheless assured that these modes of thought that I call perceptions and imaginations, inasmuch only as they are modes of thought, certainly reside in me.

And in the little that I have just said, I think I have summed up all that I really know, or at least all that hitherto I was aware that I knew. In order to try to extend my knowledge further, I shall now look around more carefully and see whether I cannot still discover in myself some other things which I have not hitherto perceived. I am certain that I am a thing which thinks; but do I not then likewise know what is requisite to render me certain of a truth? Certainly in this first knowledge there is nothing that assures me of its truth, excepting the clear and distinct perception of that which I state, which would not indeed suffice to assure me that what I say is true, if it could ever happen that a thing which I conceived so clearly and distinctly could be false; and accordingly it seems to me that already I can establish as a general rule that all things which I perceive very clearly and very distinctly are true.

At the same time I have before received and admitted many things to be very certain and manifest, which yet I afterwards recognized as being dubious. What then were these things? They were the earth, sky, stars, and all other objects which I apprehended by means of the senses. But what did I clearly perceive in them? Nothing more than that the ideas or thoughts of these things were presented to my mind. And not even now do I deny that these ideas are met with in me. But there was yet another thing which I affirmed, and which, owing to the habit which I had formed of believing it, I thought I perceived very clearly, although in truth I did not perceive it at all, to wit, that there were objects outside of me from which these ideas proceeded, and to which they were entirely similar. And it was in this that I erred, or, if perchance my judgment was correct, this was not due to any knowledge arising from my perception.

But when I took anything very simple and easy in the sphere of arithmetic or geometry into consideration, e.g. that two and three together made five, and other things of the sort, were not these present to my mind so clearly as to enable me to affirm that they were true? Certainly if I judged that since such matters could be doubted, this would not have been so for any other reason than that it came into my mind that perhaps a God might have endowed me with such a nature that I may have been deceived even concerning things which seemed to me most manifest. But every time that this preconceived opinion of the sovereign power of a God presents itself to my thought, I am constrained to confess that it is easy to Him, if He wishes it, to cause me to err, even in matters in which I believe myself to have the best evidence. And, on the other hand, always when I direct my attention to things which I believe myself to perceive very clearly, I am so persuaded of their truth that I let myself break out into words such as these: Let who will deceive me, He can never cause me to be nothing while I think that I am, or some day cause it to be true to say that I have never been, it being true now to say that I am, or that two and three make more or less than five, or any such thing in which I see a manifest contradiction. And, certainly, since I have no reason to believe that there is a God who is a deceiver, and as I have not yet satisfied myself that there is a God at all, the reason for doubt which depends on this opinion alone is very slight, and so to speak metaphysical. But in order to be able altogether to remove it, I must inquire whether there is a God as soon as the occasion presents itself; and if I find that there is a God, I must also inquire whether He may be a deceiver; for without a knowledge of these two truths I do not see that I can ever be certain of anything.

And in order that I may have an opportunity of inquiring into this in an orderly way, it is requisite that I should here divide my thoughts into certain kinds, and that I should consider in which of these kinds there is, properly speaking, truth or error to be found. Of my thoughts some are, so to speak, images of the things, and to these alone is the title "idea" properly applied; examples are my thought of a man or of a chimera, of heaven, of an angel, or of God. But other thoughts possess other forms as well. For example, in willing, fearing, approving, denying, though I always perceive something as the subject of the action of my mind, yet by this action I always add something else to the idea which I have of that thing; and of the thoughts of this kind some are called volitions or affections, and others judgments.

Now as to what concerns ideas, if we consider them only in themselves and do not relate them to anything else beyond themselves, they cannot properly speaking be false; for whether I imagine a goat or a chimera, it is not less true that I imagine the one that the other. We must not fear likewise that falsity can enter into will and into affections, for although I may desire evil things, or even things that never existed, it is not the less true that I desire them. Thus there remains no more than the judgments which we make, in which I must take the greatest care not to deceive myself. But the principal error and the commonest which we may meet with in them, consists in my judging that the ideas which are in me are similar or conformable to the things which are outside me; for without doubt if I considered the ideas only as certain modes of my thoughts, without trying to relate them to anything beyond, they could scarcely give me material for error.

But among these ideas, some appear to me to be innate, some adventitious, and others to be formed by myself; for, as I have the power of understanding what is called a thing, or a truth, or a thought, it appears to me that I hold this power from no other source than my own nature. But if I now hear some sound, if I see the sun, or feel heat, I have hitherto judged that these sensations proceeded from certain things that exist outside of me; and finally it appears to me that sirens, hippogryphs, and the like, are formed out of my own mind. But again I may possibly persuade myself that all these ideas are of the nature of those which I term adventitious, or else that they are all innate, or all fictitious: for I have not yet clearly discovered their true origin.

And my principal task in this place is to consider, in respect to those ideas which appear to me to proceed from certain objects that are outside me, what are the reasons which cause me to think them similar to these objects. It seems indeed in the first place that I am taught this lesson by nature; and, secondly, I experience in myself that these ideas do not depend on my will nor therefore on myself — for they often present themselves to my mind in spite of my will. Just now, for instance, whether I will or whether I do not will, I feel heat, and thus I persuade myself that this feeling, or at least this idea of heat, is produced in me by something which is different from me, i.e. by the heat of the fire near which I sit. And nothing seems to me more obvious than to judge that this object imprints its likeness rather than anything else upon me.

Now I must discover whether these proofs are sufficiently strong and convincing. When I say that I am so instructed by nature, I merely mean a certain spontaneous inclination which impels me to believe in this connection, and not a natural light which makes me recognize that it is true. But these two things are very different; for I cannot doubt that which the natural light causes me to believe to be true, as, for example, it has shown me that I am from the fact that I doubt, or other facts of the same kind. And I possess no other faculty whereby to distinguish truth from falsehood, which can teach me that what this light shows me to be true is not really true, and no other faculty that is equally trustworthy. But as far as natural impulses are concerned, I have frequently remarked, when I had to make active choice between virtue and vice, that they often enough led me to the part that was worse; and this is why I do not see any reason for following them in what regards truth and error.

And as to the other reason, which is that these ideas must proceed from objects outside me, since they do not depend on my will, I do not find it any the more convincing. For just as these impulses of which I have spoken are found in me, notwithstanding that they do not always concur with my will, so perhaps there is in me some faculty fitted to produce these ideas without the assistance of any external things, even though it is not yet known by me; just as, apparently, they have hitherto always been found in me during sleep without the aid of any external objects.

And finally, though they did proceed from objects different from myself, it is not a necessary consequence that they should resemble these. On the contrary, I have noticed that in many cases there was a great difference between the object and its idea. I find, for example, two completely diverse ideas of the sun in my mind; the one derives its origin from the senses, and should be placed in the category of adventitious ideas; according to this idea the sun seems to be extremely small; but the other is derived from astronomical reasonings, i.e. is elicited from certain notions that are innate in me, or else it is formed by me in some other manner; in accordance with it the sun appears to be several times greater than the earth. These two ideas cannot, indeed, both resemble the same sun, and reason makes me believe that the one which seems to have originated directly from the sun itself, is the one which is most dissimilar to it.

All this causes me to believe that until the present time it has not been by a judgment that was certain, but only by a sort of blind impulse that I believed that things existed outside of, and different from me, which, by the organs of my senses, or by some other method whatever it might be, conveyed these ideas or images to me.

But there is yet another method of inquiring whether any of the objects of which I have ideas within me exist outside of me. If ideas are only taken as certain modes of thought, I recognize among them no difference or inequality, and all appear to proceed from me in the same manner; but when we consider them as images, one representing one thing and the other another, it is clear that they are very different one from the other. There is no doubt that those which represent to me substances are something more, and contain so to speak more objective reality within them than those that simply represent modes or accidents; and that idea again by which I understand a supreme God, eternal, infinite, omniscient, omnipotent, and Creator of all things which are outside of Himself, has certainly more objective reality in itself than those ideas by which finite substances are represented.

Now it is manifest by the natural light that there must at least be as much reality in the efficient and total cause as in its effect. For, pray, from where can the effect derive its reality, if not from its cause? And in what way can this cause communicate this reality to it, unless it possessed it in itself? And from this it follows, not only that something cannot proceed from nothing, but likewise that what is more perfect — that is to say, which has more reality within itself — cannot proceed from the less perfect. And this is not only evidently true of those effects which possess actual or formal reality, but also of the ideas in which we consider merely what is termed objective reality. To take an example, the stone which has not yet existed not only cannot now commence to be unless it has been produced by something which possesses within itself, either formally or eminently, all that enters into the composition of the stone, and heat can only be produced in a subject in which it did not previously exist by a cause that is of an order at least as perfect as heat, and so in all other cases. But further, the idea of heat, or of a stone, cannot exist in me unless it has been placed within me by some cause which possesses within it at least as much reality as that which I conceive to exist in the heat or the stone. For although this cause does not transmit anything of its actual or formal reality to my idea, we must not for that reason imagine that it is necessarily a less real cause; we must remember that its nature is such that it demands of itself no other formal reality than that which it borrows from my thought, of which it is only a mode. But in order that an idea should contain some one certain objective reality rather than another, it must without doubt derive it from some cause in which there is at least as much formal reality as this idea contains of objective reality. For if we imagine that something is found in an idea which is not found in the cause, it must then have been derived from nothing; but however imperfect may be this mode of being by which a thing is objectively in the understanding by its idea, we cannot certainly say that this mode of being is nothing, nor consequently, that the idea derives its origin from nothing.

Nor must I imagine that, since the reality that I consider in these ideas is only objective, it is not essential that this reality should be formally in the causes of my ideas, but that it is sufficient that it should be found objectively. For just as this mode of objective existence pertains to ideas by their proper nature, so does the mode of formal existence pertain to the causes of those ideas (this is at least true of the first and principal) by the nature peculiar to them. And although it may be the case that one idea gives birth to another idea, that cannot continue to be so indefinitely; for in the end we must reach an idea whose cause shall be so to speak an archetype, in which the whole reality, which is so to speak objectively in these ideas, is contained formally. Thus the light of nature causes me to know clearly that the ideas in me are like images which can, in truth, easily fall short of the perfection of the objects from which they have been derived, but which can never contain anything greater or more perfect.

And the longer and the more carefully that I investigate these matters, the more clearly and distinctly do I recognize their truth. But what am I to conclude from it all in the end? It is this, that if the objective reality of any one of my ideas is of such a nature as clearly to make me recognize that it is not in me either formally or eminently, and that consequently I cannot myself be the cause of it, it follows of necessity that I am not alone in the world, but that there is another being which exists, or which is the cause of this idea. On the other hand, had no such an idea existed in me, I should have had no sufficient argument to convince me of the existence of any being beyond myself; for I have made very careful investigation everywhere and up to the present time have been able to find no other ground.

But of my ideas, beyond that which represents me to myself, as to which there can here be no difficulty, there is another which represents a God, and there are others representing corporeal and inanimate things, others angels, others animals, and others again which represent to me men similar to myself.

As regards the ideas which represent to me other men or animals, or angels, I can however easily conceive that they might be formed by an admixture of the other ideas which I have of myself, of corporeal things, and of God, even although there were apart from me neither men nor animals, nor angels, in all the world.

And in regard to the ideas of corporeal objects, I do not recognize in them anything so great or so excellent that they might not have possibly proceeded from myself; for if I consider them more closely, and examine them individually, as I yesterday examined the idea of wax, I find that there is very little in them which I perceive clearly and distinctly. Magnitude or extension in length, breadth, or depth, I do so perceive; also figure which results from a termination of this extension, the situation which bodies of different figure preserve in relation to one another, and movement or change of situation; to which we may also add substance, duration, and number. As to other things such as light, colors, sounds, scents, tastes, heat, cold, and the other tactile qualities, they are thought by me with so much obscurity and confusion that I do not even know if they are true or false, i.e. whether the ideas which I form of these qualities are actually the ideas of real objects or not. For although I have before remarked that it is only in judgments that falsity, properly speaking, or formal falsity, can be met with, a certain material falsity may nevertheless be found in ideas, i.e. when these ideas represent what is nothing as though it were something. For example, the ideas which I have of cold and heat are so far from clear and distinct that by their means I cannot tell whether cold is merely a privation of heat, or heat a privation of cold, or whether both are real qualities, or are not such. And inasmuch as there cannot be any ideas which do not appear to represent some things, if it is correct to say that cold is merely a privation of heat, the idea which represents it to me as something real and positive will not be improperly termed false, and the same holds good of other similar ideas.

To these it is certainly not necessary that I should attribute any author other than myself. For if they are false, i.e. if they represent things which do not exist, the light of nature shows me that they issue from nothing, that is to say, that they are only in me so far as something is lacking to the perfection of my nature. But if they are true, nevertheless because they exhibit so little reality to me that I cannot even clearly distinguish the thing represented from non-being, I do not see any reason why they should not be produced by myself.

As to the clear and distinct idea which I have of corporeal things, some of them seem as though I might have derived them from the idea which I possess of myself, as those which I have of substance, duration, number, and such like. For when I think that a stone is a substance, or at least a thing capable of existing of itself, and that I am a substance also, although I conceive that I am a thing that thinks and not one that is extended, and that the stone on the other hand is an extended thing which does not think, and that thus there is a notable difference between the two conceptions — they seem, nevertheless, to agree in this, that both represent substances. In the same way, when I perceive that I now exist and further recollect that I have in former times existed, and when I remember that I have various thoughts of which I can recognize the number, I acquire ideas of duration and number which I can afterwards transfer to any object that I please. But as to all the other qualities of which the ideas of corporeal things are composed, to wit, extension, figure, situation, and motion, it is true that they are not formally in me, since I am only a thing that thinks; but because they are merely certain modes of substance and because I myself am also a substance, it would seem that they might be contained in me eminently.

Hence there remains only the idea of God, concerning which we must consider whether it is something which cannot have proceeded from me myself. By the name God I understand a substance that is infinite, independent, all-knowing, all-powerful, and by which I myself and everything else, if anything else does exist, have been created. Now all these characteristics are such that the more diligently I attend to them, the less do they appear capable of proceeding from me alone; hence, from what has been already said, we must conclude that God necessarily exists.

For although the idea of substance is within me owing to the fact that I am substance, nevertheless I should not have the idea of an infinite substance — since I am finite — if it had not proceeded from some substance which was veritably infinite.

Nor should I imagine that I do not perceive the infinite by a true idea, but only by the negation of the finite, just as I perceive repose and darkness by the negation of movement and of light; for, on the contrary, I see that there is manifestly more reality in infinite substance than in finite, and therefore that in some way I have in me the notion of the infinite earlier then the finite — to wit, the notion of God before that of myself. For how would it be possible that I should know that I doubt and desire, that is to say, that something is lacking to me, and that I am not quite perfect, unless I had within me some idea of a Being more perfect than myself, in comparison with which I should recognize the deficiencies of my nature?

And we cannot say that this idea of God is perhaps materially false and that consequently I can derive it from nothing, as I have just said is the case with ideas of heat, cold, and other such things; for, on the contrary, as this idea is very clear and distinct and contains within it more objective reality than any other, there can be none which is of itself more true, nor any in which there can be less suspicion of falsehood. The idea, I say, of this Being who is absolutely perfect and infinite, is entirely true; for although, perhaps, we can imagine that such a Being does not exist, we cannot nevertheless imagine that His idea represents nothing real to me, as I have said of the idea of cold. This idea is also very clear and distinct; since all that I conceive clearly and distinctly of the real and the true, and of what conveys some perfection, is in its entirety contained in this idea. And this does not cease to be true although I do not comprehend the infinite, or though in God there is an infinitude of things which I cannot comprehend, nor possibly even reach in any way by thought; for it is of the nature of the infinite that my nature, which is finite and limited, should not comprehend it; and it is sufficient that I should understand this, and that I should judge that all things which I clearly perceive and in which I know that there is some perfection, and possibly likewise an infinitude of properties of which I am ignorant, are in God formally or eminently, so that the idea which I have of Him may become the most true, most clear, and most distinct of all the ideas that are in my mind.

But possibly I am something more than I suppose myself to be, and perhaps all those perfections which I attribute to God are in some way potentially in me, although they do not yet disclose themselves, or issue in action. As a matter of fact I am already sensible that my knowledge increases little by little, and I see nothing which can prevent it from increasing more and more into infinitude; nor do I see, after it has thus been increased, anything to prevent my being able to acquire by its means all the other perfections of the Divine nature; nor finally why the power I have of acquiring these perfections, if it really exists in me, shall not suffice to produce the ideas of them.

At the same time I recognize that this cannot be. For, in the first place, although it were true that every day my knowledge acquired new degrees of perfection, and that there were in my nature many things potentially which are not yet there actually, nevertheless these excellences do not pertain to the idea which I have of God in whom there is nothing merely potential; for it is an infallible token of imperfection in my knowledge that it increases little by little. and further, although my knowledge grows more and more, nevertheless I do not for that reason believe that it can ever be actually infinite, since it can never reach a point so high that it will be unable to attain to any greater increase. But I understand God to be actually infinite, so that He can add nothing to His supreme perfection. And finally I perceive that the objective being of an idea cannot be produced by a being that exists potentially only, which properly speaking is nothing, but only by a being which is formal or actual.

To speak the truth, I see nothing in all that I have just said which by the light of nature is not manifest to anyone who desires to think attentively on the subject; but when I slightly relax my attention, my mind, finding its vision somewhat obscured and so to speak blinded by the images of sensible objects, I do not easily recollect the reason why the idea that I possess of a being more perfect than I, must necessarily have been placed in me by a being which is really more perfect; and this is why I wish here to go on to inquire whether I, who have this idea, can exist if no such being exists.

And I ask, from whom do I then derive my existence? Perhaps from myself or from my parents, or from some other source less perfect than God; for we can imagine nothing more perfect than God, or even as perfect as He is.

But were I myself the author of my being, I should doubt nothing and I should desire nothing, and finally no perfection would be lacking to me; for I should have bestowed on myself every perfection of which I possessed any idea and should thus be God. And it must not be imagined that those things that are lacking to me are perhaps more difficult of attainment than those which I already possess; for, on the contrary, it is quite evident that it was a matter of much greater difficulty to bring to pass that I, that is to say, a thing or a substance that thinks, should emerge out of nothing, than it would be to attain to the knowledge of many things of which I am ignorant, and which are only the accidents of this thinking substance. But it is clear that if I had of myself possessed this greater perfection of which I have just spoken, I should not at least have denied myself the things which are the more easy to acquire; nor should I have deprived myself of any of the things contained in the idea which I form of God, because there are none of them which seem to me specially difficult to acquire: and if there were any that were more difficult to acquire, they would certainly appear to me to be such (supposing I myself were the origin of the other things which I possess) since I should discover in them that my powers were limited.

But though I assume that perhaps I have always existed just as I am at present, neither can I escape the force of this reasoning, and imagine that the conclusion to be drawn from this is, that I need not seek for any author of my existence. For all the course of my life may be divided into an infinite number of parts, none of which is in any way dependent on the other; and thus from the fact that I was in existence a short time ago it does not follow that I must be in existence now, unless some cause at this instant, so to speak, produces me anew, that is to say, conserves me. It is as a matter of fact perfectly clear and evident to all those who consider with attention the nature of time, that, in order to be conserved in each moment in which it endures, a substance has need of the same power and action as would be necessary to produce and create it anew, supposing it did not yet exist, so that the light of nature shows us clearly that the distinction between creation and conservation is solely a distinction of the reason.

All that I thus require here is that I should interrogate myself, if I wish to know whether I possess a power which is capable of bringing it to pass that I who now am shall still be in the future; for since I am nothing but a thinking thing, or at least since thus far it is only this portion of myself which is precisely in question at present, if such a power did reside in me, I should certainly be conscious of it. But I am conscious of nothing of the kind, and by this I know clearly that I depend on some being different from myself.

Possibly, however, this being on which I depend is not that which I call God, and I am created either by my parents or by some other cause less perfect than God. This cannot be, because, as I have just said, it is perfectly evident that there must be at least as much reality in the cause as in the effect; and thus since I am a thinking thing, and possess an idea of God within me, whatever in the end be the cause assigned to my existence, it must be allowed that it is likewise a thinking thing and that it possesses in itself the idea of all the perfections which I attribute to God. We may again inquire whether this cause derives its origin from itself or from some other thing. For if from itself, it follows by the reasons before brought forward, that this cause must itself be God; for since it possesses the virtue of self-existence, it must also without doubt have the power of actually possessing all the perfections of which it has the idea, that is, all those which I conceive as existing in God. But if it derives its existence from some other cause than itself, we shall again ask, for the same reason, whether this second cause exists by itself or through another, until from one step to another, we finally arrive at an ultimate cause, which will be God.

And it is perfectly manifest that in this there can be no regression into infinity, since what is in question is not so much the cause which formerly created me, as that which conserves me at the present time.

Nor can we suppose that several causes may have concurred in my production, and that from one I have received the idea of one of the perfections which I attribute to God, and from another the idea of some other, so that all these perfections indeed exist somewhere in the universe, but not as complete in one unity which is God. On the contrary, the unity, the simplicity or the inseparability of all things which are in God is one of the principal perfections which I conceive to be in Him. And certainly the idea of this unity of all Divine perfections cannot have been placed in me by any cause from which I have not likewise received the ideas of all the other perfections; for this cause could not make me able to comprehend them as joined together in an inseparable unity without having at the same time caused me in some measure to know what they are.

Finally, so far as my parents are concerned, although all that I have ever been able to believe of them were true, that does not make it follow that it is they who conserve me, nor are they even the authors of my being in any sense, in so far as I am a thinking being; since what they did was merely to implant certain dispositions in that matter in which the self — i.e. the mind, which alone I at present identify with myself — is by me deemed to exist. And thus there can be no difficulty in their regard, but we must of necessity conclude from the fact alone that I exist, or that the idea of a Being supremely perfect — that is of God — is in me, that the proof of God's existence is grounded on the highest evidence.

It only remains to me to examine into the manner in which I have acquired this idea from God; for I have not received it through the senses, and it is never presented to me unexpectedly, as is usual with the ideas of sensible things when these things present themselves, or seem to present themselves, to the external organs of my senses; nor is it likewise a fiction of my mind, for it is not in my power to take from or to add anything to it; and consequently the only alternative is that it is innate in me, just as the idea of myself is innate in me.

And one certainly ought not to find it strange that God, in creating me, placed this idea within me to be like the mark of the workman imprinted on his work; and it is likewise not essential that the mark shall be something different from the work itself. For from the sole fact that God created me it is most probable that in some way he has placed his image and similitude upon me, and that I perceive this similitude (in which the idea of God is contained) by means of the same faculty by which I perceive myself — that is to say, when I reflect on myself I not only know that I am something, incomplete and dependent on another, which incessantly aspires after something which is better and greater than myself, but I also know that He on whom I depend possesses in Himself all the great things toward which I aspire, and that not indefinitely or potentially alone, but really, actually and infinitely; and that thus He is God. And the whole strength of the argument which I have here made use of to prove the existence of God consists in this, that I recognize that it is not possible that my nature should be what it is, and indeed that I should have in myself the idea of a God, if God did not veritably exist — a God, I say, whose idea is in me, i.e. who possesses all those supreme perfections of which our mind may indeed have some idea but without understanding them all, who is liable to no errors or defect. From this it is manifest that He cannot be a deceiver, since the light of nature teaches us that fraud and deception necessarily proceed from some defect.

But before I examine this matter with more care, and pass on to the consideration of other truths which may be derived from it, it seems to me right to pause for a while in order to contemplate God Himself, to ponder at leisure His marvellous attributes, to consider, and admire, and adore, the beauty of this light so resplendent, at least as far as the strength of my mind, which is in some measure dazzled by the sight, will allow me to do so. For just as faith teaches us that the supreme felicity of the other life consists only in this contemplation of the Divine Majesty, so we continue to learn by experience that a similar meditation, though incomparably less perfect, causes us to enjoy the greatest satisfaction of which we are capable in this life.

Using the method of hypothetical doubt in the first two *Meditations* to discover a firm foundation for all metaphysics, Descartes reaches the point where the only fact of which he can be certain is that he himself exists as a thinking thing (*res cogitans*). At this point he cannot be certain of the existence of his body, the world, logic, or God. He is conscious only of his own thoughts and does not know whether they correspond to any external world or eternal realities. Yet among his thoughts is an idea of God. He does not know whether this idea is true or false until, applying a version of the ontological argument and the principle of denying the possibility of infinite regress, he determines that, if he exists as *res cogitans*, then his existence must be caused by God and that God would not deceive him about the existence of his body, the world, or logic. He knows that he exists, deduces from his own imperfections that he himself is not God, and therefore knows that there is a God. Moreover, he understands God's essence as the ground of *res cogitans*. To understand in depth the meaning of the superlative attributes of God is to understand that God is real. To accept the ontological argument is inseparable from awareness of the "beyond-superlative" attributes of God, and thus, as for Anselm, is Descartes's key to unlocking the secrets of God's essence.

4

Faith and Reason or Faith vs. Reason?

Any relationship between faith and reason can be categorized in a continuum of only four possibilities: Either (1) reason is primary and excludes faith, (2) reason is primary and includes faith, (3) faith is primary and includes reason, or (4) faith is primary and excludes reason. This fourfold division, since it was presented by John A. Hutchison on pages 93-104 of *Faith, Reason, and Existence* (1956) and modified in the early 1970s by Professor of Religion William D. Geoghegan for his undergraduate classes at Bowdoin College, can be called the "Hutchison-Geoghegan schema."

1. Those who maintain the primacy of reason to the exclusion of faith are not willing to accept either the phenomena or the content of faith as the proper basis of critical activity, philosophical investigation, or life in general. Adherents of this point of view are skeptical with regard to the propositions and articles of religion, believe that nothing but analytical reason is qualified to answer questions about the existence and nature of God, and claim to be able to pronounce the final judgment of this analytical reason on these questions.

Among these possible judgments are: (a) reason decides that God is not real, which is the atheism of Marx, English logician and philosopher Bertrand Russell (1872-1970), and German-American logician and philosopher Rudolf Carnap (1891-1970); (b) reason decides that God is real, and that the nature of God may be described, which is the geometrical system of Spinoza; (c) reason decides that belief without adequate reason is immoral, which is the evidentialism of Clifford; (d) reason decides that even it itself is not capable of deciding whether God is real or not, which is the comprehensive and constructive skepticism of Scottish empiricist philosopher David Hume (1711-1776); and (e) reason decides nothing, but inflicts devastating, unsystematic criticism on faith and religion, which is the radical and destructive skepticism of French gadfly François-Marie Arouet de Voltaire (1694-1778).

2. Those who hold that reason is primary and includes faith recognize the phenomena and content of faith as important enough — if not of paramount importance — to warrant reason's serious consideration. Such thinkers, even though they may adhere to the doctrines of certain religions, do not do so because they have been taught to believe catechisms or because they believe in order to understand, but rather because they have been able to satisfy themselves in their own reflections that these doctrines are reasonable, and thus true. Among them are the great philosophical monotheists who have been inspired by Plato and Aristotle, such as Pseudo-Dionysius, John Scotus Erigena, Descartes, Leibniz, Whitehead, and Hegel, as well as pagan neo-Platonist thinkers such as Plotinus and Proclus.

For some in this category, and Plotinus and Hegel would be excellent examples, the faith which reason includes is not faith in God or in special revelation, but faith in reason itself. Reason reveals that reason comes from God, and this leads, not to faith in God, but to a rational recognition of the metaphysical and ethical differences between the one and the many, and to a gradual or dialectical ascent of the finite spirit to the absolute. At the end of this spiritual journey, finite spirit knows the absolute (the one), though not in all its particulars (the many).

3. Faith primary and including reason typifies most philosophical theology, both natural and revealed. Prominent Christian theologians such as Bonaventura, Thomas Aquinas, Schleiermacher, and Tillich, who naturally maintain the primacy of faith, still recognize that they have a valuable ally, reason. These theologians will not follow either reason or faith blindly as far as it may lead them, but use reason in order to explain the mysteries of faith and to try to deepen the faith which is already present. Further, although these thinkers respect reason, they are still careful to reject or temper its conclusions whenever it either contradicts or falls short of divine revelation. Augustine and Anselm are paragons of the attitude expressed in the maxims of the latter, *credo ut intelligam* and *fides quaerens intellectum*. Also in this category would be the theory of the self-verifying belief developed by American philosopher and psychologist William James (1842-1910). Such belief arises as the result of one's exercise of the will (or right) to believe and will not happen otherwise.

For Augustine, to use reason investigate God is not sacrilegious, but rather, when pursued in the right spirit, the most sincere expression of reverence for God, the best way for a finite being to do justice to God. It is just an expansion and a reaffirmation of Augustine's definition of belief in *De praedestinatione sanctorum*, II, 5, as "thinking with assent." Even in the context of divine grace, he does not say *credere est cum assensione doceri*, i.e., "to believe is to be taught with assent," which would be the case if faith excluded reason, but rather *credere ... est ... cum assensione cogitare*, i.e., "to believe is to think with assent," which is only possible if faith includes reason. By refusing to separate the act of believing from the act of critical thinking, Augustine clearly intends that the approach of the individual to God be both self-directed and purposeful.

4. Faith primary and excluding reason characterizes not only the theocratic stances of French-Swiss Protestant reformer John Calvin (1509-1564), Iranian revolutionary Ayatollah Ruhollah Khomeini (1902-1989), *et al.*, but also the very diverse positions of Carthaginian Christian theologian Tertullian (ca. 160 - ca. 230), Persian Sufi mystic and Islamic theologian Abu Hamid Ibn Muhammad Ibn Muhammad al-Tusi al-Shafi'i al-Ghazali (1058-1111), German Protestant reformer Martin Luther (1483-1546), French mathematician and devout Roman Catholic philosopher Blaise Pascal (1623-1662), Danish philosopher and theologian Søren Kierkegaard (1813-1855), and Swiss neo-orthodox Christian theologian Karl Barth (1886-1968), all of which either deny reason completely or severely restrict its domain.

Among the most extreme forms of faith excluding reason are the fideistic intolerances of Tertullian and al-Ghazali. Tertullian believed in Christian revelation, not in spite of its absurdity, but *because* of its absurdity. He wrote in *De carne Christi*, V, 4, that the death of God's son is believable because it is absurd (*credibile est, quia ineptum est*) and that the resurrection is certain because it is impossible (*certum est, quia impossibile*). His words are often misquoted as *credo quia absurdum est* ("I believe because it is absurd"), but even the misquote accurately conveys his position. In *The Incoherence of the Philosophers*, al-Ghazali attacked all philosophical speculation as being outside the context of the Koran and thus not needed by Muslims for salvation. As the result of his single-handed effort, Islamic philosophy, which had flourished until his time, effectively ceased from then on.

Less militant examples of this standpoint are Luther's theology of justification by faith, Kierkegaard's philosophy of paradox, and Barth's neo-orthodoxy. Also involved is the opinion that while reason can indeed tell us much, it cannot tell us everything, cannot tell us the most important things, and tells us different things from what the heart tells us. Therefore, as in Pascal's *Pensées*, reason and its fruits are superseded by faith, miracles, the love of God, instinct, and "the heart's reasons, which reason does not know."

This fourfold schema is a continuum, not four rigid pigeon-holes. The borders between these categories are gray and porous, yet exhaustive. Differences among human attitudes toward the relationship between faith and reason tend to resemble differences of degree more than differences of type.

The middle two categories are really just the two sides of the same coin, insofar as they each recognize and mediate the interrelational validity of faith and reason. The first and fourth are genuine extremes, one-sided in the Hegelian sense, which means that they each fail to appreciate what is necessary to achieve any harmony, collaboration, or reconciliation between faith and reason. Thus the fourfold schema can be reduced to three: (1) reason working alone, (2) reason and faith working together, and (3) faith working alone.

In the threefold schema, only the middle is at all judicious or mediated. Most philosophical positions are somewhere between the one-sided extremes, though not always consistent or systematic harmonies of reason and faith. They typically show some degree of oscillation between these limits. In cases of such oscillation, the definitive guide could be common sense, the perhaps naive assumption that things really are as they seem to be and ought to be treated as such. To stray from common sense toward isolated reason is to deny our human character, and to stray from common sense toward isolated faith is to become gullible. Neither is acceptable. The paradox of employing common sense as the mediator of faith and reason is that our trust in common sense is *itself* an act of faith, but not an act of faith unsupported by reason.

Understanding any "-ism" is made easier by placing it within the fourfold schema. Pietism can either exclude or include reason. Secularism always excludes faith, but humanism can either exclude or include it. Not all humanism is secular, but it always includes reason.

Subjectivism involves the assertions that personal existence is the primary metaphysical category, personal perception is the ground of epistemology, emotions are essential to moral agency, and the feeling or experience of the individual is the final criterion of morals and religion. Ethically, subjectivism is almost solipsistic.

It is not the same as individualism, the rational justification of the ultimate worth and independence of the individual, not to the exclusion of other individuals. One may be a subjectivist and still feel dependent. Subjectivism, especially of the Kierkegaardian sort, always excludes reason because the subjective standpoint is grounded in feeling, which is incapable of sharing reliably or permanently any attitude of reason. Reason has the power to unite the human spirit, since its truths are equally accessible to all, even though not acknowledged by all. Feeling, on the other hand, has no such power, since its truths are essentially private, internal to a particular individual, and not in principle sharable with anyone else, except in ways distorted through language, gesture, or other means of communication.

We must either permit reason to sit in judgment of religion or refuse to permit it. If we refuse to grant reason this privilege, then we commit to any of a huge range of positions, all the way from the fundamentalism which decrees that questioning the scriptures is blasphemous because it presumes to set human reason above divine revelation, to various other types of fideism, to Schleiermacherian liberalism and its successors, and even to certain species of pantheism and atheism. On the other hand, if we allow reason to judge the content of religion, then we commit to either one of only two positions, which can be effectively presented in the paradigms of Hume and Hegel. That is, reason judging religion must either be skeptical (Hume), unwilling to accept revelations which do not accord with the usual evidence of the senses, or synthetic (Hegel), seeking under the aegis of the most overarching order of reason to bring seemingly discordant or even nonsensical revelations into harmony with rational human expectations, and even to deny the ineffability of God.

Addressing the interaction between faith and reason, Hegel wrote a provocative Foreword[1] to *Religion in its Internal Relation to Systematic Knowledge* (1822), the first book of his student, Hermann Friedrich Wilhelm Hinrichs (1794-1861):

1. The opposition of faith and reason, which for centuries has occupied the interest of not only the academy, but also the world, may seem to have lost its

---

[1] Translation adapted from *Hegel, Hinrichs, and Schleiermacher on Feeling and Reason in Religion: The Texts of Their 1821-22 Debate*, edited, translated, and with introductions by Eric von der Luft (Lewiston, New York: Edwin Mellen, 1987), pp. 245-268. The paragraph numbering and all bracketed notes and footnotes are the translator's, not Hegel's.

importance in our time, indeed almost to have disappeared. If in fact this were so, then perhaps on this account our time should only be congratulated. For that opposition is of such a nature that the human spirit can turn away from neither of its two aspects; each shows itself rather to be rooted in spirit's innermost self-consciousness, so that, if they are conceived to be in conflict, the stability of spirit is shaken and its condition is one of the most unfortunate bifurcation. However, had the conflict of faith and reason disappeared and been changed over into a reconciliation, then it would be essentially dependent on the nature of this reconciliation itself to what degree it should be congratulated.

2. For there is also a frivolous, barren, peace, indifferent to the depths of the spirit; in such a peace the annoying problem can appear removed, while it is only set aside. However, that which is only overlooked or looked down upon is not thereby overcome. On the contrary, if the deepest genuine needs were not satisfied in the reconciliation, if the sanctuary of the spirit were not to obtain its right, then the bifurcation in itself would remain, and the enmity would fester all the more deeply within; the harm, itself not acknowledged and not cognized, would only be all the more dangerous.

3. An unsatisfying peace can arise if faith has become contentless, and if nothing is left of it but the empty shell of subjective conviction — and, on the other side, reason has renounced the cognition of truth, and has left to spirit only an issue, partly of appearances, partly of feelings. How then could there be a great discord between faith and reason, if neither has objective content any longer, so that there is present no object of dispute?

4. By faith, of course, I do not understand either the merely subjective state of being convinced, which is limited to the form of certainty, and still leaves undetermined whether it has content, and if so, what content it has — or, on the other hand, only the creed, the church's confession of faith, which is set down in words and in writing, and can be admitted orally, in mental imagery, and in memory, without penetrating the inner man, without having identified itself with the certainty which a man has of himself, or with human self-consciousness. I consider faith, according to the genuine, ancient sense of the term, as involving both phases, the one just as much as the other, and I place them together, bound up in an undifferentiated unity. The ecclesiastical community is in a fortunate condition if the opposition within it restricts itself purely to the declared, formal difference, and if it is the case that the human spirit does not create out of itself a characteristic content opposed to the content of the church, and also that the ecclesiastical truth has not gone over into an external content which leaves the Holy Spirit indifferent toward it. The internal activity of the church will consist principally in the education of the human being, in the business of internalizing the truth which, at first, can be given only to mental imagery and to memory, so that the mind may become captivated and permeated with it, and self-consciousness may find itself

and its essential stability only in that truth. However, as a part of the appearance of that permanent process of education, there is a separation of immediate self-certainty from the true content, and these two aspects are united with each other neither immediately nor permanently and firmly in all of their determinations. Self-certainty is, to begin with, natural feeling and natural will, as well as the opinions and vain imaginings which correspond to this feeling and will; but the true content comes to spirit externally at first, in the word and the letter. Religious education brings about a unity of the two, so that the feelings, which are immediate to man only when they are natural, lose their force, and what was the letter grows into its own living spirit.

5. This modification and unification of what is at first external material, to be sure, instantly encounters an adversary with which it must deal: there is an immediate opponent in the natural spirit, which the modification and unification must presuppose, precisely because it is free spirit which is to be engendered, not a natural life, because free spirit exists only as a reborn spirit. Nevertheless, this natural adversary is spontaneously overcome, and free spirit set free, through the divine idea. The struggle with the natural spirit is therefore only an appearance in the finite individual. However, still another adversary proceeds from the individual, an adversary which does not have its point of departure in the mere naturalness of man, but rather in his supersensuous essence, in *thinking*, an adversary which addresses itself to the original situation of the inner man himself, to what characterizes the divine origin of man, to that through which he differentiates himself from the beasts, and to what alone, just as it is the root of his majesty, is also the root of his degradation — for beasts are capable neither of majesty nor of degradation. If thinking becomes so self-reliant that it becomes dangerous to faith, then begins an even greater and more obstinate struggle than that former one which involved only natural will and the unprejudiced consciousness which had not yet stood up for itself. Such thinking is thus what has been called human thinking, one's own understanding, finite reason, which is correctly differentiated from the thinking which, although it is in man, is yet divine; from the understanding which seeks not what is one's own, but what is universal; and from the reason which knows and contemplates only the infinite and the eternal as that which alone has being.

6. Nevertheless, it is not necessary that this finite thinking be set directly over against the doctrine of religious faith. On the contrary, it will, in the first instance, take the trouble within this doctrine, allegedly for the benefit of religion, to embellish, support, and honor the doctrine with its discoveries, curiosities, and ingenuities. In such an endeavor it may happen that the understanding ties a multitude of determinations to the doctrine of faith, as deductions or presuppositions, foundations and aims — determinations which, even though they are of finite import, are easily attributed a dignity, significance, and validity equal to that of the

eternal truth itself, because they appear in an immediate association with this truth. At the same time, since they have only finite import, and hence are suscep-tible to counterarguments and objections, they are likely to require external au-thority for their maintenance; thus they become a battlefield for human passions. Produced in the interest of what is finite, they are not supported by the testimony of the Holy Spirit, but by finite interests.

7. Absolute truth itself, however, when it appears, passes over into tem-poral configuration, and into its external conditions, associations, and circum-stances. In this way it has already surrounded itself with a multiplicity of local, his-torical, and other positive material. Because truth simply *is*, it must appear and it must have appeared; this manifestation of truth belongs to its eternal nature itself, which is inseparable from it, to such a degree that this separation would destroy it by degrading its content to an empty abstraction. However, the aspect of the momentary, local, external, ancillary essence must be well differentiated from the eternal appearance which inheres in the essence of truth, in order not to confuse the finite with the infinite, or the indifferent with the substantial. Within this aspect, new latitude is opened up for the understanding, for its exertions, and for its augmentation of finite material; and the understanding, by its association with this ancillary essence, finds immediate inducement to raise up the individualities of this ancillary essence to the dignity of the truly divine, and the frame to the dig-nity of the work of art enclosed within it, in order to promote the same reverence for, and the same *faith* in, finite histories, events, circumstances, mental images, commandments, etc., as there is for, and in, that which is absolute Being and eternal history.

8. It is in these aspects, then, that the *formal significance of faith* begins to achieve prominence — the significance that faith is generally a *taking-as-true*; what is claimed to be true may be organized according to its inner nature, in any way whatever. It is this same taking-as-true which is and is valid in its place within the everyday things of ordinary life, its conditions, relations, events, or other natural existences, properties, and qualities. If the criteria on the basis of which faith in such things emerges are sensuous external direct beholding, or internal immediate feeling, the testimonies of others, and trust in their witness, etc., then doubtless hereby a conviction as a taking-as-true mediated through *grounds* can be differentiated from faith as such. But this differentiation is too insignificant to maintain that such a conviction has an advantage over mere faith; for the so-called grounds are nothing but the indicated sources of what is here called faith.

9. Of another sort, however, is a difference, regarding this universal taking-as-true, which refers to the material and in particular to the use which is made of that material. Since those finite and external histories and circumstances which lie on the periphery of religious faith are, of course, associated with eternal history, which constitutes the objective basis of religion, piety thus derives from

this material its multifarious agitations, edifications, and instructions with regard to worldly relations, individual fates and postures; and piety finds its mental imagery and the entire extent of its organizing structure joined, either for the most part or completely, with that sphere of histories and doctrines which surrounds the eternal truth. In any case such a sphere — from which, as from a popular novel, people have generally derived their consciousness of all further relations involving their minds and lives, indeed, which is even the medium through which they raise their actuality up to the religious viewpoint — deserves, at the very least, the greatest attention and a respectful treatment.

10. Now it is one thing if such a sphere is innocently taken by pious sentiment alone, and used for the sake of this sentiment; but it is something else if it is grasped by one understanding, and offered to another understanding in the way in which it is grasped and fixed by the first understanding, so as to be valid to the second understanding as a standard and as a solid basis for the taking-as-true; in so doing this second understanding is supposed to subjugate itself only to the first understanding, provided that this subjugation is demanded in the name of divine truth.

11. In fact, such a demand accomplishes the opposite of its own aim; since it is not the divine spirit of faith, but the understanding, which claims to subjugate the understanding to itself, it is thus rather through this subjugation that the understanding is justified in having the last word in matters pertaining to God. Over against such content of the letter and of the sterile erudition of orthodoxy, the better sense has a divine right. For it so happens that the more this finite wisdom boasts about matters pertaining to God, and the more stress it lays on external narrative and on the invention of its own sagacity, the more it has worked against both the divine truth and itself. It has generated and recognized the principle which is contrary to the divine truth, disclosed and prepared a quite different foundation for cognizing; and on this foundation the infinite energy, which the principle of cognizing possesses within itself and, at the same time, is that in which rests the deeper possibility of its future reconciliation with true faith, will, against constraint, attend to that finite realm of the understanding, and destroy this realm's pretensions of wanting to be the Kingdom of Heaven.

12. It is the better sense which is shocked at letting the contradiction of such arrogance, finitudes, and externalities be recognized and worshipped as the divine; it is the better sense which is equipped with the weapon of finite thinking, which, on the one hand as *enlightenment*, established and maintained the *freedom of the spirit*, the principle of a spiritual religion, but on the other hand as only abstract thinking, *has not known how to effect any difference* between determinations of a merely finite content and determinations *of the truth* itself. This abstract understanding has thus turned against all determinacy, emptied truth throughout of all content, and kept nothing for itself except, on the one hand, the pure

negative itself, the *caput mortuum* of a merely abstract *essence*, and on the other hand, finite material, which is in part, according to its nature, finite and external, but in part also that which the abstract understanding has obtained from the divine content, the material itself which this understanding has degraded to the externality of merely common narrative events, to parochial opinions and particular views of the time. — But thinking cannot, in general, be inactive. There is nothing to be caught or recovered, either inside or outside of that God, for God has already been made hollow within Himself. He is the non-cognizable, for cognizing has to do with content, determination, and movement; but hollowness is lacking in content, indeterminate, without life and action in itself. The doctrine of truth is no more and no less than this: to be a doctrine of God, and to have revealed His nature and occupation. The understanding, however, since it has dissolved all this content, has again enveloped God and degraded Him to that which He was earlier in the time of mere yearning, i.e., the Unknown. Therefore no material remains for thinking activity, except that previously mentioned finite material, but *accompanied by the consciousness and the determination* that it is nothing but temporal and finite material. This activity is thus confined to indulging in such material, finding satisfaction in vanity, configuring and changing the vain in many ways, and bringing before itself, in a scholarly manner, a huge measure of the vain.

13. To spirit, however, which does not endure this vanity, is left only longing; for that in which it wants to satisfy itself is something *otherworldly* which is lacking in configuration, content, and determination. But only through configuration, content, and determination does anything exist for spirit, is anything reason, actuality, life, is anything in and for itself. That finite material, however, is only something subjective, and unable to furnish import for the empty eternity. The need which lies in spirit seeking again religion has accordingly demanded directly the determination which would be an import in and for itself, and a truth which would not appertain to the opining or to the peculiar arrogance of the understanding, but which would be *objective*. The only thing that remains for such a need, if it is to attain satisfaction, is *to be driven back into feeling*. Feeling is still the only way in which religion can exist. Reflection always has an interest in the higher configurations of religion's existence, and in the mode of *mental imagery* and of the *taking-as-true* of a content; and reflection has driven itself to the point of negating every objective determination.

14. These are, in brief, the main features of the procedure which formal reflection has followed in religion. The system of subtle, metaphysical, casuistical differentiations and determinations, in which the understanding has dispersed the compact content of religion, and on which it has bestowed the same authority as resides in eternal truth, is the foremost evil which originates within religion itself. But the other evil, however much it may appear, in the first instance, as an opposite, is in fact grounded in the first standpoint, and is only a further development

of it. It is the evil caused when thinking becomes self-reliant and turns against itself with the formal weapons to which that mass of sterile lack of import owes its origin, the weapons which thinking itself owes to its first transaction; and thinking finds its final principle, pure abstraction itself, the highest essence which lacks determination. Thinking is interested in philosophical contemplation, to note precisely this sudden shift, which reflection itself had not expected, into something hostile to its own work — a sudden shift which in fact is only a determination inherent in this reflection itself.

15. Following what has been said, the evil into which the Enlightenment has brought *religion* and *theology* may be defined as a privation *of known truth, of an objective content, and of a doctrine of religious faith.* Yet properly it can be only be said of religion that it suffers such a privation, for there is no longer any theology if there is no longer any such content. Theology is reduced to historical erudition, and then to the insufficient exposition of certain subjective feelings. The declared result, however, is that what is done on the part of religion tends toward the reconciliation of faith and reason. It must now also be mentioned that *philosophy,* too, for its part, has in fact offered its services in the same way toward such a settlement.

16. For the privation into which philosophy has fallen shows itself also as a privation of *objective content.* Philosophy is the systematic knowledge of thinking reason — as religious faith is the consciousness and the absolute taking-as-true of the reason which is accepted as mental imagery — and the material for this systematic knowledge has become as flimsy as it has for faith.

17. The philosophy by which, first of all, the standpoint of the universal organization of thought has recently been established, and which has named itself, and rightly so, the *"critical"* philosophy, has done nothing other than reduce to its simple formula the business of the Enlightenment, which had chiefly been directed toward concrete mental images and objects; this philosophy has no other content or result than that which has emerged from that argumentative understanding. The *critical* or *Kantian* philosophy, to be sure, like the *Enlightenment,* is something which its *name* discloses as obsolete; and trouble would come to one who today would still brand as Kantian philosophy whatever might appear to be philosophy in the writings of those authors who call themselves philosophers, moreover the academic authors who write about matters of theology, religion, morals, and even those who write about political affairs, laws, and constitutional questions; and just as much trouble would come to one who would ascribe an *Enlightenment* view to the argumentative theologians, and more especially, to those [such as Schleiermacher] among them who locate religion in subjective feelings. Who has not refuted Kantian philosophy, or improved it? Who among these does not continue to stand as a knight to defend it? Who has not progressed further? But if one would examine the achievements of these authors' philosophical,

moral, and theological works, the last named of which resists nothing so strongly as it resists the wish to be something philosophical, then one would instantly cognize only the same principles and results which, however, appear here already as *presuppositions* and as *recognized truths*. "You will know them by their fruits" [Mt. 7:16]. The circumstance of being situated wholly and exclusively on the highway of contemporary mental images and prejudices does not prevent this peculiar arrogance from opining that its trivialities, ladled out of the universal flow, are completely original views and new discoveries in the field of spirit and systematic knowledge.

18. That which is in and for itself, and that which is finite and temporal, are the two basic determinations which must be included in a doctrine of truth; and the import of such a doctrine is dependent upon how these two aspects are grasped and established, and upon what disposition toward them is assigned to spirit. Let us, with this in mind, consider the truths of the philosophy of our time — truths which are claimed to be so widely recognized that one need waste no further words over them.

19. One of the absolute presuppositions of the culture of our time is that man *knows nothing about truth*. The understanding of the Enlightenment has not so much brought this result to consciousness and articulation as it has simply given rise to this result. The understanding, as mentioned above, has proceeded by liberating thinking from those shackles of the other understanding which would plant its finitudes in the soil of the divine teaching itself and would use the absolute authority of God for these, its rampant weeds, and by establishing the freedom which has been won by the religion of truth and made into this religion's home. Thus above all it has had the will to assault error and superstition; and what it truly succeeded in destroying was certainly not religion, but that pharisaic understanding which has meant to be clever, in the manner of this world, about the things of another world, and has even intended to be able to call its cleverness "religious doctrine." It has wanted to eliminate error, only in order to make room for *truth*; it has sought and recognized eternal truths, and, furthermore, it has located the dignity of man in the fact that, *for him*, and for him alone, not for beasts, *such truths exist*. On this view, these truths should be something fixed and objective, over against subjective opinion and the impulses of feeling; and the opinion-forming process, as well as the feelings, should be essentially conformable to, subjugated under, and guided by, the insight of reason, if they are to have any justification.

20. The *consistent* and *self-reliant* development of the principle of the understanding leads, however, to a grasping of all determination and with it all content as something that is only finite, thus annihilating the configuration and determination of the divine. Through this "improvement," objective truth, which should be the goal, has been brought down more unconsciously to the sparse-

ness and dryness which Kantian philosophy has now had only to bring to consciousness and to articulate as the determination of the goal of reason. Consequently the *identity of the understanding* is declared by this philosophy to be the highest principle, the ultimate result, both for the cognizing process itself and for its object — the *void* of atomistic philosophy, determinationless God, without any predicates or properties, lifted up into the *otherworldly realm* of knowledge, or rather brought down to contentlessness. This philosophy has given this understanding the correct consciousness of itself: that it is unable to cognize truth. But while it has interpreted spirit only as this understanding, it has brought consciousness to the universal proposition that man — as if there could really be absolute objects and a truth outside of God — can know nothing at all about God or about whatever *is in itself.* If religion places the honor and the redemption of man in the cognizing of God, and places its beneficence in having this cognition of God communicated to man and the unknown essence of God disclosed to him; then in this philosophy, in the most enormous opposition to religion, spirit has degenerated to the unpretentiousness of cattle, as its highest determination, except that spirit, unfortunately, still has the prerogative of being conscious of its ignorance, whereas cattle, in fact, possess in their ignorance a much purer, genuine, i.e., completely disinterested, unpretentiousness. One might well now regard this result as, with few exceptions, having become a universal prejudice of our culture. It does no good to have refuted Kantian philosophy, or to scorn it; the advances beyond it, and the presumptions of such advances, may have done much in their own way, but they are only the same worldly wisdom as that described above, for they deny to spirit the capacity and the vocation for objective truth.

21. The *other* principle, herewith immediately associated with this wisdom, is that spirit, while it is certainly cognizant, though truth is denied to it, can have to do only with appearances, with finitudes. The church and piety have frequently viewed the varieties of worldly systematic knowledge as suspicious and dangerous, often indeed as hostile toward them, and as leading to atheism. A famous astronomer is supposed to have said that he searched heaven through and through, but could find no God there.[2] In fact, worldly systematic knowledge addresses itself to the cognizing of the *finite,* since it strives to penetrate into the interior of the finite, causes and grounds are the ultimate thing in which it finds reassurance. However, these causes and grounds are essentially something analo-

---

[2] This "famous astronomer" was likely Joseph Jérôme Le Français de Lalande (1732-1807), director of the Paris Observatory from 1768 until his death. The claim resembles the infamous Soviet "cosmonautological" argument for the non-existence of God, wherein Soviet cosmonauts reported on their earliest space voyages in the 1960s that they had seen no God in heaven, and thus there is no God.

gous to what is to be explained, and thus it is only finite forces which fall within its domain. If now, similarly, these varieties of systematic knowledge do not carry their cognitions over into the region of the eternal — which is not just something supersensuous, for those causes and forces, too, as well as the interior which is generated by the reflective understanding and cognized in its way, are not anything sensuous — because this mediation is not the business of these types of systematic knowledge, then indeed nothing prevents the systematic knowledge of the finite from admitting a divine sphere. Confronted with such a higher sphere, it is quite prepared to recognize as a content that which is nothing in and for itself, but which is only appearance, and which comes to consciousness only through the senses and through reflection at the level of understanding. If, however, there is a general renunciation of the cognition of truth, then cognizing has only *one basis*, the basis of appearance. From this standpoint, even in the efforts of cognition, concerned with a doctrine which cognition recognizes as divine, the concern cannot be with the *doctrine itself*, but only with its external surroundings. The doctrine for itself remains outside of the interest of spiritual activity and no insight, faith, or conviction concerning it can be sought, for its content is assumed to be unattainable. Thus the intelligence, when occupied with religious doctrines, must restrict itself to their aspects as appearances, throw itself into their external circumstances, and become interested in their *narrative*, where spirit has to do with things past, with something remote from itself *in which spirit itself is not present*. What the serious effort of scholarship, diligence, sagacity, etc., discloses is likewise called truth, and an ocean of such truths is brought to light and propagated; but these are not truths of the kind which the serious spirit of religion demands for its satisfaction.

22. Now if that which is *thisworldly* and has *presence for spirit* is this broad realm of vanity and appearance, but that which is in and for itself is removed from spirit and is something empty and otherworldly for spirit, then where can spirit find a place in which the substantial could encounter it, in which the eternal world would come near it, in which it could achieve union with these things, and in which it could attain certainty and the enjoyment of this certainty? It is only into the *region of feeling* that the instinct toward truth can flee. Only in the muffled way of sensation is consciousness able to endure that which is rich in import, that which is unwavering in the face of reflection. This form lacks the objectivity and determinacy which knowledge and self-conscious faith require, but which the understanding has known how to destroy. Just because of this danger, religiosity merely trembles in fear of determinacy, and on this account withdraws into the sheltered seclusion which seems to offer to thinking no aspect against which to mount a dialectical attack. In such religiosity, if it arises out of an authentic need, the soul can find its required peace, since it strives to make up in intensity and internality what it lacks in content and in the extent of faith.

23. One may still adduce, however, as the *third universal prejudice*, the assumption that feeling is the genuine and even the only form in which religiosity may retain its authenticity.

24. Of course, such religiosity is no longer unbiased. Spirit generally demands, since it is spirit, that what exists in feeling also be available for it in mental imagery, that something sensed accord with sensation, and that the vivacity of sensation not remain a motionless concentration, but still be a pursuit of objective truths. Spirit further demands that what happens in a cult extend to actions which not only attest to the communality of spirits in religion, but also, like the pursuit of truths, nourish religious sentiment, preserve it in truth, and grant to this sentiment the enjoyment of this truth. But such expansion toward a cult, as toward a bulk of doctrines of religious faith, is no longer compatible with the form of feeling — on the contrary, religiosity, in the configuration considered here, has escaped from development and objectivity into feeling, and has polemically declared this feeling to be the exclusive or predominant form.

25. It is here, then, that the danger of this standpoint begins, along with the turning over of this standpoint into the opposite of what religiosity seeks in it. This is an aspect of greatest importance, but to which we shall refer only briefly; and in so doing I must concern myself only with what is most universal, without here being able to investigate further the nature of feeling. But then there can be no doubt that feeling is a base which, undetermined for itself, contains within it at the same time what is most diverse and most contrary. Feeling, for itself, is natural subjectivity, which is just as capable of being good as of being evil, just as capable of being pious as of being godless. Accordingly, if what was once called reason, which however was in fact the finite understanding and its argumentation, has been made into something which passes judgment on what I take as true, as well as on what is supposed to be for me a rule of conduct; and if feeling is supposed to be that from which the judgment of what I am and of what I value is supposed to emerge, then even the illusion of objectivity has disappeared, an illusion which rests, at least, in the principle of the understanding. For, according to the understanding, what should have value for me should indeed depend on a universally valid ground, on something which exists in and for itself. Even more determinately, however, that which is divine, eternal, and rational, which has being in and for itself, is valid as an *objective law* in all religion as well as in all ethical living together among people, in the family and in the state; and this objective law is thus the *foremost thing*, through which alone feeling obtains its support and its true bearing. The natural feelings are supposed rather to be determined, corrected, and purified through the doctrines and the exercise of religion and through the firm principles of the ethical order of life; and brought from these foundations only into the feeling which *makes* itself into a correct, *religious, moral feeling*.

26. "*Natural man* perceives nothing of the spirit of God and cannot re-

cognize it, for it must be spiritually ordered." Natural man, however, is man in his natural feelings, and it is such a man who, according to the doctrine of subjectivity, is supposed to cognize nothing at all, but still is supposed to be the only one who, insofar as he is natural man, perceives the spirit of God. Among the feelings of natural man there is indeed *also* a feeling of the divine; but the natural feeling of the divine is one thing, and the spirit of God another. But what other feelings are not found besides in the human heart? Feeling, as natural feeling, does not even include the claim that that natural feeling is a feeling of the divine; the divine exists only within spirit and for spirit, and spirit, as was said above, is not to be a natural life, but a reborn spirit. If feeling constitutes the basic determination of the essence of man, then man is established as the equivalent of the beast, for it is characteristic of the beast to have its determination or vocation in feeling, and to live according to feeling. If religion in man is based only on a feeling, then such a feeling rightly has no further determination than to be the *feeling of his dependence*, and the dog would then be the best Christian, for the dog feels this most strongly in himself and lives mainly within this feeling. The dog also has feelings of redemption, whenever his hunger is satisfied by a bone.[3] But spirit, on the contrary, has in religion its liberation and the feeling of its divine freedom; only free spirit has religion or can have religion. What is constrained in religion is the natural feeling of the heart, particular subjectivity; what is liberated in religion, and precisely by means of religion, is spirit. In the worst religions — those in which servitude and thus superstition are most powerful — man's raising himself up to God is the place wherein he feels, directly beholds, and enjoys his freedom, infinity, and universality, i.e., the higher things which originate not from feeling as such but from spirit.

27. When one speaks of religious, ethical, etc. feelings, one must of course say that these are authentic feelings; and then when, as we have come thenceforth to this standpoint, we have arrived at the mistrust of, or rather the contempt for and hatred of, thinking — the misology of which Plato spoke long ago [in the *Phaedo*] — one is quite ready to locate what is authentic and divine in feelings for themselves. It would certainly not be necessary, to begin with, particularly with reference to the Christian religion, to see only a choice between un-

---

[3] Contrary to the usual opinion, this slogan of Hegel's sharp attack on Schleiermacher is not the main point of the Foreword. Rather, the "dog" metaphor is only an easily remembered image, while the real crux of the essay is the theme of the progressive "rebirth" of spirit from an abstract state of mere naturalness toward a mediated state of genuine freedom which enables spirit to know and express divine truth and thus to become reconciled with God. Hegel's basic purpose is chiefly dialectical and systematic rather than confrontational, although confrontation with the more subjectivist wing of romanticism was surely part of Hegel's plan.

derstanding and feeling as the origin of religion and truth; and one must already have eliminated what the Christian religion declares to be its source, the higher divine revelation, to be limited to that choice, and then, after having rejected the understanding, and furthermore, thought in general, to want to base a Christian doctrine on feelings. — But since feeling is generally supposed to be the seat and source of what is genuine, one thus overlooks the essential nature of feeling, namely, that it is, for itself, a *mere form*, for itself undetermined, and can include any content. There is nothing which cannot be felt, and is not felt. God, truth, and duty are felt; evil, falsehood, and injustice just as much; all human conditions and relations are felt; all mental images of the relation of oneself to spiritual and natural things become feelings. From religious feeling, the feeling of duty, of sympathy, etc., to envy, hatred, pride, vanity, etc., to joy, pain, sorrow, etc. — who would want to try to name and enumerate all the feelings?[4] From the very diversity, but even more from the opposition and contradiction of feelings, there follows, even for ordinary thinking, the correct conclusion that feeling is something purely formal and cannot be a principle for a genuine determination. Moreover, it is just as correct to conclude that, if *feeling* is made into such a principle, then its only concern will be to relinquish to the *subject the choice of which* feelings the *subject* wants to have. Feeling is the absolute indeterminacy which acknowledges itself as a standard and as a justification, i.e., the arbitrary will and the inclination to be and do whatever it pleases, and to make itself into an oracle of what has worth and of what kinds of religion, duty, and law have exalted value.

    28. Religion, like duty and law, shall become and even should become a matter of feeling, and lodge in the heart, as freedom also generally lowers itself into feeling and becomes in man a feeling of freedom. But it is entirely something else whether such content, created out of feeling, as God, truth, and freedom, whether such objects should have feeling for their justification; or whether, conversely, such objective content, valid in and for itself, comes to lodge in the heart and in feeling, and feelings, rather, come to receive their content as well as their determination, rectification, and justification from this objective content. Everything depends upon *this difference of attitude*. On it rests the separation of old-fashioned honesty and ancient faith, of genuine religiosity and the ethical order of life which establishes God, truth, and duty as *foremost*, from the perversity, the peculiar arrogance, and the absolute selfishness which has arisen in our time and which makes willfulness, peculiar opining and peculiar inclination into the rule of religiosity and law. Obedience, discipline, faith in the ancient sense of the word, reverence for God and truth, are the sentiments which are associated with the first attitude and which emerge from it; vanity, peculiar arrogance, shallowness, and pride, are the feelings which emerge from the second attitude, or rather it is out of

---

[4] Possibly a reference to Descartes or Spinoza.

these feelings of the merely natural man that this attitude originates.

29. The previous remarks might have furnished the material for a long exposition which I have already provided elsewhere [in the *Encyclopedia of the Philosophical Sciences* and the *Philosophy of Right*] dealing with a few aspects of the issue, but here is not the place for such a project. Let those remarks be only reminders of the viewpoints which have been suggested in order to designate more precisely what constitutes the malady *of our time*, and with it, the *requirement of our time*. This *malady*, the *contingency* and *arbitrary will* of *subjective* feeling and its opining, combined with the *culture of reflection* which claims that spirit is *incapable* of the *knowledge of truth*, has since ancient times been called "*sophistry*." It is what deserves the nickname which Mr. Friedrich von Schlegel has recently selected afresh, "*worldly wisdom*"; for it is a wisdom in and of what is usually called the *world*, a wisdom which concerns the contingent, the untrue, and the temporal. It is the vanity which elevates the vain, the contingency of feeling, and the inclination of opining, to serve as the absolute principle of what is to count as law and duty, faith and truth. We must indeed often hear these sophistical presentations called "philosophy"; but for all that, this theory contradicts itself in using the name of philosophy for these presentations, since it is often heard to claim *that it has nothing to do with philosophy*. This theory is correct in wanting to know nothing of philosophy; it thereby expresses the consciousness of what in fact it is and wants. From time immemorial philosophy has struggled against sophistry, which can borrow from philosophy only the formal weapon, the culture of reflection, but has nothing in common with it as far as content is concerned; for it is precisely this: to flee from all objectivity of truth. Not even the other source of truth — insofar as truth is an affair of religion — the revelation of the Holy Scriptures, can serve to gain a content for sophistry; for this teaching recognizes no ground except the peculiar vanity of what it itself holds and "reveals."

30. But regarding the *requirement* of our time, it is the case that the *common* requirement of *religion* and *philosophy* is *directed* toward a *substantial, objective content of truth*. As religion on its part and along its way would regain for its content esteem, reverence, and authority over against the arbitrary system of opinion, and would establish itself as a bond of objective faith, doctrine, and worship, this intrinsically very extensive inquiry would at the same time have to consider thoroughly our contemporary empirical situation in its multifarious tendencies; and thus such an inquiry would be out of place here, since in general it would not be of a purely philosophical sort. But in one segment of the business of satisfying this requirement the two spheres of religion and philosophy coincide. For it can at least be mentioned that the development of the spirit of the times has induced thinking, and the manner of viewing which is associated with thinking, to have grown, for consciousness, into an *unavoidable stipulation* of *what* should be granted and recognized *as true*. It is not a matter of concern here to decide to

what extent only a part of the religious community would no longer live, i.e., no longer be capable of existing spiritually, without the freedom of thinking spirit; or, on the contrary, to what extent there are whole communities in which this higher principle has become visible, for which the form of thinking, developed to whatever level, is now an indispensable demand of their faith. Development and the return to principles may occur at many different levels; for, in order to express itself popularly, thinking can be composed in reducing particular cases, propositions, etc., to one *immanent, universal proposition* which, in a relative sense, is the *axiom* for the material made dependent on it in consciousness. Whatever is an axiom, an ultimate firm foundation, at a given level of the development of thought, needs, for another level, an even further reduction to still more universal, deeper axioms. But the axioms are a content which consciousness holds fast in conviction, a content for which its spirit has given testimony, and a content which now is not separate from thinking or from peculiar selfhood. If the axioms are surrendered to argumentation, then this leads to the deviation, mentioned above, in which such argumentation puts subjective opinion and arbitrary will in the place of axiomatic propositions, and culminates in sophistry.

31. But the mode of conviction which occurs in religion can remain firm in the configuration of what is properly called *faith*; however, when this happens one must not fail to note that faith is not to be mentally imagined as something external, as something to be offered mechanically, but rather, as essentially needing the testimony of the indwelling spirit of truth, and as having to be fixed in one's own heart, so that it may be something lively, and not servitude. If, however, the element of axiomatic propositions has infiltrated the religious requirement, then that requirement is no longer separate from the requirement and activity of thought, and religion demands, according to this aspect, a *systematic knowledge* of religion — a theology. This systematic knowledge has in common with philosophy whatever in it is more than, or only deserves to be more than, the universal acquaintance with religion which appertains to every member of every culture. Thus *scholastic theology* was produced in the Middle Ages — a systematic knowledge which religion cultivated from the side of thinking and reason, in an effort to comprehend in thought the deepest doctrines of revealed religion. Compared with the sublime orientation of such a systematic knowledge, that method of theology is quite backwards which locates its systematic difference from universal religious doctrine merely in the historical element with which, in its length and breadth, in its boundless individual details, this theology supplements religion. The absolute content of religion is essentially something present, and therefore it is not in the external addition of scholarly historical material, but rather only in rational cognition, that spirit can find something further present and free for it and which is able to satisfy its eternal requirement to think and thus to add the infinite form to the infinite content of religion.

32. Given the prejudice against which philosophizing on the subject of religion in our time has to fight, namely the prejudice that the divine cannot be *conceived*, or rather, that even the concept and the cognition which conceives degrade God and the divine attributes to the domain of finitude, and by so doing, annihilate them, — this prejudice, fortunately, scholastic theology did not yet have to fight; the honor and worth of the cognition which thinks were not undervalued to such an extent, but on the contrary, they were left untouched, even impartial. It was only modern philosophy itself which brought its own element, the concept, to be so badly misunderstood and into such discredit. This philosophy has not cognized the infinity of the concept, and has confused it with finite reflection and with understanding — to such an extent that only the understanding is supposed to be able to think, whereas reason is not supposed to be able to think, but only to know immediately, i.e., only to behold directly and to feel, and consequently is supposed to be able to *know* only *in a sensory way*.

33. According to the mental image of divine justice provided by the ancient Greek poets, the gods hate and strike down whatever raises itself up, whatever is fortunate or distinguished. Purer thought about the divine has banished this mental image; Plato and Aristotle teach that *God* is *not jealous*, and that He does not withhold the cognition of Himself and of truth from human beings. It would be nothing other than *jealousy* if God denied the knowledge of God to consciousness; by so doing, God would have denied all truth to consciousness, for God alone is what is true; whatever else is true and appears to be something without divine content is true only insofar as it is grounded in God and is cognized through God; all the rest is temporal appearance. The cognition of God and of truth is the only thing that raises man up above the beasts, sets man apart, makes man happy, or rather, according to Plato and Aristotle, as well as Christian doctrine — makes man blessed.

34. It is the quite symptomatic appearance of our time to have reverted, at the pinnacle of its culture, to that old mental image which holds that God is uncommunicative and does not reveal His nature to the human spirit. This assertion of the jealousy of God must be so much the more conspicuous within the sphere of the Christian religion, because this religion is and wants to be nothing other than the *revelation* of what God is, and the Christian community is supposed to be nothing other than the community into which the spirit of God is sent and in which this spirit — just that spirit which, because it is spirit, is not sensuousness and feeling, not a mental imagining of something sensuous, but rather, thinking, knowing, cognizing; and because it is the divine Holy Spirit, is only the thinking, knowing and cognizing of God — guides its members toward the cognition of God. What ever would the Christian community be without this cognition? What is a theology without a cognition of God? Precisely what a philosophy is without a cognition of God: a resounding brass and a tinkling cymbal! [Cf. 1 Cor. 13:1.]

5

What is Religious Experience?

Climbing the neo-Platonic ladder of reason to mystical awareness, giving oneself to an organized religion, conducting a metaphysical investigation, or meditating on the conflict between faith and reason are not the only ways to learn about God. There is also, for want of a better term, "religious experience," the individual's spontaneous knowledge of the transcendent, or perhaps of unaccountable facts which, under normal circumstances, the individual could not know.

Among the classic works on religious experience are *I and Thou* by Austrian Hasidic mystic Martin Buber (1878-1965), various books of Eliade and Swiss physician and philosopher Carl Gustav Jung (1875-1961), *Religious Experience* by Columbia University Professor of Religion Wayne Proudfoot, and various spiritual autobiographies, such as Augustine's *Confessions*, al-Ghazali's *Deliverance from Error*, Kierkegaard's *The Point of View for My Work as an Author*, *Apologia Pro Vita Sua* by Roman Catholic Cardinal John Henry Newman (1801-1890), and *The Seven Storey Mountain* by American Trappist monk Thomas Merton (1915-1968).

Buber distinguishes between the "I-It" relationship, the usual subject-object dualism, and the "I-Thou" relationship, in which dualism is overcome and the perceived permeates the perceiver's entire being to the extent that, for the perceiver, the two become spiritually one. The "I-Thou" is the basis and essence of all religious experience. Proudfoot's focus is likewise on the subjective phenomena of religious experience rather than on the possible objective truth of whatever is experienced. Religious experience is valid if it is honest and intense, not if it is accurate. In a persuasive analogy, Proudfoot writes: "If someone is afraid of a bear, his fear cannot be accurately described without mentioning the bear. This remains true regardless of whether or not the bear actually exists outside his mind. He may mistakenly perceive a fallen tree trunk on the trail ahead of him as a bear, but his fear is properly described as fear of a bear. To describe it as fear of a log would be to misidentify his emotion and reduce it to something other than it is" (pp. 192-193). The hiker's experience of fear, not the identity of the object of his fear, is what is important. Similarly, in genuine religious experience, one's awe of the numinous, the sacred, what Otto calls the *mysterium tremendum et fascinans*, or what Schleiermacher calls the pious "feeling of utter dependence," is all that matters.

Because of the richness of religious experience, there are at least eight scholarly paths by which to study religion: (1) anthropological, (2) sociological, (3) historical/biographical, (4) psychological, (5) phenomenological, (6) theological/doctrinal, (7) literary, and (8) philosophical. The anthropological method studies religion in its respective settings in the various cultures of all times and places. The sociological approach does the same with regard to our own culture. The history of religions and the biographies of religious leaders and specialists tend to produce an appreciation of the chronological development of religion. Psychology, especially in the wake of Jung, may study the conscious or unconscious motivations of believers, the unconscious awareness of universal religious symbols or archetypes, or the emotional manifestations of religious experience. The phenomenological tactic would most generally focus on the external trappings of religion, such as shrine architecture, prescribed rituals, or sacred music, and may compare phenomena among religions, usually without judgment. Scrutiny of the theologies or doctrines of various religions leads to knowledge of their common spiritual threads and emphases as well as of their apparent differences. The literary study of religion includes not only the very fruitful "higher criticism" of scripture that was invented by German scholars in the nineteenth century, but also the impartial investigation of folklore, oral traditions, spiritual memoirs, and relevant texts of all kinds from all cultures. These seven are all data for the eighth approach, the philosophical.

Religious experience often takes the form of either "theophany," a self-revelation of God, or "hierophany," a revelation that something is holy. For Moses, to use an example from the Hebrew Bible, his encounter with the burning bush was a hierophany and his reception of the Ten Commandments was a theophany; but for the Hebrew people, these experiences of Moses only contributed to establish him as the medium of God's message, and their subsequent studies of this message became a species of revealed theology. The people themselves, even though they eventually accepted Moses's word about God, did not experience either hierophany or theophany. Religious experience is not easily transmitted or communicated in its full force from the original knower to anyone else. Hearing or reading about it, no matter how receptive the hearer or reader is, is not as powerful as living through it or feeling it.

Religious people who do not themselves have the advantage of direct religious experience typically demand symbols, signs, relics, and even personifications of someone else's religious experience in order to simulate or aspire to enlightenment and thus to try to uplift their own spirituality. They demand deified heroes or spiritual celebrities who can be worshipped for their personality rather than for the content of their message. German sociologist Max Weber (1864-1920) called this phenomenon "the routinization of charisma" and its detractors sneer at it as "mysticism for the masses." Every religious movement in history has examples of this dilution of spiritual truth from the one who actually experiences it to those many who wish they knew it. The clearest example is the early development of Buddhism. According to the story, Indian Prince Siddhartha Gautama (ca. 563 - ca. 483 B.C.E.) sat meditating under the fig tree at Bodhgaya until he achieved full enlightenment and thereby became the Buddha, "The Enlightened One." The result of his meditation was essentially a philosophical system of ethics with little or no emphasis on God; but his followers demanded the supernatural, and within only a few generations they populated his system with deities, thus shifting the emphasis of Buddhism from asceticism to worship.

At best, religious experience receives a revelation that can lead to someone not just knowing (*wissen, savoir*), but "knowing" (*kennen, connaître*) God. It can legitimately become the foundation of a religious system. But, at the same time, since whatever is received is received according to the receiver, hard questions must arise whenever the perceived original content of religious experience is transmitted in any way to secondary receivers, who did not themselves have this, or any, religious experience. After the charismatic person preaches the content of religious experience and acquires followers, so that a formal religion is begun and charisma is routinized, an impartial critique should include questions such as: Is religion just a way of speaking? What is the nature of religious language? Do the sentences "God led me across the street" and "I crossed the street" mean the same thing?

Revelation and its reception entail a certain way of seeing. Saul of Tarsus on the road to Damascus notwithstanding, nothing is revealed to anyone who is unable or unwilling to receive as revelation the content of what God intends to be revealed. Whatever is revealed must be revealed *to* a consciousness, otherwise it is not revealed at all. A receptive human consciousness is more important for the process of revelation than that which is taken to be the source of what is revealed. This does not mean that finite human perceivers are more important on an absolute scale than God, but only that, while God sends any number of things as potential revelation into the world, whether or not they will ever be perceived as revelation is left for humans to determine.

A revelation of the divine nature can be found in a child's loving eyes, a rock, a symphony, a mathematical equation, a t-bone steak, or even a murder, just as well as in the Bible or in a miracle. Even though religious experience is often involuntary, humans can become prone to seeing the world as revelation. This does not mean scouring the plethora of worldly phenomena in search of evidence to support preconceived notions about the nature of God; rather, it means only turning around (converting) our usual way of seeing the world so that we learn to appreciate it *sub specie aeternitatis*.

The purpose of seeing the world as revelation is to provide the individual with a useful and coherent integration of the world, i.e., to bring some order into that individual's life. Toward this end, the individual subconsciously translates the primitive content of revelation into explanatory categories which then serve that person as a moral and social conscience, a general guide for orderly action. If one's conscience is best developed toward fostering orderly action by belief in miracles, while another's is best so developed by disbelief in miracles, then that difference must be respected, leaving each free to see the world in his or her own way.

In 1902 William James published a groundbreaking work in the philosophy of religion, *The Varieties of Religious Experience*, transcribed from his lectures at the University of Edinburgh, which examined the psychology of the believer. This selection is from the first chapter, "Religion and Neurology":

As regards the manner in which I shall have to administer this lectureship, I am neither a theologian, nor a scholar learned in the history of religions, nor an anthropologist. Psychology is the only branch of learning in which I am particularly versed. To the psychologist the religious propensities of man must be at least as interesting as any other of the facts pertaining to his mental constitution. It would seem, therefore, that, as a psychologist, the natural thing for me would be to invite you to a descriptive survey of those religious propensities.

If the inquiry be psychological, not religious institutions, but rather religious feelings and religious impulses must be its subject, and I must confine myself to those more developed subjective phenomena recorded in literature produced by articulate and fully self-conscious men, in works of piety and autobiography. Interesting as the origins and early stages of a subject always are, yet when one seeks earnestly for its full significance, one must always look to its more completely evolved and perfect forms. It follows from this that the documents that will most concern us will be those of the men who were most accomplished in the religious life and best able to give an intelligible account of their ideas and motives. These men, of course, are either comparatively modern writers, or else such earlier ones as have become religious classics. The *documents humains* which we shall find most instructive need not then be sought for in the haunts of special erudition — they lie along the beaten highway; and this circumstance, which flows so naturally from the character of our problem, suits admirably also your lecturer's lack of special theological learning. I may take my citations, my sentences and paragraphs of personal confession, from books that most of you at some time will have had already in your hands, and yet this will be no detriment to the value of my conclusions. It is true that some more adventurous reader and investigator, lecturing here in future, may unearth from the shelves of libraries documents that will make a more delectable and curious entertainment to listen to than mine. Yet I doubt whether he will necessarily, by his control of so much more out-of-the-way material, get much closer to the essence of the matter in hand.

The question, What are the religious propensities? and the question, What is their philosophic significance? are two entirely different orders of question from the logical point of view; and, as a failure to recognize this fact distinctly may breed confusion, I wish to insist upon the point a little before we enter into the documents and materials to which I have referred.

In recent books on logic, distinction is made between two orders of inquiry concerning anything. First, what is the nature of it? how did it come about? what is its constitution, origin, and history? And second, What is its importance, meaning, or significance, now that it is once here? The answer to the one question is given in an *existential judgment* or proposition. The answer to the other is a *proposition of value*, what the Germans call a *Werthurtheil* [value judgment], or what we may, if we like, denominate a *spiritual judgment*. Neither judgment can be deduced immediately from the other. They proceed from diverse intellectual preoccupations, and the mind combines them only by making them first separately, and then adding them together.

In the matter of religions it is particularly easy to distinguish the two orders of question. Every religious phenomenon has its history and its derivation from natural antecedents. What is nowadays called the higher criticism of the

Bible is only a study of the Bible from this existential point of view, neglected too much by the earlier church. Under just what biographic conditions did the sacred writers bring forth their various contributions to the holy volume? And what had they exactly in their several individual minds, when they delivered their utterances? These are manifestly questions of historical fact, and one does not see how the answer to them can decide offhand the still further question: of what use should such a volume, with its manner of coming into existence so defined, be to us as a guide to life and a revelation? To answer this other question we must have already in our mind some sort of a general theory as to what the peculiarities in a thing should be which give it value for purposes of revelation; and this theory itself would be what I just called a spiritual judgment. Combining it with our existential judgment, we might indeed deduce another spiritual judgment as to the Bible's worth. Thus if our theory of revelation-value were to affirm that any book, to possess it, must have been composed automatically or not by the free caprice of the writer, or that it must exhibit no scientific and historic errors and express no local or personal passions, the Bible would probably fare ill at our hands. But if, on the other hand, our theory should allow that a book may well be a revelation in spite of errors and passions and deliberate human composition, if only it be a true record of the inner experiences of great-souled persons wrestling with the crises of their fate, then the verdict would be much more favorable. You see that the existential facts by themselves are insufficient for determining the value; and the best adepts of the higher criticism accordingly never confound the existential with the spiritual problem. With the same conclusions of fact before them, some take one view, and some another, of the Bible's value as a revelation, according as their spiritual judgment as to the foundation of values differs.

I make these general remarks about the two sorts of judgment, because there are many religious persons — some of you now present, possibly, are among them — who do not yet make a working use of the distinction, and who may therefore feel at first a little startled at the purely existential point of view from which in the following lectures the phenomena of religious experience must be considered. When I handle them biologically and psychologically as if they were mere curious facts of individual history, some of you may think it a degradation of so sublime a subject, and may even suspect me, until my purpose gets more fully expressed, of deliberately seeking to discredit the religious side of life.

Such a result is of course absolutely alien to my intention; and since such a prejudice on your part would seriously obstruct the due effect of much of what I have to relate, I will devote a few more words to the point.

There can be no doubt that as a matter of fact a religious life, exclusively pursued, does tend to make the person exceptional and eccentric. I speak not now of your ordinary religious believer, who follows the conventional observances of his country, whether it be Buddhist, Christian, or Mohammedan. His religion has been made for him by others, communicated to him by tradition, determined to fixed forms by imitation, and retained by habit. It would profit us little to study this second-hand religious life. We must make search rather for the original experiences which were the pattern-setters to all this mass of suggested feeling and imitated conduct. These experiences we can only find in individuals for whom religion exists not as a dull habit, but as an acute fever rather. But such individuals are "geniuses" in the religious line; and like many other geniuses who have brought forth fruits effective enough for commemoration in the pages of biography, such religious geniuses have often shown symptoms of nervous instability. Even more perhaps than other kinds of genius, religious leaders have been subject to abnormal psychical visitations. Invariably they have been creatures of exalted emotional sensibility. Often they have led a discordant inner life, and had melancholy during a part of their career. They have known no measure, been liable to obsessions and fixed ideas; and frequently they have fallen into trances, heard voices, seen visions, and presented all sorts of peculiarities which are ordinarily classed as pathological. Often, moreover, these pathological features in their career have helped to give them their religious authority and influence.

If you ask for a concrete example, there can be no better one than is furnished by the person of George Fox. The Quaker religion which he founded is something which it is impossible to overpraise. In a day of shams, it was a religion of veracity rooted in spiritual inwardness, and a return to something more like the original gospel truth than men had ever known in England. So far as our Christian sects today are evolving into liberality, they are simply reverting in essence to the position which Fox and the early Quakers so long ago assumed. No one can pretend for a moment that in point of spiritual sagacity and capacity, Fox's mind was unsound. Every one who confronted him personally, from Oliver Cromwell down to county magistrates and jailers, seems to have acknowledged his superior power. Yet from the point of view of his nervous constitution, Fox was a psychopath or *détraqué* of the deepest dye. ...

Bent as we are on studying religion's existential conditions, we cannot possibly ignore these pathological aspects of the subject. We must describe and name them just as if they occurred in non-religious men. It is true that we instinctively recoil from seeing an object to which our emotions and affections are committed handled by the intellect as any other object is handled. The first thing the intellect does with an object is to class it along with something else. But any object that is infinitely important to us and awakens our devotion feels to us also as if it must be *sui generis* and unique. Probably a crab would be filled with a sense of personal outrage if it could hear us class it without ado or apology as a crustacean, and thus dispose of it. "I am no such thing," it would say; "I am MYSELF, MYSELF alone."

The next thing the intellect does is to lay bare the causes in which the thing originates. Spinoza says: "I will analyze the actions and appetites of men as if it were a question of lines, of planes, and of solids." And elsewhere he remarks that he will consider our passions and their properties with the same eye with which he looks on all other natural things, since the consequences of our affections flow from their nature with the same necessity as it results from the nature of a triangle that its three angles should be equal to two right angles. Similarly M[onsieur Hippolyte] Taine, in the introduction to his history of English literature, has written: "Whether facts be moral or physical, it makes no matter. They always have their causes. There are causes for ambition, courage, veracity, just as there are for digestion, muscular movement, animal heat. Vice and virtue are products like vitriol and sugar." When we read such proclamations of the intellect bent on showing the existential conditions of absolutely everything, we feel — quite apart from our legitimate impatience at the somewhat ridiculous swagger of the program, in view of what the authors are actually able to perform — menaced and negated in the springs of our innermost life. Such cold-blooded assimilations threaten, we think, to undo our soul's vital secrets, as if the same breath which should succeed in explaining their origin would simultaneously explain away their significance, and make them appear of no more preciousness, either, than the useful groceries of which M. Taine speaks.

Perhaps the commonest expression of this assumption that spiritual value is undone if lowly origin be asserted is seen in those comments which unsentimental people so often pass on their more sentimental acquaintances. Alfred believes in immortality so strongly because his temperament is so emotional. Fanny's extraordinary conscientiousness is merely a matter of over-instigated nerves. William's melancholy about the universe is due to bad digestion — probably his liver is torpid. Eliza's delight in her church is a symptom of her hysterical constitution. Peter would be less troubled about his soul if he would take more exercise in the open air, etc. A more fully developed example of the same kind of reasoning is the fashion, quite common nowadays among certain writers, of criticising the religious emotions by showing a connection between them and the sexual life. Conversion is a crisis of puberty and adolescence. The macerations of saints, and the devotion of missionaries, are only instances of the parental instinct of self-sacrifice gone astray. For the hysterical nun, starving for natural life, Christ is but an imaginary substitute for a more earthly object of affection. And the like. ...

We are surely all familiar in a general way with this method of discrediting states of mind for which we have an antipathy. We all use it to some degree in criticising persons whose states of mind we regard as overstrained. But when other people criticise our own more exalted soul-flights by calling them "nothing but" expressions of our organic disposition, we feel outraged and hurt, for we know that, whatever be our organism's peculiarities, our mental states have their substantive value as revelations of the living truth; and we wish that all this medical materialism could be made to hold its tongue.

Medical materialism seems indeed a good appellation for the too simple-minded system of thought which we are considering. Medical materialism finishes up Saint Paul by calling his vision on the road to Damascus a discharging lesion of the occipital cortex, he being an epileptic. It snuffs out Saint Teresa as an hysteric, Saint Francis of Assisi as an hereditary degenerate. George Fox's discontent with the shams of his age, and his pining for spiritual veracity, it treats as a symptom of a disordered colon. Carlyle's organ-tones of misery it accounts for by a gastro-duodenal catarrh. All such mental over-tensions, it says, are, when you come to the bottom of the matter, mere affairs of diathesis (auto-intoxications most probably), due to the perverted action of various glands which physiology will yet discover.

And medical materialism then thinks that the spiritual authority of all such personages is successfully undermined. ...

Let us ourselves look at the matter in the largest possible way. Modern psychology, finding definite psycho-physical connections to hold good, assumes as a convenient hypothesis that the dependence of mental states upon bodily conditions must be thorough-going and complete. If we adopt the assumption, then of course what medical materialism insists on must be true in a general way, if not in every detail: Saint Paul certainly had once an epileptoid, if not an epileptic seizure; George Fox was an hereditary degenerate; Carlyle was undoubtedly auto-intoxicated by some organ or other, no matter which, — and the rest. But now, I ask you, how can such an existential account of facts of mental history decide in one way or another upon their spiritual significance? According to the general postulate of psychology just referred to, there is not a single one of our states of mind, high or low, healthy or morbid, that has not some organic process as its condition. Scientific theories are organically conditioned just as much as religious emotions are; and if we only knew the facts intimately enough, we should doubt-less see "the liver" determining the dicta of the sturdy atheist as decisively as it does those of the Methodist under conviction anxious about his soul. When it alters in one way the blood that percolates it, we get the Methodist, when in another way, we get the atheist form of mind. So of all our raptures, and our drynesses, our longings and pantings, our questions and beliefs. They are equally organically founded, be they of religious or of non-religious content.

To plead the organic causation of a religious state of mind, then, in re-futation of its claim to possess superior spiritual value, is quite illogical and ar-bitrary, unless one have already worked out in advance some psycho-physical theory connecting spiritual values in general with determinate sorts of physiologi-cal change. Otherwise none of our thoughts and feelings, not even our scientific doctrines, not even our *dis*-beliefs, could retain any value as revelations of the

truth, for every one of them without exception flows from the state of their pos-
sessor's body at the time.

It is needless to say that medical materialism draws in point of fact no
such sweeping skeptical conclusion. It is sure, just as every simple man is sure,
that some states of mind are inwardly superior to others, and reveal to us more
truth, and in this it simply makes use of an ordinary spiritual judgment. It has no
physiological theory of the production of these its favorite states, by which it may
accredit them; and its attempt to discredit the states which it dislikes, by vaguely
associating them with nerves and liver, and connecting them with names con-
noting bodily affliction, is altogether illogical and inconsistent.

Let us play fair in this whole matter, and be quite candid with ourselves
and with the facts. When we think certain states of mind superior to others, is it
ever because of what we know concerning their organic antecedents? No! It is always for two entirely different reasons. It is either because we take an immediate
delight in them; or else it is because we believe them to bring us good conse-
quential fruits for life. When we speak disparagingly of "feverish fancies," surely
the fever-process as such is not the ground of our disesteem — for aught we
know to the contrary, 103 degrees or 104 degrees Fahrenheit might be a much
more favorable temperature for truths to germinate and sprout in, than the more
ordinary blood-heat of 97 or 98 degrees. It is either the disagreeableness itself of
the fancies, or their inability to bear the criticisms of the convalescent hour. When
we praise the thoughts which health brings, health's peculiar chemical metabolisms have nothing to do with determining our judgment. We know in fact almost
nothing about these metabolisms. It is the character of inner happiness in the
thoughts which stamps them as good, or else their consistency with our other
opinions and their serviceability for our needs, which make them pass for true in
our esteem.

Now the more intrinsic and the more remote of these criteria do not always hang together. Inner happiness and serviceability do not always agree. What
immediately feels most "good" is not always most "true," when measured by the
verdict of the rest of experience. The difference between Philip drunk and Philip
sober is the classic instance in corroboration. If merely "feeling good" could decide, drunkenness would be the supremely valid human experience. But its revelations, however acutely satisfying at the moment, are inserted into an environment which refuses to bear them out for any length of time. The consequence of
this discrepancy of the two criteria is the uncertainty which still prevails over so
many of our spiritual judgments. There are moments of sentimental and mystical
experience — we shall hereafter hear much of them — that carry an enormous
sense of inner authority and illumination with them when they come. But they
come seldom, and they do not come to every one; and the rest of life makes
either no connection with them, or tends to contradict them more than it confirms

them. Some persons follow more the voice of the moment in these cases, some prefer to be guided by the average results. Hence the sad discordancy of so many of the spiritual judgments of human beings; a discordancy which will be brought home to us acutely enough before these lectures end.

It is, however, a discordancy that can never be resolved by any merely medical test. ... the medical line of attack either confines itself to such secular productions as every one admits to be intrinsically eccentric, or else addresses itself exclusively to religious manifestations. And then it is because the religious manifestations have been already condemned because the critic dislikes them on internal or spiritual grounds.

In the natural sciences and industrial arts it never occurs to any one to try to refute opinions by showing up their author's neurotic constitution. Opinions here are invariably tested by logic and by experiment, no matter what may be their author's neurological type. It should be no otherwise with religious opinions. Their value can only be ascertained by spiritual judgments directly passed upon them, judgments based on our own immediate feeling primarily; and secondarily on what we can ascertain of their experiential relations to our moral needs and to the rest of what we hold as true.

Immediate luminousness, in short, *philosophical reasonableness*, and *moral helpfulness* are the only available criteria. Saint Teresa might have had the nervous system of the placidest cow, and it would not now save her theology, if the trial of the theology by these other tests should show it to be contemptible. And conversely if her theology can stand these other tests, it will make no difference how hysterical or nervously off her balance Saint Teresa may have been when she was with us here below.

You see that at bottom we are thrown back upon the general principles by which the empirical philosophy has always contended that we must be guided in our search for truth. Dogmatic philosophies have sought for tests for truth which might dispense us from appealing to the future. Some direct mark, by noting which we can be protected immediately and absolutely, now and forever, against all mistake — such has been the darling dream of philosophic dogmatists. It is clear that the *origin* of the truth would be an admirable criterion of this sort, if only the various origins could be discriminated from one another from this point of view, and the history of dogmatic opinion shows that origin has always been a favorite test. Origin in immediate intuition; origin in pontifical authority; origin in supernatural revelation, as by vision, hearing, or unaccountable impression; origin in direct possession by a higher spirit, expressing itself in prophecy and warning; origin in automatic utterance generally, — these origins have been stock warrants for the truth of one opinion after another which we find represented in religious history. The medical materialists are therefore only so many belated dogmatists, neatly turning the tables on their predecessors by using the criterion of origin in a destructive instead of an accreditive way.

They are effective with their talk of pathological origin only so long as supernatural origin is pleaded by the other side, and nothing but the argument from origin is under discussion. But the argument from origin has seldom been used alone, for it is too obviously insufficient. ...

[The] final test of a belief ... is our own empiricist criterion; and this criterion the stoutest insisters on supernatural origin have also been forced to use in the end. Among the visions and messages some have always been too patently silly, among the trances and convulsive seizures some have been too fruitless for conduct and character, to pass themselves off as significant, still less as divine. In the history of Christian mysticism the problem how to discriminate between such messages and experiences as were really divine miracles, and such others as the demon in his malice was able to counterfeit, thus making the religious person twofold more the child of hell he was before, has always been a difficult one to solve, needing all the sagacity and experience of the best directors of conscience. In the end it had to come to our empiricist criterion: By their fruits ye shall know them, not by their roots. Jonathan Edwards's *Treatise on Religious Affections* is an elaborate working out of this thesis. The *roots* of a man's virtue are inaccessible to us. No appearances whatever are infallible proofs of grace. Our practice is the only sure evidence, even to ourselves, that we are genuinely Christians. ...

Catholic writers are equally emphatic. The good dispositions which a vision, or voice, or other apparent heavenly favor leave behind them are the only marks by which we may be sure they are not possible deceptions of the tempter. ...

I fear I may have made a longer excursus than was necessary, and that fewer words would have dispelled the uneasiness which may have arisen among some of you as I announced my pathological program. At any rate you must all be ready now to judge the religious life by its results exclusively, and I shall assume that the bugaboo of morbid origin will scandalize your piety no more.

Still, you may ask me, if its results are to be the ground of our final spiritual estimate of a religious phenomenon, why threaten us at all with so much existential study of its conditions? Why not simply leave pathological questions out?

To this I reply in two ways: First, I say, irrepressible curiosity imperiously leads one on; and I say, secondly, that it always leads to a better understanding of a thing's significance to consider its exaggerations and perversions, its equivalents and substitutes and nearest relatives elsewhere. Not that we may thereby swamp the thing in the wholesale condemnation which we pass on its inferior congeners, but rather that we may by contrast ascertain the more precisely in what its merits consist, by learning at the same time to what particular dangers of corruption it may also be exposed.

Insane conditions have this advantage, that they isolate special factors of the mental life, and enable us to inspect them unmasked by their more usual surroundings. They play the part in mental anatomy which the scalpel and the microscope play in the anatomy of the body. To understand a thing rightly we need to see it both out of its environment and in it, and to have acquaintance with the whole range of its variations. The study of hallucinations has in this way been for psychologists the key to their comprehension of normal sensation, that of illusions has been the key to the right comprehension of perception. Morbid impulses and imperative conceptions, "fixed ideas," so called, have thrown a flood of light on the psychology of the normal will; and obsessions and delusions have performed the same service for that of the normal faculty of belief.

Similarly, the nature of genius has been illuminated by the attempts, of which I already made mention, to class it with psychopathical phenomena. Borderland insanity, crankiness, insane temperament, loss of mental balance, psychopathic degeneration (to use a few of the many synonyms by which it has been called), has certain peculiarities and liabilities which, when combined with a superior quality of intellect in an individual, make it more probable that he will make his mark and affect his age, than if his temperament were less neurotic. There is of course no special affinity between crankiness as such and superior intellect, ... for most psychopaths have feeble intellects, and superior intellects more commonly have normal nervous systems. But the psychopathic temperament, whatever be the intellect with which it finds itself paired, often brings with it ardor and excitability of character. The cranky person has extraordinary emotional susceptibility. He is liable to fixed ideas and obsessions. His conceptions tend to pass immediately into belief and action; and when he gets a new idea, he has no rest till he proclaims it, or in some way "works it off." "What shall I think of it?" a common person says to himself about a vexed question but in a "cranky" mind "What must I do about it?" is the form the question tends to take. In the autobiography of that high-souled woman, Mrs. Annie Besant, I read the following passage: "Plenty of people wish well to any good cause, but very few care to exert themselves to help it, and still fewer will risk anything in its support. 'Some one ought to do it, but why should I?' is the ever re-echoed phrase of weak-kneed amiability. 'Some one ought to do it, so why not I?' is the cry of some earnest servant of man, eagerly forward springing to face some perilous duty. Between these two sentences lie whole centuries of moral evolution." True enough! and between these two sentences lie also the different destinies of the ordinary sluggard and the psychopathic man. Thus, when a superior intellect and a psychopathic temperament coalesce — as in the endless permutations and combinations of human faculty, they are bound to coalesce often enough — in the same individual, we have the best possible condition for the kind of effective genius that gets into the biographical dictionaries. Such men do not remain mere critics and understanders with their intellect. Their ideas possess them, they inflict them, for better or worse, upon their companions or their age. ...

To pass now to religious phenomena, take the melancholy which, as we shall see, constitutes an essential moment in every complete religious evolution. Take the happiness which achieved religious belief confers. Take the trance-like states of insight into truth which all religious mystics report. ... These are each and all of them special cases of kinds of human experience of much wider scope. Religious melancholy, whatever peculiarities it may have *qua* religious, is at any rate melancholy. Religious happiness is happiness. Religious trance is trance. And the moment we renounce the absurd notion that a thing is exploded away as soon as it is classed with others, or its origin is shown; the moment we agree to stand by experimental results and inner quality, in judging of values, — who does not see that we are likely to ascertain the distinctive significance of religious melancholy and happiness, or of religious trances, far better by comparing them as conscientiously as we can with other varieties of melancholy, happiness, and trance, than by refusing to consider their place in any more general series, and treating them as if they were outside of nature's order altogether?

I hope that the course of these lectures will confirm us in this supposition. As regards the psychopathic origin of so many religious phenomena, that would not be in the least surprising or disconcerting, even were such phenomena certified from on high to be the most precious of human experiences. No one organism can possibly yield to its owner the whole body of truth. Few of us are not in some way infirm, or even diseased; and our very infirmities help us unexpectedly. In the psychopathic temperament we have the emotionality which is the *sine qua non* of moral perception; we have the intensity and tendency to emphasis which are the essence of practical moral vigor; and we have the love of metaphysics and mysticism which carry one's interests beyond the surface of the sensible world. What, then, is more natural than that this temperament should introduce one to regions of religious truth, to corners of the universe, which your robust Philistine type of nervous system, forever offering its biceps to be felt, thumping its breast, and thanking Heaven that it hasn't a single morbid fibre in its composition, would be sure to hide forever from its self-satisfied possessors?

If there were such a thing as inspiration from a higher realm, it might well be that the neurotic temperament would furnish the chief condition of the requisite receptivity. And having said thus much, I think that I may let the matter of religion and neuroticism drop.

The mass of collateral phenomena, morbid or healthy, with which the various religious phenomena must be compared in order to understand them better, forms what in the slang of pedagogics is termed "the apperceiving mass" by which we comprehend them. The only novelty that I can imagine this course of lectures to possess lies in the breadth of the apperceiving mass. I may succeed in discussing religious experiences in a wider context than has been usual in university courses.

6

Who is Religious and What is Faith?

The average believer has no need of the theistic proofs, would likely not understand them with any amount of study, came to believe in God through entirely different means, and may even regard applying reason to matters of faith as anti-religious. Such believers are characteristically fervent, unshakable in their faith, without benefit of any of the rational foundations of religion. They believe because they either inherit their faith from their parents or community, artlessly feel the presence of God in their hearts, fear eternal damnation or other consequences of not believing, or consciously snub cool reason to embrace hot religious passion. The intellectual aspect of religion means nothing to them.

But if there is no intellectual certainty that God is real, then why believe? At least some of the teachings of each religion run counter to reason, evidence, and experience. God demands faith, but does faith entail rejecting reason, denying evidence, and ignoring experience in order to gain favor with God?

Pascal analyzed religious belief into four possibilities and expressed it in the form of a wager. Either (1) we believe, and God is real; (2) we believe, but God is not real; (3) we do not believe, but God is real; or (4) we do not believe, and God is not real. For Pascal, we have everything to gain and nothing to lose by believing, but critics say that if (2) is true, then the believer's life has been wasted.

Pascal's scattered manuscript fragments for his envisioned defense of Christianity were discovered in the nineteenth century by French eclectic philosopher Victor Cousin (1792-1867) and thereafter compiled and published as *Pensées* ("Thoughts") in at least four separate arrangements by Léon Brunschvicg, Louis Lafuma, Jean Mesnard, and Philippe Sellier, respectively. Since these numbering systems have all survived, it is important when citing Pascal to say which is being used. Pascal's famous wager occurs in Brunschvicg fragment number 233, given here in the 1908 translation of William Finlayson Trotter:

Infinite — nothing. — Our soul is cast into a body, where it finds number, time, dimension. Thereupon it reasons, and calls this nature, necessity, and can believe nothing else.

Unity joined to infinity adds nothing to it, no more than one foot to an infinite measure. The finite is annihilated in the presence of the infinite, and becomes a pure nothing. So our spirit before God, so our justice before divine justice. There is not so great a disproportion between our justice and that of God as between unity and infinity.

The justice of God must be vast like His compassion. Now justice to the outcast is less vast, and ought less to offend our feelings than mercy towards the elect.

We know that there is an infinite, and are ignorant of its nature. As we know it to be false that numbers are finite, it is therefore true that there is an infinity in number. But we do not know what it is. It is false that it is even, it is false that it is odd; for the addition of a unit can make no change in its nature. Yet it is a number, and every number is odd or even (this is certainly true of every finite number). So we may well know that there is a God without knowing what He is. Is there not one substantial truth, seeing there are so many things which are not the truth itself?

We know then the existence and nature of the finite, because we also are finite and have extension. We know the existence of the infinite, and are ignorant of its nature, because it has extension like us, but not limits like us. But we know neither the existence nor the nature of God, because He has neither extension nor limits.

But by faith we know His existence; in glory we shall know His nature. Now, I have already shown that we may well know the existence of a thing, without knowing its nature.

Let us now speak according to natural lights.

If there is a God, He is infinitely incomprehensible, since, having neither parts nor limits, He has no affinity to us. We are then incapable of knowing either what He is or if He is. This being so, who will dare to undertake the decision of the question? Not we, who have no affinity to Him.

Who then will blame Christians for not being able to give a reason for their belief, since they profess a religion for which they cannot give a reason? They declare, in expounding it to the world, that it is a foolishness ... and then you complain that they do not prove it! If they proved it, they would not keep their word; it is in lacking proofs, that they are not lacking in sense. "Yes, but although this excuses those who offer it as such, and takes away from them the blame of putting it forward without reason, it does not excuse those who receive it." Let us then examine this point, and say, "God is, or He is not." But to which side shall we incline? Reason can decide nothing here. There is an infinite chaos which separated us. A game is being played at the extremity of this infinite distance where heads or tails will turn up. What will you wager? According to reason, you can do neither the one thing nor the other; according to reason, you can defend neither of the propositions.

Do not then reprove for error those who have made a choice; for you know nothing about it. "No, but I blame them for having made, not this choice, but a choice; for again both he who chooses heads and he who chooses tails are equally at fault, they are both in the wrong. The true course is not to wager at all."

Yes; but you must wager. It is not optional. You are embarked. Which will you choose then? Let us see. Since you must choose, let us see which interests you least. You have two things to lose, the true and the good; and two things to stake, your reason and your will, your knowledge and your happiness; and your nature has two things to shun, error and misery. Your reason is no more shocked in choosing one rather than the other, since you must of necessity choose. This is one point settled. But your happiness? Let us weigh the gain and the loss in wagering that God is. Let us estimate these two chances. If you gain, you gain all; if you lose, you lose nothing. Wager, then, without hesitation that He is. — "That is very fine. Yes, I must wager; but I may perhaps wager too much." — Let us see. Since there is an equal risk of gain and of loss, if you had only to gain two lives, instead of one, you might still wager. But if there were three lives to gain, you would have to play (since you are under the necessity of playing), and you would be imprudent, when you are forced to play, not to chance your life to gain three at a game where there is an equal risk of loss and gain. But there is an eternity of life and happiness. And this being so, if there were an infinity of chances, of which one only would be for you, you would still be right in wagering one to win two, and you would act stupidly, being obliged to play, by refusing to stake one life against three at a game in which out of an infinity of chances there is one for you, if there were an infinity of an infinitely happy life to gain. But there is here an infinity of an infinitely happy life to gain, a chance of gain against a finite number of chances of loss, and what you stake is finite. It is all divided; wherever the infinite is and there is not an infinity of chances of loss against that of gain, there is no time to hesitate, you must give all. And thus, when one is forced to play, he must renounce reason to preserve his life, rather than risk it for infinite gain, as likely to happen as the loss of nothingness.

For it is no use to say it is uncertain if we will gain, and it is certain that we risk, and that the infinite distance between the *certainty* of what is staked and the *uncertainty* of what will be gained, equals the finite good which is certainly staked against the uncertain infinite. It is not so, as every player stakes a certainty to gain an uncertainty, and yet he stakes a finite certainty to gain a finite uncertainty, without transgressing against reason. There is not an infinite distance between the certainty staked and the uncertainty of the gain; that is untrue. In truth, there is an infinity between the certainty of gain and the certainty of loss. But the uncertainty of the gain is proportioned to the certainty of the stake according to the proportion of the chances of gain and loss. Hence it comes that, if there are as many risks on one side as on the other, the course is to play even; and then the certainty of the stake is equal to the uncertainty of the gain, so far is it from fact that there is an infinite distance between them. And so our proposition is of infinite force, when there is the finite to stake in a game where there are equal risks of gain and of loss, and the infinite to gain. This is demonstrable; and if men are capable of any truths, this is one.

"I confess it, I admit it. But, still, is there no means of seeing the faces of the cards?" Yes, Scripture and the rest, etc. "Yes, but I have my hands tied and my mouth closed; I am forced to wager, and am not free. I am not released, and am so made that I cannot believe. What, then, would you have me do?"

True. But at least learn your inability to believe, since reason brings you to this, and yet you cannot believe. Endeavour then to convince yourself, not by increase of proofs of God, but by the abatement of your passions. You would like to attain faith, and do not know the way; you would like to cure yourself of unbelief, and ask the remedy for it. Learn of those who have been bound like you, and who now stake all their possessions. These are people who know the way which you would follow, and who are cured of an ill of which you would be cured. Follow the way by which they began; by acting as if they believed, taking the holy water, having masses said, etc. Even this will naturally make you believe, and deaden your acuteness. "But this is what I am afraid of." — And why? What have you to lose?

But to show you that this leads you there, it is this which will lessen the passions, which are your stumbling-blocks.

The end of this discourse. — Now, what harm will befall you in taking this side? You will be faithful, humble, grateful, generous, a sincere friend, truthful. Certainly you will not have those poisonous pleasures, glory and luxury; but will you not have others? I will tell you that you will thereby gain in this life, and that, at each step you take on this road, you will see so great certainty of gain, so much nothingness in what you risk, that you will at last recognise that you have wagered for something certain and infinite, for which you have given nothing.

"Ah! This discourse transports me, charms me," etc.

If this discourse pleases you and seems impressive, know that it is made by a man who has knelt, both before and after it, in prayer to that Being, infinite and without parts, before whom he lays all he has, for you also to lay before Him all you have for your own good and for His glory, that so strength may be given to lowliness.

A skeptic, apostate, or Aristotelian might argue that we lose our self-respect by wagering as Pascal recommends. That is, if we choose to believe in God against our better judgment or rational inclination, only in hope of gaining eternal happiness in heaven, then we have in effect abandoned reason, that which raises us above the animals and makes us human, and have become no better than the dog who grovels at its master's feet in hope of gaining indefinite food, favor, and petting in the master's house. Such a critic stands in need of the theistic proofs, and cannot be helped by any religion of the heart.

Against Pascal, Clifford wrote "The Ethics of Belief," which appeared in the *Contemporary Review* (1877) and, shortly after his untimely death from tuberculosis, in his *Lectures and Essays* (1879):

A shipowner was about to send to sea an emigrant-ship. He knew that she was old, and not over-well built at the first; that she had seen many seas and climes,, and often had needed repairs. Doubts had been suggested to him that possibly she was not seaworthy. These doubts preyed upon his mind, and made him unhappy; he thought that perhaps he ought to have her thoroughly overhauled and refitted, even though this should put him at great expense. Before the ship sailed, however, he succeeded in overcoming these melancholy reflections. He said to himself that she had gone safely through so many voyages and weathered so many storms that it was idle to suppose she would not come safely home from this trip also. He would put his trust in Providence, which could hardly fail to protect all these unhappy families that were leaving their fatherland to seek for better times elsewhere. He would dismiss from his mind all ungenerous suspicions about the honesty of builders and contractors. In such ways he acquired a sincere and comfortable conviction that his vessel was thoroughly safe and seaworthy; he watched her departure with a light heart, and benevolent wishes for the success of the exiles in their strange new home that was to be; and he got his insurance-money when she went down in mid-ocean and told no tales.

What shall we say of him? Surely this, that he was verily guilty of the death of those men. It is admitted that he did sincerely believe in the soundness of his ship; but the sincerity of his conviction can in no wise help him, because *he had no right to believe on such evidence as was before him.* He had acquired his belief not by honestly earning it in patient investigation, but by stifling his doubts. And although in the end he may have felt so sure about it that he could not think otherwise, yet inasmuch as he had knowingly and willingly worked himself into that frame of mind, he must be held responsible for it.

Let us alter the case a little, and suppose that the ship was not unsound after all; that she made her voyage safely, and many others after it. Will that diminish the guilt of her owner? Not one jot. When an action is once done, it is right or wrong for ever; no accidental failure of its good or evil fruits can possibly alter that. The man would not have been innocent, he would only have been not found out. The question of right or wrong has to do with the origin of his belief, not the matter of it; not what it was, but how he got it; not whether it turned out to be true or false, but whether he had a right to believe on such evidence as was before him.

There was once an island in which some of the inhabitants professed a religion teaching neither the doctrine of original sin nor that of eternal punishment. A suspicion got abroad that the professors of this religion had made use of unfair means to get their doctrines taught to children. They were accused of wresting the laws of their country in such a way as to remove children from the care of their natural and legal guardians; and even of stealing them away and keeping them concealed from their friends and relations. A certain number of men formed themselves into a society for the purpose of agitating the public about this matter. They published grave accusations against against individual citizens of the highest position and character, and did all in their power to injure these citizens in their exercise of their professions. So great was the noise they made, that a Commission was appointed to investigate the facts; but after the Commission had carefully inquired into all the evidence that could be got, it appeared that the accused were innocent. Not only had they been accused of insufficient evidence, but the evidence of their innocence was such as the agitators might easily have obtained, if they had attempted a fair inquiry. After these disclosures the inhabitants of that country looked upon the members of the agitating society, not only as persons whose judgment was to be distrusted, but also as no longer to be counted honourable men. For although they had sincerely and conscientiously believed in the charges they had made, *yet they had no right to believe on such evidence as was before them*. Their sincere convictions, instead of being honestly earned by patient inquiring, were stolen by listening to the voice of prejudice and passion.

Let us vary this case also, and suppose, other things remaining as before, that a still more accurate investigation proved the accused to have been really guilty. Would this make any difference in the guilt of the accusers? Clearly not; the question is not whether their belief was true or false, but whether they entertained it on wrong grounds. They would no doubt say, "Now you see that we were right after all; next time perhaps you will believe us." And they might be believed, but they would not thereby become honourable men. They would not be innocent, they would only be not found out. Every one of them, if he chose to examine himself *in foro conscientiae*, would know that he had acquired and nourished a belief, when he had no right to believe on such evidence as was before him; and therein he would know that he had done a wrong thing.

It may be said, however, that in both these supposed cases it is not the belief which is judged to be wrong, but the action following upon it. The shipowner might say, "I am perfectly certain that my ship is sound, but still I feel it my duty to have her examined, before trusting the lives of so many people to her." And it might be said to the agitator, "However convinced you were of the justice of your cause and the truth of your convictions, you ought not to have made a public attack upon any man's character until you had examined the evidence on both sides with the utmost patience and care."

In the first place, let us admit that, so far as it goes, this view of the case is right and necessary; right, because even when a man's belief is so fixed that he cannot think otherwise, he still has a choice in the action suggested by it, and so cannot escape the duty of investigating on the ground of the strength of his convictions; and necessary, because those who are not yet capable of controlling their feelings and thoughts must have a plain rule dealing with overt acts.

But this being premised as necessary, it becomes clear that it is not sufficient, and that our previous judgment is required to supplement it. For it is not possible so to sever the belief from the action it suggests as to condemn the one without condemning the other. No man holding a strong belief on one side of a question, or even wishing to hold a belief on one side, can investigate it with such fairness and completeness as if he were really in doubt and unbiased; so that the existence of a belief not founded on fair inquiry unfits a man for the performance of this necessary duty.

Nor is it that truly a belief at all which has not some influence upon the actions of him who holds it. He who truly believes that which prompts him to an action has looked upon the action to lust after it, he has committed it already in his heart. If a belief is not realized immediately in open deeds, it is stored up for the guidance of the future. It goes to make a part of that aggregate of beliefs which is the link between sensation and action at every moment of all our lives, and which is so organized and compacted together that no part of it can be isolated from the rest, but every new addition modifies the structure of the whole. No real belief, however trifling and fragmentary it may seem, is ever truly insignificant; it prepares us to receive more of its like, confirms those which resembled it before, and weakens others; and so gradually it lays a stealthy train in our inmost thoughts, which may someday explode into overt action, and leave its stamp upon our character for ever.

And no one man's belief is in any case a private matter which concerns himself alone. Our lives are guided by that general conception of the course of things which has been created by society for social purposes. Our words, our phrases, our forms and processes and modes of thought, are common property, fashioned and perfected from age to age; an heirloom which every succeeding generation inherits as a precious deposit and a sacred trust to be handled on to the next one, not unchanged but enlarged and purified, with some clear marks of its proper handiwork. Into this, for good or ill, is woven every belief of every man who has speech of his fellows. A awful privilege, and an awful responsibility, that we should help to create the world in which posterity will live.

In the two supposed cases which have been considered, it has been judged wrong to believe on insufficient evidence, or to nourish belief by suppressing doubts and avoiding investigation. The reason of this judgment is not far to seek: it is that in both these cases the belief held by one man was of great importance to other men. But for as much as no belief held by one man, however seemingly trivial the belief, and however obscure the believer, is ever actually insignificant or without its effect on the fate of mankind, we have no choice but to extend our judgment to all cases of belief whatever. Belief, that sacred faculty which prompts the decisions of our will, and knits into harmonious working all the compacted energies of our being, is ours not for ourselves, but for humanity. It is rightly used on truths which have been established by long experience and waiting toil, and which have stood in the fierce light of free and fearless questioning. Then it helps to bind men together, and to strengthen and direct their common action. It is desecrated when given to unproved and unquestioned statements, for the solace and private pleasure of the believer; to add a tinsel splendour to the plain straight road of our life and display a bright mirage beyond it; or even to drown the common sorrows of our kind by a self-deception which allows them not only to cast down, but also to degrade us. Whoso would deserve well of his fellows in this matter will guard the purity of his belief with a very fanaticism of jealous care, lest at any time it should rest on an unworthy object, and catch a stain which can never be wiped away.

It is not only the leader of men, statesman, philosopher, or poet, that owes this bounden duty to mankind. Every rustic who delivers in the village alehouse his slow, infrequent sentences, may help to kill or keep alive the fatal superstitions which clog his race. Every hard-worked wife of an artisan may transmit to her children beliefs which shall knit society together, or rend it in pieces. No simplicity of mind, no obscurity of station, can escape the universal duty of questioning all that we believe.

It is true that this duty is a hard one, and the doubt which comes out of it is often a very bitter thing. It leaves us bare and powerless where we thought that we were safe and strong. To know all about anything is to know how to deal with it under all circumstances. We feel much happier and more secure when we think we know precisely what to do, no matter what happens, than when we have lost our way and do not know where to turn. And if we have supposed ourselves to know all about anything, and to be capable of doing what is fit in regard to it, we naturally do not like to find that we are really ignorant and powerless, that we have to begin again at the beginning, and try to learn what the thing is and how it is to be dealt with — if indeed anything can be learnt about it. It is the sense of power attached to a sense of knowledge that makes men desirous of believing, and afraid of doubting.

This sense of power is the highest and best of pleasures when the belief on which it is founded is a true belief, and has been fairly earned by investigation. For then we may justly feel that it is common property, and hold good for others as well as for ourselves. Then we may be glad, not that *I* have learned secrets by which I am safer and stronger, but that *we men* have got mastery over more of the world; and we shall be strong, not for ourselves but in the name of Man and in his strength. But if the belief has been accepted on insufficient evidence, the pleasure is a stolen one. Not only does it deceive ourselves by giving us a sense of power which we do not really possess, but it is sinful, because it is stolen in defiance of our duty to mankind. That duty is to guard ourselves from such beliefs as from pestilence, which may shortly master our own body and then spread to the rest of the town. What would be thought of one who, for the sake of a sweet fruit, should deliberately run the risk of delivering a plague upon his family and his neighbours?

And, as in other such cases, it is not the risk only which has to be considered; for a bad action is always bad at the time when it is done, no matter what happens afterwards. Every time we let ourselves believe for unworthy reasons, we weaken our powers of self-control, of doubting, of judicially and fairly weighing evidence. We all suffer severely enough from the maintenance and support of false beliefs and the fatally wrong actions which they lead to, and the evil born when one such belief is entertained is great and wide. But a greater and wider evil arises when the credulous character is maintained and supported, when a habit of believing for unworthy reasons is fostered and made permanent. If I steal money from any person, there may be no harm done from the mere transfer of possession; he may not feel the loss, or it may prevent him from using the money badly. But I cannot help doing this great wrong towards Man, that I make myself dishonest. What hurts society is not that it should lose its property, but that it should become a den of thieves, for then it must cease to be society. This is why we ought not to do evil, that good may come; for at any rate this great evil has come, that we have done evil and are made wicked thereby. In like manner, if I let myself believe anything on insufficient evidence, there may be no great harm done by the mere belief; it may be true after all, or I may never have occasion to exhibit it in outward acts. But I cannot help doing this great wrong towards Man, that I make myself credulous. The danger to society is not merely that it should believe wrong things, though that is great enough; but that it should become credulous, and lose the habit of testing things and inquiring into them; for then it must sink back into savagery.

The harm which is done by credulity in a man is not confined to the fostering of a credulous character in others, and consequent support of false beliefs. Habitual want of care about what I believe leads to habitual want of care in others about the truth of what is told to me. Men speak the truth of one another when each reveres the truth in his own mind and in the other's mind; but how shall my friend revere the truth in my mind when I myself am careless about it, when I believe things because I want to believe them, and because they are comforting and pleasant? Will he not learn to cry, "Peace," to me, when there is no peace? By such a course I shall surround myself with a thick atmosphere of falsehood and fraud, and in that I must live. It may matter little to me, in my cloud-castle of sweet illusions and darling lies; but it matters much to Man that I have made my neighbours ready to deceive. The credulous man is father to the liar and the cheat; he lives in the bosom of this his family, and it is no marvel if he should become even as they are. So closely are our duties knit together, that whoso shall keep the whole law, and yet offend in one point, he is guilty of all.

To sum up: it is wrong always, everywhere, and for anyone, to believe anything upon insufficient evidence.

If a man, holding a belief which he was taught in childhood or persuaded of afterwards, keeps down and pushes away any doubts which arise about it in his mind, purposely avoids the reading of books and the company of men that call into question or discuss it, and regards as impious those questions which cannot easily be asked without disturbing it – the life of that man is one long sin against mankind.

If this judgment seems harsh when applied to those simple souls who have never known better, who have been brought up from the cradle with a horror of doubt, and taught that their eternal welfare depends on *what* they believe, then it leads to the very serious question, *Who hath made Israel to sin?* It may be permitted me to fortify this judgment with the sentence of Milton — "A man may be a heretic in the truth; and if he believe things only because his pastor says so, or the assembly so determine, without knowing other reason, though his belief be true, yet the very truth he holds becomes his heresy." And with this famous aphorism of Coleridge — "He who begins by loving Christianity better than Truth, will proceed by loving his own sect or Church better than Christianity, and end loving himself better than all."

Inquiry into the evidence of a doctrine is not to be made once for all, and then taken as finally settled. It is never lawful to stifle a doubt; for either it can be honestly answered by means of the inquiry already made, or else it proves that the inquiry was not complete.

"But," says one, "I am a busy man; I have no time for the long course of study which would be necessary to make me in any degree a competent judge of certain questions, or even able to understand the nature of the arguments." Then he should have no time to believe.

Against both Clifford and Pascal, James published *The Will to Believe and Other Essays in Popular Philosophy* in 1897:

In Pascal's Thoughts there is a celebrated passage known in literature as Pascal's wager. In it he tries to force us into Christianity by reasoning as if our concern with truth resembled our concern with the stakes in a game of chance. ... Why should you not? At bottom, what have you to lose?

You probably feel that when religious faith expresses itself thus, in the language of the gaming-table, it is put to its last trumps. Surely Pascal's own personal belief in masses and holy water had far other springs; and this celebrated page of his is but an argument for others, a last desperate snatch at a weapon against the hardness of the unbelieving heart. We feel that a faith in masses and holy water adopted wilfully after such a mechanical calculation would lack the inner soul of faith's reality; and if we were ourselves in the place of the Deity, we should probably take particular pleasure in cutting off believers of this pattern from their infinite reward. It is evident that unless there be some pre-existing tendency to believe in masses and holy water, the option offered to the will by Pascal is not a living option. ...

The talk of believing by our volition seems, then, from one point of view, simply silly. From another point of view it is worse than silly, it is vile. When one turns to the magnificent edifice of the physical sciences, and sees how it was reared; what thousands of disinterested moral lives of men lie buried in its mere foundations; what patience and postponement, what choking down of preference, what submission to the icy laws of outer fact are wrought into its very stones and mortar; how absolutely impersonal it stands in its vast augustness, — then how besotted and contemptible seems every little sentimentalist who comes blowing his voluntary smoke-wreaths, and pretending to decide things from out of his private dream! Can we wonder if those bred in the rugged and manly school of science should feel like spewing such subjectivism out of their mouths? ... And that delicious *enfant terrible* Clifford ...

All this strikes one as healthy, even when expressed, as by Clifford, with somewhat too much of robustious pathos in the voice. Free-will and simple wishing do seem, in the matter of our credences, to be only fifth wheels to the coach. Yet if any one should thereupon assume that intellectual insight is what remains after wish and will and sentimental preference have taken wing, or that pure reason is what then settles our opinions, he would fly quite as directly in the teeth of the facts.

It is only our already dead hypotheses that our willing nature is unable to bring to life again. But what has made them dead for us is for the most part a previous action of our willing nature of an antagonistic kind. When I say "willing nature," I do not mean only such deliberate volitions as may have set up habits of belief that we cannot now escape from, — I mean all such factors of belief as fear and hope, prejudice and passion, imitation and partisanship, the circum-pressure of our caste and set. As a matter of fact we find ourselves believing, we hardly know how or why. ... Our reason is quite satisfied, in nine hundred and ninety-nine cases out of every thousand of us, if it can find a few arguments that will do to recite in case our credulity is criticised by some one else. Our faith is faith in some one else's faith, and in the greatest matters this is most the case. Our belief in truth itself, for instance, that there is a truth, and that our minds and it are made for each other,—what is it but a passionate affirmation of desire, in which our social system backs us up? We want to have a truth; we want to believe that our experiments and studies and discussions must put us in a continually better and better position towards it; and on this line we agree to fight out our thinking lives. But if a pyrrhonistic sceptic asks us *how we know* all this, can our logic find a reply? No! certainly it cannot. It is just one volition against another, — we willing to go in for life upon a trust or assumption which he, for his part, does not care to make.

As a rule we disbelieve all facts and theories for which we have no use. Clifford's cosmic emotions find no use for Christian feelings. Huxley belabors the bishops because there is no use for sacerdotalism in his scheme of life. New-man, on the contrary, goes over to Romanism, and finds all sorts of reasons good for staying there, because a priestly system is for him an organic need and delight. Why do so few "scientists" even look at the evidence for telepathy, so called? Because they think, as a leading biologist, now dead, once said to me, that even if such a thing were true, scientists ought to band together to keep it suppressed and concealed. It would undo the uniformity of Nature and all sorts of other things without which scientists cannot carry on their pursuits. But if this very man had been shown something which as a scientist he might *do* with telepathy, he might not only have examined the evidence, but even have found it good enough. This very law which the logicians would impose upon us — if I may give the name of logicians to those who would rule out our willing nature here — is based on nothing but their own natural wish to exclude all elements for which they, in their professional quality of logicians, can find no use.

Evidently, then, our non-intellectual nature does influence our convic-tions. There are passional tendencies and volitions which run before and others which come after belief, and it is only the latter that are too late for the fair; and they are not too late when the previous passional work has been already in their own direction. Pascal's argument, instead of being powerless, then seems a regular clincher, and is the last stroke needed to make our faith in masses and holy water complete. The state of things is evidently far from simple; and pure insight and logic, whatever they might do ideally, are not the only things that really do produce our creeds.

Our next duty, having recognized this mixed-up state of affairs, is to ask whether it be simply reprehensible and pathological, or whether, on the contrary, we must treat it as a normal element in making up our minds. The thesis I defend is, briefly stated, this: *Our passional nature not only lawfully may, but must, decide an option between propositions, whenever it is a genuine option that cannot by its nature be decided on intellectual grounds; for to say, under such circumstances, "Do not decide, but leave the question open," is itself a passional decision, — just like deciding yes or no, — and is attended with the same risk of losing the truth. ...*

Now, let us consider what the logical elements of this situation are *in case the religious hypothesis in both its branches be really true.* ... So proceeding, we see, first, that religion offers itself as a *momentous* option. We are supposed to gain, even now, by our belief, and to lose by our nonbelief, a certain vital good. Secondly, religion is a *forced* option, so far as that good goes. We cannot escape the issue by remaining sceptical and waiting for more light, because, although we do avoid error in that way *if religion be untrue*, we lose the good, *if it be true*, just as certainly as if we positively chose to disbelieve. It is as if a man should hesitate indefinitely to ask a certain woman to marry him because he was not perfectly sure that she would prove an angel after he brought her home. Would he not cut himself off from that particular angel-possibility as decisively as if he went and married some one else? Scepticism, then, is not avoidance of option; it is option of a certain particular kind of risk. *Better risk loss of truth than chance of error,* — that is your faith-vetoer's exact position. He is actively playing his stake as much as the believer is; he is backing the field against the religious hypothesis, just as the believer is backing the religious hypothesis against the field. To preach scepticism to us as a duty until "sufficient evidence" for religion be found, is tantamount therefore to telling us, when in presence of the religious hypothesis, that to yield to our fear of its being error is wiser and better than to yield to our hope that it may be true. It is not intellect against all passions, then; it is only intellect with one passion laying down its law. And by what, forsooth, is the supreme wisdom of this passion warranted? Dupery for dupery, what proof is there that dupery through hope is so much worse than dupery through fear? I, for one, can see no proof; and I simply refuse obedience to the scientist's command to imitate his kind of option, in a case where my own stake is important enough to give me the right to choose my own form of risk. If religion be true and the evidence for it be still insufficient, I do not wish, by putting your extinguisher upon my nature (which feels to me as if it had after all some business in this matter), to forfeit my sole chance in life of getting upon the winning side, — that chance depending, of course, on my willingness to run the risk of acting as if my passional need of taking the world religiously might be prophetic and right.

In "Is Life Worth Living?", an address to the Harvard Young Men's Christian Association published in the *International Journal of Ethics* (1895), James defined the concept of the "self-verifying belief," i.e., a belief which is true only if it is believed:

A man's religious faith (whatever more special items of doctrine it may involve) means ... essentially his faith in the existence of an unseen order of some kind in which the riddles of the natural order may be found explained. ...

It is a fact of human nature, that men can live and die by the help of a sort of faith that goes without a single dogma or definition. ...

It is only by risking our persons from one hour to another that we live at all. And often enough our faith beforehand in an uncertified result *is the only thing that makes the result come true.* Suppose, for instance, that you are climbing a mountain, and have worked yourself into a position from which the only escape is by a terrible leap. Have faith that you can successfully make it, and your feet are nerved to its accomplishment. But mistrust yourself, and think of all the sweet things you have heard the scientists say of *maybes,* and you will hesitate so long that, at last, all unstrung and trembling, and launching yourself in a moment of despair, you roll in the abyss. In such a case (and it belongs to an enormous class) the part of wisdom as well as of courage, is to *believe what is in the line of your needs,* for only by such belief is the need fulfilled. Refuse to believe, and you shall indeed be right, for you shall irretrievably perish. But believe, and again you shall be right, for you shall save yourself. You make one or the other of two possible universes true by your trust or mistrust, — both universes having been only *maybes,* in this particular, before you contributed your act.

James's famous metaphor of the endangered mountain climber is the linchpin of his case against Pascal. The climber has a clear and obvious reason to believe, i.e., an existential emergency, to save his life; but Pascal's wagerer merely surrenders to a chance that depends on an assumption of church doctrine.

Pascal, Kierkegaard, Tertullian, and their fellow fideists hold that we cannot be truly religious without being energetic and boldly proactive. But for those who are more likely to incorporate reason into their religious belief, religious people need not be ecstatic knights of faith or daring believers. They could also be commonplace members of organized religions, routinized followers, gregarious spiritual workers for the greater immediate good of humankind, solitary contemplatives such as Whitehead encourages in *Religion in the Making,* or serene mystics such as Buber supports in *I and Thou.* We need not abandon reason in order to recognize the holy or to feel the spirit in nature.

7

What is God?

Traditionally, in most religions, God is believed to have superlative attributes such as omnipotence, omnipresence, omnibenevolence, eternity, omniscience including absolute foreknowledge, immutability, infallibility, immortality, and perfection in general. But, as is clear from negative theology, assigning attributes to God, even superlative attributes, makes God less than God actually is, or limits God by restricting the divine to human understanding. As Anselm wrote in *Proslogium* XV, God is indeed greater than anything we finite beings can say or think about what is divine. To account for this inconceivable "beyond-perfection" of God, Hinduism posits an unknowable God without attributes, Brahman Nirguna, behind the trinity of Brahma, Vishnu, and Shiva, who are collectively known as Brahman Saguna, or Brahman with attributes. Similarly, Western neo-Platonic Christian mystics such as Meister Eckhart (1260?-1327?) follow the lead of Pseudo-Dionysius by referring to the "Godhead" (*Gottheit*) as the unknowable "beyond-God" without attributes that is the source of and greater than the Christian trinity of Father, Son, and Holy Spirit, all of whom have definite, recognizable attributes as individuals. Moreover, Hartshorne challenged the entire notion of divine attributes because they render God static, unable to evolve or improve.

None of the theistic proofs show the reality of any named God, such as Yahweh, Allah, Brahman, *et al.*, over against any other named God. They show only that there must be an ultimate ground of being. Thus the proofs do not serve the purposes of any particular religion because they do not say anything about the doctrine-specific nature or characteristics of this ground of being. Even the design argument, which depicts God as the supremely intelligent creator in a Judeo-Christian context, is equally applicable to Islam, Hinduism, *et al*. The individual traits of the Gods of particular religions are matters of theological doctrine, not philosophical speculation.

All of God's attributes are controversial. If God is immutable, how is divine action possible? If God is all good, why is there evil? Does God have, as Spinoza claims, infinite attributes, and if so, what does this mean?

Among the most controversial questions surrounding the divine attributes is how to reconcile divine foreknowledge with human free will. This is a topic in *The Consolation of Philosophy* by Roman philosopher Boethius (ca. 480-524), a dialogue between him and his imagined Lady Philosophy as he sits in the prison of Ostrogothic King Theodoric in 524 awaiting execution on unjust charges. She acquaints him with the nature of God and thus prepares him to meet his fate with courage and serenity. This excerpt from Book Five is adapted from Wilbraham Villiers Cooper's 1902 translation:

[Lady Philosophy]: "If chance is defined as an outcome of random influence, produced by no sequence of causes, I am sure that there is no such thing as chance, and I consider that it is but an empty word, beyond showing the meaning of the matter which we have in hand. For what place can be left for anything happening at random, so long as God controls everything in order? It is a true saying that nothing can come out of nothing. None of the old philosophers has denied that, though they did not apply it to the effective principle, but to the matter operated upon, that is to say, to nature; and this was the foundation upon which they built all their reasoning. If anything arises from no causes, it will appear to have risen out of nothing. But if this is impossible, then chance also cannot be anything of that sort, which is stated in the definition which we mentioned."

"Then is there nothing which can be justly called chance, nor anything that happens by chance?" I asked. "Or is there anything which common people know not, but to which those words refer?"

"My philosopher, Aristotle, defined chance in his *Physics* briefly and well nigh truly."

"How?" I asked.

"Whenever anything is done with one intention, but something else, other than was intended, results from certain causes, that is called chance. For instance, if a man digs the ground for the sake of cultivating it, and finds a heap of buried gold, such a thing is believed to have happened by chance. But it does not come from nothing, for it has its own causes, whose unforeseen and unexpected coincidence seem to have brought about a chance. For if the cultivator did not dig the ground, if the owner had not buried his money, the gold would not have been found. These are the causes of the chance piece of good fortune, which comes about from the causes which meet it, and move along with it, not from the intention of the actor. For neither the burier nor the tiller intended that the gold should be found; but, as I said, it was a coincidence, and it happened that the one dug up what the other buried. We may therefore define chance as an unexpected result from the coincidence of certain causes in matters where there was another purpose. The order of the universe, advancing with its inevitable sequences, brings about this coincidence of causes. This order itself emanates from its source, which is Providence, and disposes all things in their proper time and place." ...

"I have listened to you," I said, "and agree that it is as you say. But in this close sequence of causes, is there any freedom for our judgment or does this chain of fate bind the very feelings of our minds too?"

"There is free will," she answered. "Nor could there be any reasoning nature without freedom of judgment. For any being that can use its reason by nature, has a power of judgment by which it can without further aid decide each point, and so distinguish between objects to be desired and objects to be shunned. Each therefore seeks what it deems desirable, and flies from what it considers should be shunned. Wherefore all who have reason have also freedom of desiring and refusing in themselves. But I do not lay down that this is equal in all beings. Heavenly and divine beings have with them a judgment of great insight, an imperturbable will, and a power which can effect their desires. But human spirits must be more free when they keep themselves safe in the contemplation of the mind of God; but less free when they sink into bodies, and less still when they are bound by their earthly members. The last stage is mere slavery, when the spirit is given over to vices and has fallen away from the possession of its reason. For when the mind turns its eyes from the light of truth on high to lower darkness, soon they are dimmed by the clouds of ignorance, and become turbid through ruinous passions. By yielding to these passions and consenting to them, men increase the slavery which they have brought upon themselves, and their true liberty is lost in captivity. But God, looking upon all out of the infinite, perceives the views of Providence, and disposes each as its destiny has already fated for it according to its merits." ...

Then I said, "Again am I plunged in yet more doubt and difficulty."

"What is it?" she asked, "though I have already my idea of what your trouble is?"

"There seems to be," I said, "incompatibility between God's universal foreknowledge and that of any freedom of will or judgment. For if God foresees all things and cannot in anything be mistaken, that, which His Providence sees will happen, must result. Wherefore if it knows beforehand not only men's deeds but even their designs and wishes, there will be no freedom of judgment For there can neither be any deed done, nor wish formed, except such as the infallible Providence of God has foreseen. For if matters could ever so be turned that they resulted otherwise than was foreseen of Providence, this foreknowledge would cease to be sure. But, rather than knowledge, it is opinion which is uncertain; and that, I deem, is not applicable to God. Further, I cannot approve of an argument by which some men think that they can cut this knot; for they say that a result does not come to pass for the reason that Providence has foreseen it, but the opposite rather, namely, that because it is about to come to pass, therefore it cannot be hidden from God's Providence. In that way it seems to me that the argument must resolve itself into an argument on the other side. For in that case it is not necessary that that which is foreseen should happen, but that that which is about to happen should be foreseen; as though, indeed, our question was whether God's foreknowledge is the certain cause of future events, or whether the certainty of future events is the cause of Providence. But let our aim be to prove that, whatever be the shape which this series of causes takes, the fulfillment of God's foreknowledge is necessary, even if this knowledge may not seem to induce the necessity for the occurrence of future events. For instance, if a man sits down, it must be that the opinion, which conjectures that he is sitting, is true; but conversely, if the opinion concerning the man is true because he is sitting, he must be sitting down. There is therefore necessity in both cases: the man must be sitting, and the opinion must be true. But he does not sit because the opinion is true, but rather the opinion is true because his sitting down has preceded it. Thus, though the cause of the truth of the opinion proceeds from the other fact, yet there is a common necessity on both parts. In like manner we must reason of Providence and future events. For even though they are foreseen because they are about to happen, yet they do not happen because they are foreseen. None the less it is necessary that either God should foresee what is about to happen, or that what has been foreseen should happen; and this alone is enough to destroy all free will. Yet how absurd it is to say that the result of temporal affairs is the cause of eternal foreknowledge! To think that God foresees future events because they are about to happen, is nothing else than to hold events of past time to be the cause of that highest Providence. Besides, just as, when I know a present fact, that fact must be so; so also when I know of something that will happen, that must come to pass. Thus it follows that the fulfillment of a foreknown event must be inevitable.

"Lastly, if anyone believes that any matter is otherwise than the fact is, he not only does not know, but his opinion is false also, and that is very far from the truth of knowledge. For if any future event is such that its fulfillment is not sure or necessary, how can it possibly be known beforehand that it will occur? Just as absolute knowledge has no taint of falsity, so also that which knowledge conceives cannot be otherwise than as it is conceived. That is the reason why knowledge cannot lie, because each matter must be just as knowledge knows it. How then can God know beforehand these uncertain future events? For if He deems inevitable the fulfillment of such things as may possibly not result, He is wrong; and we may not believe that, nor even utter it rightly. But if He perceives that they will result as they are in such a manner that He knows only that they may or may not occur, equally, how is this foreknowledge, which knows nothing for sure, nothing absolutely? How is such a foreknowledge different from the absurd prophecy which Horace puts in the mouth of Tiresias: 'Whatever I shall say, will either come to pass, or it will not.'? How, too, would God's Providence be better than man's opinion, if, as men do, He only sees to be uncertain such things as have an uncertain result? But if there can be no uncertainty with God, the most sure source of all things, then the fulfillment of all that He has surely foreknown, must be certain. Thus we are led to see that there is no freedom for the intentions or actions of men, since the mind of God, foreseeing all things without error or deception, binds all together and controls their results. When we have once allowed this, it is plain how complete is the fall of all human actions in consequence. In vain are rewards or punishments set before good or bad, for there is no free or voluntary action of the mind to deserve them and what we just now determined was most fair, will prove to be most unfair of all, namely to punish the dishonest or reward the honest, since their own will does not put them in the way of honesty or dishonesty, but the unfailing necessity of development constrains them. Thus neither virtues nor vices are anything, but there is rather an indiscriminate confusion of all deserts. Nothing could be more vicious than this. Since the whole order of events comes from Providence, and nothing is left to human intention, it follows that our crimes, as well as our good deeds, must all be held due to the author of all good. Hence it is unreasonable to hope or to pray. For what could any man hope for or pray against, if an undeviating chain links together all that we can desire? Thus will the only understanding between God and man, the right of prayer, be taken away. ...

Then she replied, "This is the old complaint about Providence that was so strongly urged by Cicero when treating of divination, and you yourself have often and at length questioned the same subject. But so far, none of you have explained it with enough diligence or certainty. The cause of this obscurity is that the working of human reason cannot approach the directness of divine foreknowledge. ...

"Tell me why you think abortive the reasoning of those who ... argue that foreknowledge cannot be held to be a cause for the necessity of future results, and therefore free will is not in any way shackled by foreknowledge. From where do you draw your proof of the necessity of future results, if not from the fact that such things as are known beforehand cannot but come to pass? If, then, as you yourself admitted just now, foreknowledge brings no necessity to bear upon future events, how is it that the voluntary results of such events are bound to find a fixed end? Now for the sake of the argument, that you may turn your attention to what follows, let us suppose that there is no foreknowledge at all. Then, are the events which are determined by free will bound by any necessity in this regard?"

[Boethius]: "Of course not."

[Lady Philosophy]: "Secondly, let us suppose that foreknowledge exists, but brings no necessity to bear upon events; then, I think, the same free will will be left, intact and absolute. ...

"Since all that is known is known ... not according to its own nature but according to the nature of the knower, let us examine, so far as we lawfully may, the nature of the divine being, so that we may be able to learn what its knowledge is. The common opinion ... is that God is eternal. Let us therefore consider what is eternity. For eternity will, I think, make clear to us at the same time the divine nature and knowledge.

"Eternity is the simultaneous and complete possession of infinite life. This will appear more clearly if we compare it with temporal things. All that lives under the conditions of time moves through the present from the past to the future; there is nothing set in time which can at one moment grasp the whole space of its lifetime. It cannot yet comprehend tomorrow; yesterday it has already lost. In this life of today your life is no more than a changing, passing moment. ... What we should rightly call eternal is that which grasps and possesses wholly and simultaneously the fullness of unending life, which lacks nothing of the future, and has lost nothing of the fleeting past; and such an existence must be ever present in itself to control and aid itself, and also must keep present with itself the infinity of changing time. ...

"Further, God should not be regarded as older than His creations by any period of time, but rather by the peculiar property of His own single nature. For the infinite changing of temporal things tries to imitate the ever simultaneously present immutability of His life: it cannot succeed in imitating or equalling this, but sinks from immutability into change, and falls from the single directness of the present into an infinite space of future and past. Since this temporal state cannot possess its life completely and simultaneously, but it does in the same manner exist for ever without ceasing, it therefore seems to try in some degree to rival that which it cannot fulfill or represent, for it binds itself to some sort of present time out of this small and fleeting moment; but inasmuch as this temporal present bears a certain appearance of that abiding present, it somehow makes those, to whom it comes, seem to be in truth what they imitate. But since this imitation could not be abiding, the unending march of time has swept it away, and thus we find that it has bound together, as it passes, a chain of life, which it could not by abiding embrace in its fullness. Thus ... we can say, following Plato, that God is eternal, but the universe is continual.

"Since all judgment apprehends the objects of its thought according to its own nature, and God has a condition of ever present eternity, therefore His knowledge, which passes over every change of time, embracing infinite lengths of past and future, views in its own direct comprehension everything as though it were taking place in the present. If you would weigh the foreknowledge by which God distinguishes all things, you will more rightly hold it to be a knowledge of a never failing constancy in the present, than a foreknowledge of the future. ...

"If one may not unworthily compare this present time with the divine, just as you can see things in this your temporal present, so God sees all things in His eternal present. Wherefore this divine foreknowledge does not change the nature or individual qualities of things. It sees things present in its understanding just as they will result some time in the future. It makes no confusion in its distinctions, and with one view of its mind it discerns all that shall come to pass whether of necessity or not. For instance, when you see at the same time a man walking on the earth and the sun rising in the heavens, you see each sight simultaneously, yet you distinguish between them, and decide that one is moving voluntarily, the other of necessity. In like manner the perception of God looks down upon all things without disturbing at all their nature, though they are present to Him but future under the conditions of time. Hence this foreknowledge is not opinion but knowledge resting upon truth, since He knows that a future event is, though He knows too that it will not occur of necessity. If you answer here that what God sees about to happen, cannot but happen, and that what cannot but happen is bound by necessity, you fasten me down to the word necessity, I will grant that we have a matter of most firm truth, but it is one to which scarce any man can approach unless he be a contemplator of the divine. For I shall answer that such a thing will occur of necessity, when it is viewed from the point of divine knowledge; but when it is examined in its own nature, it seems perfectly free and unrestrained. ... God looks in His present upon those future things which come to pass through free will. Therefore if these things be looked at from the point of view of God's insight, they come to pass of necessity under the condition of divine knowledge; if, on the other hand, they are viewed by themselves, they do not lose the perfect freedom of their nature. Without doubt, then, all things that God foreknows do come to pass, but some of them proceed from free will; and though they result by coming into existence, yet they do not lose their own nature, because before they came to pass they could also not have come to pass. ...

"You can change your purpose, but since the truth of Providence knows in its present that you can do so, and whether you do so, and in what direction you may change it, therefore you cannot escape that divine foreknowledge: just as you cannot avoid the glance of a present eye, though you may by your free will turn yourself to all kinds of different actions. ... divine insight precedes all future things, turning them back and recalling them to the present time of its own peculiar knowledge. It does not change, as you may think, between this and that alternation of foreknowledge. It is constant in preceding and embracing by one glance all your changes. God does not receive this ever present grasp of all things and vision of the present at the occurrence of future events, but from His own unique directness. Thus also is that difficulty solved which you laid down a little while ago, that it was not worthy to say that our future events were the cause of God's knowledge. For this power of knowledge, ever in the present and embracing all things in its perception, does itself constrain all things, and owes nothing to subsequent events from which it has received nothing. Thus, therefore , mortal men have their freedom of judgment intact. ..."

Subtly different from Boethius on this issue, Descartes discussed divine foreknowledge in his January 1646 letter to Princess Elisabeth of Bohemia, newly translated by Diane Davis Luft:

I proceed to the difficulty Your Highness raises concerning free will, which I will try to clarify by a comparison to show both its dependence and its freedom. What if a certain king, who has outlawed duels, knows for a fact that two gentlemen of his kingdom, living in different towns, are quarreling and so angry with each other that nothing will prevent their fighting should they ever meet? If this king charges one of them to go on a certain day to the town where the other lives, and charges the other to go on the same day to the place where the first one lives, he knows for certain that they will encounter each other and fight, and thus disobey his order, but nevertheless he does not force them to do so, and his knowledge, and even his will to set them in motion in this manner, does not stop their fighting from being voluntary and free, just as if they had met on some other occasion of which he was completely unaware, and they can thus be justly punished for violating the prohibition. Now what a king can do regarding certain free acts of his subjects, God, possessed of infinite foreknowledge and power, does infallibly regarding all the actions of men. And before He sent us into this world, He knew precisely what would be all the inclinations of our will; it is He who gave them to us, it is He who has so disposed all other things outside ourselves in order that such and such objects would present themselves to our senses at such and such times, on which occasion He knew that our free will would bring about such or such a thing; and He willed it thus, but He did not thereby will to constrain our wills. One can distinguish in this king two different degrees of will, one by which he willed that these gentlemen should fight, since he brought about their meeting, and the other by which he did not so will, since he prohibited duels. Likewise theologians distinguish in the will of God both an absolute and independent will, by which He wills all things to happen as they do, and another will which is relative, and concerns the worthiness or unworthiness of men, by which He wills them to obey His laws.

8

Does Religion Need the Supernatural?

What effect does believing something without proof have on believers? What kinds of predispositions lead people to accept counterintuitive propositions with neither proof nor strong evidence? Besides the possible deleterious influence on civilization that Clifford alleges, psychological changes may occur in believers such that they become smug, self-righteous, intolerant, and less likely to consider rational counterarguments to their convictions. The psychology of the believer is an important component of the philosophy of religion. Discussions of it are found in the works of thinkers as diverse as German individualist philosopher Friedrich Nietzsche (1844-1900), Austrian psychoanalyst Sigmund Freud (1856-1939), Jung, Fromm, Tillich, Eliade, Otto, Schleiermacher, and Augustine.

It may be that these adverse psychological characteristics of believers would abate if the aspect and influence of the supernatural were minimized in religion. Such religion would emphasize ethics rather than devotion and would seek to improve this world rather than give up on it in order to expect happiness only in the next world. Accordingly, all religions can generally, if oversimply, be classified as either thisworldly or otherworldly. Detractors of religion, such as Nietzsche, typically focus on its supernaturalism and claim that otherworldliness is pessimistic for seeing this world as spiritually incorrigible and for thus refusing to work at bettering earthly civilization.

Questions about the place of the supernatural in religion — the import of calling anything "holy" or "sacred" or identifying it as mana, tabu, spirit, numen loci, etc.; the existential consequences of holiness; how believers behave in the presence of the holy; what it means for a human being to interact with the "wholly other" or the "completely different"; the reason for obedience; the extent to which one believes that God is active in human history; whether religion can be reduced to morality — are best answered by psychology, anthropology, sociology, or philosophical anthropology, the inexact science that, from empirical evidence of the character and environment of individuals, deduces or predicts their actions and attitudes. For example, one of a protective temperament is more likely to be a right-winger in politics, while one more naive is more likely to be a leftist. Correlations between suspicion and conservatism and between trust and liberalism are not absolute, but are a good guide. A leading philosophical anthropologist was Kant. Following is a new translation of portions of Part Four, "On Service and Pseudo-Service Under the Control of the Good Principle, or, on Religion and Clericalism," from his *Religion Within the Bounds of Mere Reason*:

Subjectively considered, *religion* is the knowledge that all our duties are divine commands. The religion in which I must know (*wissen*) in advance that something is a divine command in order to recognize it as my duty, is *revealed* religion (or one that needs a revelation). On the other hand, the religion in which I must first know (*wissen*) that something is my duty before I can accept it as a divine command is *natural religion*. Whoever explains natural religion merely as a moral necessity, i.e., as duty, can be called *rationalist* (in matters of faith). If he denies the actuality of all supernatural divine revelation, he is called a *naturalist*. If indeed he allows revelation, but maintains that to know (*kennen*) it and accept it as actual is not necessarily required for religion, he could be called a *pure rationalist*. But if he holds that belief in revelation is necessary for universal religion, he could be called a pure *supernaturalist* in matters of faith.

The rationalist, by virtue of this title of his, must of course voluntarily confine himself within the limits of human insight. Hence he will never argue dogmatically from the naturalist standpoint and never dispute either the inner possibility of revelation in general or the necessity of a revelation as a divine means of introducing true religion, since no human can make anything of these matters through reason. Thus the controversy can concern only the reciprocal claims of the pure rationalist and the supernaturalist in matters of faith, or what the one or the other accepts as necessary and sufficient or merely contingent for the one true religion. ...

The worship of powerful, invisible beings, which was extorted from helpless man through natural fear grounded in his consciousness of his powerlessness, did not start so much with religion as with a slavish service to a God (or idols), which, once it had obtained a certain openly legalized form, became *service to a temple*, and became *service to a church* only after human moral culture was gradually tied to these laws. Historical faith lay at the root of both kinds of service until man finally began to see such faith as merely provisional, as the symbolic presentation of pure religious faith, and as the means of promoting it. ...

Now the man who uses actions, which for themselves contain nothing that satisfies God, i.e., nothing moral, as the very means to gain God's immediate satisfaction with him and thereby the fulfillment of his wishes, is deluded to believe that he possesses the knack of accomplishing a supernatural effect by entirely natural means. We can label such attempts *magic*, but (since this word also connotes the related concept of partnership with the evil principle, while these attempts can be thought of as undertaken with good moral intent, albeit through misunderstanding) we prefer to exchange it for the elsewhere familiar word, *fetish-making*. A supernatural result produced by a man would only be possible, as he thinks, because he supposedly has an effect on God and uses God as a means to bring forth in the world a result toward which his own powers and even his insight into whether it may satisfy God would not, for themselves, suffice. But this is already nonsense even in its concept.

But if the man, not only by that which makes him immediately an object of divine satisfaction (by being actively disposed toward a good way of life) but also by means of certain formalities, seeks to make himself *worthy* of the revival of his powerlessness by supernatural assistance, and, with this purpose, by obser-vances that indeed have no immediate value but yet serve as the means of fur-thering that moral disposition, if he means to make himself merely receptive to reaching the object of his good moral wishes, then indeed he counts on some-thing *supernatural* to revive his natural powerlessness, but indeed not on any-thing humanly *wrought* (by influencing God's will), rather on what he receives, which he can hope for but cannot bring forth. But, for him, if actions contain in themselves, as far as we can see, nothing moral or satisfying to God, yet never-theless, in his opinion, are supposed to serve as a means, or even a condition, by which he expects to obtain his wishes immediately from God, then he is deluded. His delusion is that, even though he has neither any physical power nor any moral influence over this supernaturalness, yet he can — through *natural* actions which are still in no way compatible in themselves with morality (actions whose practice requires no conviction satisfying to God and which can be performed by the worst people just as well as by the best), through invocative formulas, through confes-sing a faith from which he expects reward, through churchy observances, and so on — cause these effects and thus, as it were, *magically compel* the assistance of the Godhead. For, according to any law of which reason can think, there is no con-nection at all between merely physical means and a morally effective cause, such that the latter could be represented as determinable through the former toward certain operations.

Thus whoever puts obeying statutory laws first, laws that require a reve-lation as necessary to religion, and sees this obedience not merely as a means to moral conviction, but as the objective condition of becoming immediately satis-fying to God; and whoever puts striving toward a good way of life behind this his-torical faith (and must be governed by this faith, which can satisfy God only *in a conditional way*, instead of by this striving, which alone *utterly* satisfies God); such a person transforms the service of God into a mere *fetish-making* and practices a pseudo-service which makes all cooperative efforts toward true religion retrogressive. When we wish to combine two good things, so much depends on the order in which they are combined! —— In this very distinction consists true *enlightenment*; thereby the service of God becomes above all a free and consequently a moral service. ...

Clericalism is thus the constitution of a church to the extent that a *fetish-service* rules within it. This state of affairs is always found where statutory commands, rules of faith, and observances, instead of principles of an ethical order of life (*Sittlichkeit*), comprise the basic and essential elements of the service. ...

Now there is a practical cognition which, although it depends solely on reason and requires no historical teaching, lies indeed so near to everyone, even the most simple people, as if it were written in their hearts. If we only name this law, we are instantly in agreement with everyone about its authority, and it carries with it in everyone's consciousness an *unconditional* obligation, namely, the law of morality. Moreover, this cognition leads either by and for itself alone to faith in God or at least only determines the concept of God as that of a moral lawgiver. Hence it guides us to a pure religious faith, which is not only conceivable by everyone, but also sacred in the highest degree. Indeed, faith leads to this point so naturally that, if one wants to make the attempt, one will find that it can be entirely obtained by questioning anyone without that person ever having been taught anything about it. Thus not only beginning with this cognition, and letting the historical faith which harmonizes with it be derived from it, is acting wisely, but also, making this cognition the foremost, the only condition by which we can hope to participate in the salvation that a religious faith may promise us, is our duty. Of course, only according to the interpretation which pure religious faith gives of historical faith can we regard the latter as universally binding or may we be allowed to value it (because it contains universally valid teaching). Meanwhile, that moral believers remain open to historical faith, inasmuch as they find it conducive to the revival of their pure religious conviction, is the only way in which historical faith has any pure moral worth, because it is free and not forced by any threat (whereby it could never be sincere).

Now even inasmuch as the service of God in a church is chiefly aimed at the pure moral veneration of God, in accordance with laws prescribed to humankind in general, we can still ask whether, in this service, the *teaching of godliness* alone or also the *teaching* of pure *virtue*, or either in particular, should constitute the content of religious discourse. ...

Whatever good, according to the laws of freedom, humans can do for themselves, compared with their power that is possible only through supernatural assistance, can be called *nature*, as distinguished from *grace*. Not as if we understand by nature a physical property distinguished from freedom, but only because we at least discern the *laws* (of *virtue*) as this power, and thereby because reason, as an analogue of nature, thus has a visible and comprehensible guide to nature; on the contrary, whether, if, what, and how much *grace* will work in us remains completely hidden from us, and on this account reason is left with just the supernatural in general (to which morality, as *holiness*, belongs), but without any knowledge of the laws by which the supernatural might occur.

The concept of a supernatural accession to our moral, though deficient, power and even to our not fully purified and in all cases weak conviction to do all our duty sufficiently, is transcendent and a mere idea, the reality of which no experience can convince us. Even if accepted as an idea with a merely practical intention, it is very risky, and hardly compatible with reason, because what should be ascribed to us as good ethical behavior must occur not through alien influence but only through the best possible use of our own powers. Yet the impossibility of that (i.e., of both occurring side by side) indeed does not allow itself to be proved, because freedom itself, although it contains nothing supernatural in its concept, remains nevertheless, according to its possibility, just as inconceivable to us as the supernatural, which some would like to embrace as a substitute for the self-acting but deficient determination of freedom.

But while we know (*kennen*) at least the (moral) *laws* of freedom, laws according to which freedom is to be determined, we cannot cognize even the minimum about supernatural assistance, whether a certain moral strength, perceived in us, actually comes from the supernatural, or indeed, in which cases and under what conditions it may be expected. So, outside the universal presupposition that grace will effect in us what nature cannot if only we have used our own powers as much as possible, we cannot make any further use of this idea at all, neither how (beyond the constant striving toward a good way of life) we draw its cooperation to us, nor how we could determine in which cases we can expect it. This idea is entirely extravagant, and moreover, to hold it at a reverential distance as a holy thing is even beneficial. With that, not deluded that we perform miracles ourselves or perceive miracles within us, we make ourselves unfit to use any kind of reason, or we even allow ourselves to be tempted into the laziness of expecting from above, in passive leisure, what we should be seeking within ourselves.

Now all the intermediate causes that humans have in *their power* are *means* toward actualizing thereby a certain purpose; and there is (and can be) no other way to become worthy of heavenly assistance than serious striving to better their ethical character to the greatest extent possible and thereby to make themselves receptive to the perfection — which is not in their power — of the suitability of this character to satisfy God; because that divine assistance, which they expect, itself has no other proper purpose than their ethical order (*Sittlichkeit*). But it was already well to be expected *a priori* that the ignoble man would not seek such assistance there, but rather in certain sensuous contrivances (which of course he has in his power, but which however cannot in themselves make a man better, and yet are supposed to produce this very result in a supernatural way) — and this in fact is just what happens. The concept of a so-called *means of grace*, although it is self-contradictory in itself (according to what was said above), still serves here as a means of self-deception, which is as common as it is detrimental to true religion.

The true (moral) service of God, which the faithful must perform as subjects belonging to God's realm neither more nor less than (under the laws of freedom) as citizens of the realm, is indeed, like the realm itself, invisible, i.e., a *service of the heart* (in spirit and in truth); and can consist only in the conviction of obeying all true duties as divine commands, not in actions determined exclusively for God. But, for humans, the invisible needs to be represented through something visible (something sensuous); indeed, and what is more, it needs to be accompanied by the visible for the purpose of practicality, and although it is intellectual, it must be made, as it were (according to a certain analogy), intuitive. All this is, even though totally indispensable, simply a means of presenting to ourselves our duty in the service of God, but a means that is at the same time quite subject to the danger of misinterpretation. Through a *delusion* that creeps up on us, it is lightly taken for the *service of God* itself and is indeed commonly so called. ...

Every beginning in matters of religion, if we do not consider it merely morally, but rather as something which *in itself* makes us satisfying to God and therefore, through God, grasps the means of gratifying all our wishes, is *fetish-faith*, which is a persuasion that what can do nothing at all by either *natural* laws or the moral laws of reason, will indeed nevertheless, by itself, produce what is wished, if we only believe firmly that such things will be done, and then if we bind up certain formalities with this faith. Otherwise, where the firm persuasion that everything here depends on ethical goodness, which can arise only from action, has already prevailed, the sensuous man still indeed seeks a sneaky way for himself to evade that troublesome condition, namely, if he only follows the custom (the formality), God would of course accept it for the deed itself. ...

There can of course be three kinds of *delusional faith* that involve possibly transgressing the bounds of our reason in consideration of the supernatural (which, according to the laws of reason, is not an object of either theoretical or practical use): *First*, faith in cognizing through experience something that we ourselves can indeed admit to be impossible if it happens according to the objective laws of experience (faith in *miracles*). *Second*, the delusion that, as necessary to our moral best, we must assimilate even within our rational concepts that of which we cannot formulate any rational concept (faith in *mysteries*). *Third*, the delusion that, through the use of merely natural means, we can bring forth an effect which for us is a mystery, namely, God's influence on our ethical order (*Sittlichkeit*) (faith in a *means of grace*). ...

9

Do Miracles Occur?

Miracles are entirely a matter of belief or disbelief. We cannot either verify that miracles exist or demonstrate that they do not — as, for example, we verify that county fairs exist and demonstrate that square circles do not. The question of miracles is not for either science or philosophy to decide, since both are powerless to do so.

The two main antagonists in the unending debate about miracles are Hume and University of Oxford philosopher Richard Swinburne (b. 1934), author of *The Concept of Miracle* (1971) and editor of *Miracles* (1989). Swinburne argues that accepting the existence of miracles by believing either scriptural authority, historical testimony, or direct evidence in their favor does not break any laws of logic. He agrees with Hume and other disbelievers in miracles that "miracle" may be defined as a violation of the laws of nature, but maintains against Hume that the creator of these laws can violate them at will and expect devotees to believe in these divine interventions. We regard any violation of the laws of nature as an extraordinary, unique, unrepeated occurrence. If an apparent miracle were subsequently discovered to have recurred in similar circumstances elsewhere or at another time, then it would likely not be a genuine miracle, but only a prodigious event, and may require revising our understanding of the laws of nature in order to accommodate it. But until a second, similar event is found, there is no reason to assume that a stunning revelation is merely marvellous and repeatable rather than truly miraculous and unique. For Swinburne, then, theistic belief in unique, God-caused violations of laws of nature is not at all irrational, given the premises of theism itself.

Hume's essay, "Of Miracles," comprises Section 10 of the 1777 revised edition of his *Enquiry Concerning Human Understanding*. The numbering and footnotes are Hume's:

86. There is, in Dr. Tillotson's writings, an argument against the *real presence*, which is as concise, and elegant, and strong as any argument can possibly be

supposed against a doctrine, so little worthy of a serious refutation. It is acknowledged on all hands, says that learned prelate, that the authority, either of the
scripture or of tradition, is founded merely in the testimony of the apostles, who
were eye-witnesses to those miracles of our Saviour, by which he proved his divine mission. Our evidence, then, for the truth of the *Christian* religion is less than
the evidence for the truth of our senses; because, even in the first authors of our
religion, it was no greater; and it is evident it must diminish in passing from them
to their disciples; nor can any one rest such confidence in their testimony, as in
the immediate object of his senses. But a weaker evidence can never destroy a
stronger; and therefore, were the doctrine of the real presence ever so clearly
revealed in scripture, it were directly contrary to the rules of just reasoning to give
our assent to it. It contradicts sense, though both the scripture and tradition, on
which it is supposed to be built, carry not such evidence with them as sense; when
they are considered merely as external evidences, and are not brought home to
every one's breast, by the immediate operation of the Holy Spirit.

Nothing is so convenient as a decisive argument of this kind, which must
at least *silence* the most arrogant bigotry and superstition, and free us from their
impertinent solicitations. I flatter myself, that I have discovered an argument of a
like nature, which, if just, will, with the wise and learned, be an everlasting check to
all kinds of superstitious delusion, and consequently, will be useful as long as the
world endures. For so long, I presume, will the accounts of miracles and prodigies
be found in all history, sacred and profane.

87. Though experience be our only guide in reasoning concerning matters of fact; it must be acknowledged, that this guide is not altogether infallible,
but in some cases is apt to lead us into errors. One, who in our climate, should
expect better weather in any week of June than in one of December, would reason
justly, and conformably to experience; but it is certain, that he may happen, in the
event, to find himself mistaken. However, we may observe, that, in such a case, he
would have no cause to complain of experience; because it commonly informs us
beforehand of the uncertainty, by that contrariety of events, which we may learn
from a diligent observation. All effects follow not with like certainty from their supposed causes. Some events are found, in all countries and all ages, to have been
constantly conjoined together: Others are found to have been more variable, and
sometimes to disappoint our expectations; so that, in our reasonings concerning
matter of fact, there are all imaginable degrees of assurance, from the highest
certainty to the lowest species of moral evidence.

A wise man, therefore, proportions his belief to the evidence. In such
conclusions as are founded on an infallible experience, he expects the event with
the last degree of assurance, and regards his past experience as a full *proof* of
the future existence of that event. In other cases, he proceeds with more caution:
He weighs the opposite experiments: He considers which side is supported by the

greater number of experiments: to that side he inclines, with doubt and hesitation; and when at last he fixes his judgement, the evidence exceeds not what we properly call *probability.* All probability, then, supposes an opposition of experiments and observations, where the one side is found to overbalance the other, and to produce a degree of evidence, proportioned to the superiority. A hundred instances or experiments on one side, and fifty on another, afford a doubtful expectation of any event; though a hundred uniform experiments, with only one that is contradictory, reasonably beget a pretty strong degree of assurance. In all cases, we must balance the opposite experiments, where they are opposite, and deduct the smaller number from the greater, in order to know the exact force of the superior evidence.

88. To apply these principles to a particular instance; we may observe that there is no species of reasoning more common, more useful, and even necessary to human life, than that which is derived from the testimony of men, and the reports of eye-witnesses and spectators. This species of reasoning, perhaps, one may deny to be founded on the relation of cause and effect. I shall not dispute about a word. It will be sufficient to observe that our assurance in any argument of this kind is derived from no other principle than our observation of the veracity of human testimony, and of the usual conformity of facts to the reports of witnesses. It being a general maxim, that no objects have any discoverable connexion together, and that all the inferences, which we can draw from one to another, are founded merely on our experience of their constant and regular conjunction; it is evident that we ought not to make an exception to this maxim in favour of human testimony, whose connexion with any event seems, in itself, as little necessary as any other. Were not the memory tenacious to a certain degree; had not men commonly an inclination to truth and a principle of probity; were they not sensible to shame, when detected in a falsehood: Were not these, I say, discovered by *experience* to be qualities, inherent in human nature, we should never repose the least confidence in human testimony. A man delirious, or noted for falsehood and villany, has no manner of authority with us.

And as the evidence, derived from witnesses and human testimony, is founded on past experience, so it varies with the experience, and is regarded either as a *proof or a probability,* according as the conjunction between any particular kind of report and any kind of object has been found to be constant or variable. There are a number of circumstances to be taken into consideration in all judgements of this kind; and the ultimate standard, by which we determine all disputes, that may arise concerning them, is always derived from experience and observation. Where this experience is not entirely uniform on any side, it is attended with an unavoidable contrariety in our judgements, and with the same opposition and mutual destruction of argument as in every other kind of evidence. We frequently hesitate concerning the reports of others. We balance the opposite circumstances, which cause any doubt or uncertainty; and when we discover a superiority on any side, we incline to it; but still with a diminution of assurance, in proportion to the force of its antagonist.

89. This contrariety of evidence, in the present case, may be derived from several different causes; from the opposition of contrary testimony; from the character or number of the witnesses; from the manner of their delivering their testimony; or from the union of all these circumstances. We entertain a suspicion concerning any matter of fact, when the witnesses contradict each other; when they are but few, or of a doubtful character; when they have an interest in what they affirm; when they deliver their testimony with hesitation, or on the contrary, with too violent asseverations. There are many other particulars of the same kind, which may diminish or destroy the force of any argument, derived from human testimony.

Suppose, for instance, that the fact, which the testimony endeavours to establish, partakes of the extraordinary and the marvellous; in that case, the evidence, resulting from the testimony, admits of a diminution, greater or less, in proportion as the fact is more or less unusual. The reason why we place any credit in witnesses and historians, is not derived from any *connexion*, which we perceive *a priori*, between testimony and reality, but because we are accustomed to find a conformity between them. But when the fact attested is such a one as has seldom fallen under our observation, here is a contest of two opposite experiences; of which the one destroys the other, as far as its force goes, and the superior can only operate on the mind by the force, which remains. The very same principle of experience, which gives us a certain degree of assurance in the testimony of witnesses, gives us also, in this case, another degree of assurance against the fact, which they endeavour to establish; from which contradiction there necessarily arises a counterpoize, and mutual destruction of belief and authority.

I should not believe such a story were it told me by Cato, was a proverbial saying in Rome, even during the lifetime of that philosophical patriot. The incredibility of a fact, it was allowed, might invalidate so great an authority.

The Indian prince, who refused to believe the first relations concerning the effects of frost, reasoned justly; and it naturally required very strong testimony to engage his assent to facts, that arose from a state of nature, with which he was unacquainted, and which bore so little analogy to those events, of which he had had constant and uniform experience. Though they were not contrary to his experience, they were not conformable to it.[1]

---

[1] No Indian, it is evident, could have experience that water did not freeze in cold climates. This is placing nature in a situation quite unknown to him; and it is impossible for him to tell *a priori* what will result from it. It is making a new experiment, the consequence of which is always uncertain. One may sometimes conjecture from analogy what

90. But in order to encrease the probability against the testimony of witnesses, let us suppose, that the fact, which they affirm, instead of being only marvellous, is really miraculous; and suppose also, that the testimony considered apart and in itself, amounts to an entire proof; in that case, there is proof against proof, of which the strongest must prevail, but still with a diminution of its force, in proportion to that of its antagonist.

A miracle is a violation of the laws of nature; and as a firm and unalterable experience has established these laws, the proof against a miracle, from the very nature of the fact, is as entire as any argument from experience can possibly be imagined. Why is it more than probable, that all men must die; that lead cannot, of itself, remain suspended in the air; that fire consumes wood, and is extinguished by water; unless it be, that these events are found agreeable to the laws of nature, and there is required a violation of these laws, or in other words, a miracle to prevent them? Nothing is esteemed a miracle, if it ever happen in the common course of nature. It is no miracle that a man, seemingly in good health, should die on a sudden: because such a kind of death, though more unusual than any other, has yet been frequently observed to happen. But it is a miracle, that a dead man should come to life; because that has never been observed in any age or country. There must, therefore, be a uniform experience against every miraculous event, otherwise the event would not merit that appellation. And as a uniform experience amounts to a proof, there is here a direct and full *proof*, from the nature of the fact, against the existence of any miracle; nor can such a proof be destroyed, or the miracle rendered credible, but by an opposite proof, which is superior.[2]

---

will follow; but still this is but conjecture. And it must be confessed, that, in the present case of freezing, the event follows contrary to the rules of analogy, and is such as a rational Indian would not look for. The operations of cold upon water are not gradual, according to the degrees of cold; but whenever it comes to the freezing point, the water passes in a moment, from the utmost liquidity to perfect hardness. Such an event, therefore, may be denominated *extraordinary*, and requires a pretty strong testimony to render it credible to people in a warm climate: But still it is not *miraculous*, nor contrary to uniform experience of the course of nature in cases where all the circumstances are the same. The inhabitants of Sumatra have always seen water fluid in their own climate, and the freezing of their rivers ought to be deemed a prodigy: But they never saw water in Muscovy during the winter; and therefore they cannot reasonably be positive what would there be the consequence.

[2] Sometimes an event may not, *in itself, seem* to be contrary to the laws of nature, and yet, if it were real, it might, by reason of some circumstances, be denominated a miracle; because, in *fact*, it is contrary to these laws. Thus if a person, claiming a divine authority, should command a sick person to be well, a healthful man to fall down dead, the clouds

91. The plain consequence is (and it is a general maxim worthy of our attention), "That no testimony is sufficient to establish a miracle, unless the testimony be of such a kind, that its falsehood would be more miraculous, than the fact, which it endeavours to establish; and even in that case there is a mutual destruction of arguments, and the superior only gives us an assurance suitable to that degree of force, which remains, after deducting the inferior." When anyone tells me, that he saw a dead man restored to life, I immediately consider with myself, whether it be more probable, that this person should either deceive or be deceived, or that the fact, which he relates, should really have happened. I weigh the one miracle against the other; and according to the superiority, which I discover, I pronounce my decision, and always reject the greater miracle. If the falsehood of his testimony would be more miraculous, than the event which he relates; then, and not till then, can he pretend to command my belief or opinion.

Part II

92. In the foregoing reasoning we have supposed, that the testimony, upon which a miracle is founded, may possibly amount to an entire proof, and that the falsehood of that testimony would be a real prodigy: But it is easy to shew, that we have been a great deal too liberal in our concession, and that there never was a miraculous event established on so full an evidence.

For *first*, there is not to be found, in all history, any miracle attested by a sufficient number of men, of such unquestioned good-sense, education, and learning, as to secure us against all delusion in themselves; of such undoubted integrity, as to place them beyond all suspicion of any design to deceive others; of such credit and reputation in the eyes of mankind, as to have a great deal to lose in case of their being detected in any falsehood; and at the same time, attesting facts performed in such a public manner and in so celebrated a part of the world, as to render the detection unavoidable: All which circumstances are requisite to

---

to pour rain, the winds to blow, in short, should order many natural events, which immediately follow upon his command; these might justly be esteemed miracles, because they are really, in this case, contrary to the laws of nature. For if any suspicion remain, that the event and command concurred by accident, there is no miracle and no transgression of the laws of nature. If this suspicion be removed, there is evidently a miracle, and a transgression of these laws; because nothing can be more contrary to nature than that the voice or command of a man should have such an influence. A miracle may be accurately defined, *a transgression of a law of nature by a particular volition of the Deity, or by the interposition of some invisible agent.* A miracle may either be discoverable by men or not. This alters not its nature and essence. The raising of a house or ship into the air is a visible miracle. The raising of a feather, when the wind wants ever so little of a force requisite for that purpose, is as real a miracle, though not so sensible with regard to us.

give us a full assurance in the testimony of men.

93. *Secondly.* We may observe in human nature a principle which, if strictly examined, will be found to diminish extremely the assurance, which we might, from human testimony, have, in any kind of prodigy. The maxim, by which we commonly conduct ourselves in our reasonings, is, that the objects, of which we have no experience, resemble those, of which we have; that what we have found to be most usual is always most probable; and that where there is an opposition of arguments, we ought to give the preference to such as are founded on the greatest number of past observations. But though, in proceeding by this rule, we readily reject any fact which is unusual and incredible in an ordinary degree; yet in advancing farther, the mind observes not always the same rule; but when anything is affirmed utterly absurd and miraculous, it rather the more readily admits of such a fact, upon account of that very circumstance, which ought to destroy all its authority. The passion of *surprise* and *wonder*, arising from miracles, being an agreeable emotion, gives a sensible tendency towards the belief of those events, from which it is derived. And this goes so far, that even those who cannot enjoy this pleasure immediately, nor can believe those miraculous events, of which they are informed, yet love to partake of the satisfaction at second-hand or by rebound, and place a pride and delight in exciting the admiration of others.

With what greediness are the miraculous accounts of travellers received, their descriptions of sea and land monsters, their relations of wonderful adventures, strange men, and uncouth manners? But if the spirit of religion join itself to the love of wonder, there is an end of common sense; and human testimony, in these circumstances, loses all pretensions to authority. A religionist may be an enthusiast, and imagine he sees what has no reality: he may know his narrative to be false, and yet persevere in it, with the best intentions in the world, for the sake of promoting so holy a cause: or even where this delusion has not place, vanity, excited by so strong a temptation, operates on him more powerfully than on the rest of mankind in any other circumstances; and self-interest with equal force. His auditors may not have, and commonly have not, sufficient judgement to canvass his evidence: what judgement they have, they renounce by principle, in these sublime and mysterious subjects: or if they were ever so willing to employ it, passion and a heated imagination disturb the regularity of its operations. Their credulity increases his impudence: and his impudence overpowers their credulity.

Eloquence, when at its highest pitch, leaves little room for reason or reflection; but addressing itself entirely to the fancy or the affections, captivates the willing hearers, and subdues their understanding. Happily, this pitch it seldom attains. But what a Tully or a Demosthenes could scarcely effect over a Roman or Athenian audience, every *Capuchin*, every itinerant or stationary teacher can perform over the generality of mankind, and in a higher degree, by touching such gross and vulgar passions.

The many instances of forged miracles, and prophecies, and supernatural events, which, in all ages, have either been detected by contrary evidence, or which detect themselves by their absurdity, prove sufficiently the strong propensity of mankind to the extraordinary and the marvellous, and ought reasonably to beget a suspicion against all relations of this kind. This is our natural way of thinking, even with regard to the most common and most credible events. For instance: There is no kind of report which rises so easily, and spreads so quickly, especially in country places and provincial towns, as those concerning marriages; insomuch that two young persons of equal condition never see each other twice, but the whole neighbourhood immediately join them together. The pleasure of telling a piece of news so interesting, of propagating it, and of being the first reporters of it, spreads the intelligence. And this is so well known, that no man of sense gives attention to these reports, till he find them confirmed by some greater evidence. Do not the same passions, and others still stronger, incline the generality of mankind to believe and report, with the greatest vehemence and assurance, all religious miracles?

94. *Thirdly.* It forms a strong presumption against all supernatural and miraculous relations, that they are observed chiefly to abound among ignorant and barbarous nations; or if a civilized people has ever given admission to any of them, that people will be found to have received them from ignorant and barbarous ancestors, who transmitted them with that inviolable sanction and authority, which always attend received opinions. When we peruse the first histories of all nations, we are apt to imagine ourselves transported into some new world; where the whole frame of nature is disjointed, and every element performs its operations in a different manner, from what it does at present. Battles, revolutions, pestilence, famine and death, are never the effect of those natural causes, which we experience. Prodigies, omens, oracles, judgements, quite obscure the few natural events, that are intermingled with them. But as the former grow thinner every page, in proportion as we advance nearer the enlightened ages, we soon learn, that there is nothing mysterious or supernatural in the case, but that all proceeds from the usual propensity of mankind towards the marvellous, and that, though this inclination may at intervals receive a check from sense and learning, it can never be thoroughly extirpated from human nature.

It is strange, a judicious reader is apt to say, upon the perusal of these wonderful historians, *that such prodigious events never happen in our days*. But it is nothing strange, I hope, that men should lie in all ages. You must surely have seen instances enough of that frailty. You have yourself heard many such marvellous relations started, which, being treated with scorn by all the wise and judicious, have at last been abandoned even by the vulgar. Be assured, that those renowned lies, which have spread and flourished to such a monstrous height, arose from like beginnings; but being sown in a more proper soil, shot up at last into prodigies almost equal to those which they relate.

It was a wise policy in that false prophet, Alexander, who though now forgotten, was once so famous, to lay the first scene of his impostures in Paphlagonia, where, as Lucian tells us, the people were extremely ignorant and stupid, and ready to swallow even the grossest delusion. People at a distance, who are weak enough to think the matter at all worth enquiry, have no opportunity of receiving better information. The stories come magnified to them by a hundred circumstances. Fools are industrious in propagating the imposture; while the wise and learned are contented, in general, to deride its absurdity, without informing themselves of the particular facts, by which it may be distinctly refuted. And thus the impostor above mentioned was enabled to proceed, from his ignorant Paphlagonians, to the enlisting of votaries, even among the Grecian philosophers, and men of the most eminent rank and distinction in Rome: nay, could engage the attention of that sage emperor Marcus Aurelius; so far as to make him trust the success of a military expedition to his delusive prophecies.

The advantages are so great, of starting an imposture among an ignorant people, that, even though the delusion should be too gross to impose on the generality of them (*which, though seldom, is sometimes the case*) it has a much better chance for succeeding in remote countries, than if the first scene had been laid in a city renowned for arts and knowledge. The most ignorant and barbarous of these barbarians carry the report abroad. None of their countrymen have a large correspondence, or sufficient credit and authority to contradict and beat down the delusion. Men's inclination to the marvellous has full opportunity to display itself. And thus a story, which is universally exploded in the place where it was first started, shall pass for certain at a thousand miles distance. But had Alexander fixed his residence at Athens, the philosophers of that renowned mart of learning had immediately spread, throughout the whole Roman empire, their sense of the matter; which, being supported by so great authority, and displayed by all the force of reason and eloquence, had entirely opened the eyes of mankind. It is true; Lucian, passing by chance through Paphlagonia, had an opportunity of performing this good office. But, though much to be wished, it does not always happen, that every Alexander meets with a Lucian, ready to expose and detect his impostures.

95. I may add as a *fourth* reason, which diminishes the authority of prodigies, that there is no testimony for any, even those which have not been expressly detected, that is not opposed by an infinite number of witnesses; so that not only the miracle destroys the credit of testimony, but the testimony destroys itself. To make this the better understood, let us consider, that, in matters of religion, whatever is different is contrary; and that it is impossible the religions of ancient Rome, of Turkey, of Siam, and of China should, all of them, be established on any solid foundation. Every miracle, therefore, pretended to have been wrought in

any of these religions (and all of them abound in miracles), as its direct scope is to establish the particular system to which it is attributed; so has it the same force, though more indirectly, to overthrow every other system. In destroying a rival system, it likewise destroys the credit of those miracles, on which that system was established; so that all the prodigies of different religions are to be regarded as contrary facts, and the evidences of these prodigies, whether weak or strong, as opposite to each other. According to this method of reasoning, when we believe any miracle of Mahomet or his successors, we have for our warrant the testimony of a few barbarous Arabians: And on the other hand, we are to regard the authority of Titus Livius, Plutarch, Tacitus, and, in short, of all the authors and witnesses, Grecian, Chinese, and Roman Catholic, who have related any miracle in their particular religion; I say, we are to regard their testimony in the same light as if they had mentioned that Mahometan miracle, and had in express terms contradicted it, with the same certainty as they have for the miracle they relate. This argument may appear over subtile and refined; but is not in reality different from the reasoning of a judge, who supposes that the credit of two witnesses, maintaining a crime against any one, is destroyed by the testimony of two others, who affirm him to have been two hundred leagues distant, at the same instant when the crime is said to have been committed.

96. One of the best attested miracles in all profane history, is that which Tacitus reports of Vespasian, who cured a blind man in Alexandria, by means of his spittle, and a lame man by the mere touch of his foot; in obedience to a vision of the god Serapis, who had enjoined them to have recourse to the Emperor, for these miraculous cures. The story may be seen in that fine historian; where every circumstance seems to add weight to the testimony, and might be displayed at large with all the force of argument and eloquence, if any one were now concerned to enforce the evidence of that exploded and idolatrous superstition. The gravity, solidity, age, and probity of so great an emperor, who, through the whole course of his life, conversed in a familiar manner with his friends and courtiers, and never affected those extraordinary airs of divinity assumed by Alexander and Demetrius. The historian, a contemporary writer, noted for candour and veracity, and withal, the greatest and most penetrating genius, perhaps, of all antiquity; and so free from any tendency to credulity, that he even lies under the contrary imputation, of atheism and profaneness: The persons, from whose authority he related the miracle, of established character for judgement and veracity, as we may well presume; eye-witnesses of the fact, and confirming their testimony, after the Flavian family was despoiled of the empire, and could no longer give any reward, as the price of a lie. *Utrumque, qui interfuere, nunc quoque memorant, postquam nullum mendacio pretium* [Those who were there still tell of these incidents, and now lying about them is no longer worthwhile]. To which if we add the public nature of the facts, as related, it will appear, that no evidence can well be

supposed stronger for so gross and so palpable a falsehood.

There is also a memorable story related by Cardinal de Retz, which may well deserve our consideration. When that intriguing politician fled into Spain, to avoid the persecution of his enemies, he passed through Saragossa, the capital of Arragon, where he was shewn, in the cathedral, a man, who had served seven years as a doorkeeper, and was well known to every body in town, that had ever paid his devotions at that church. He had been seen, for so long a time, wanting a leg; but recovered that limb by the rubbing of holy oil upon the stump; and the cardinal assures us that he saw him with two legs. This miracle was vouched by all the canons of the church; and the whole company in town were appealed to for a confirmation of the fact; whom the cardinal found, by their zealous devotion, to be thorough believers of the miracle. Here the relater was also contemporary to the supposed prodigy, of an incredulous and libertine character, as well as of great genius; the miracle of so *singular* a nature as could scarcely admit of a counterfeit, and the witnesses very numerous, and all of them, in a manner, spectators of the fact, to which they gave their testimony. And what adds mightily to the force of the evidence, and may double our surprise on this occasion, is, that the cardinal himself, who relates the story, seems not to give any credit to it, and consequently cannot be suspected of any concurrence in the holy fraud. He considered justly, that it was not requisite, in order to reject a fact of this nature, to be able accurately to disprove the testimony, and to trace its falsehood, through all the circumstances of knavery and credulity which produced it. He knew, that, as this was commonly altogether impossible at any small distance of time and place; so was it extremely difficult, even where one was immediately present, by reason of the bigotry, ignorance, cunning, and roguery of a great part of mankind. He therefore concluded, like a just reasoner, that such an evidence carried falsehood upon the very face of it, and that a miracle, supported by any human testimony, was more properly a subject of derision than of argument.

There surely never was a greater number of miracles ascribed to one person, than those, which were lately said to have been wrought in France upon the tomb of Abbé Paris, the famous Jansenist, with whose sanctity the people were so long deluded. The curing of the sick, giving hearing to the deaf, and sight to the blind, were every where talked of as the usual effects of that holy sepulchre. But what is more extraordinary; many of the miracles were immediately proved upon the spot, before judges of unquestioned integrity, attested by witnesses of credit and distinction, in a learned age, and on the most eminent theatre that is now in the world. Nor is this all: a relation of them was published and dispersed every where; nor were the *Jesuits*, though a learned body, supported by the civil magistrate, and determined enemies to those opinions, in whose favour the miracles were said to have been wrought, ever able distinctly to refute or detect them. Where shall we find such a number of circumstances, agreeing to the corroboration of one fact? And what have we to oppose to such a cloud of witnesses, but the absolute impossibility or miraculous nature of the events, which they relate? And this surely, in the eyes of all reasonable people, will alone be regarded as a sufficient refutation.

97. Is the consequence just, because some human testimony has the utmost force and authority in some cases, when it relates the battle of Philippi or Pharsalia for instance; that therefore all kinds of testimony must, in all cases, have equal force and authority? Suppose that the Caesarean and Pompeian factions had, each of them, claimed the victory in these battles, and that the historians of each party had uniformly ascribed the advantage to their own side; how could mankind, at this distance, have been able to determine between them? The contrariety is equally strong between the miracles related by Herodotus or Plutarch, and those delivered by Mariana, Bede, or any monkish historian.

The wise lend a very academic faith to every report which favours the passion of the reporter; whether it magnifies his country, his family, or himself, or in any other way strikes in with his natural inclinations and propensities. But what greater temptation than to appear a missionary, a prophet, an ambassador from heaven? Who would not encounter many dangers and difficulties, in order to attain so sublime a character? Or if, by the help of vanity and a heated imagination, a man has first made a convert of himself, and entered seriously into the delusion; who ever scruples to make use of pious frauds, in support of so holy and meritorious a cause?

The smallest spark may here kindle into the greatest flame; because the materials are always prepared for it. The *avidum genus auricularum* ["the human genus, eager for hearsay," paraphrasing Lucretius], the gazing populace, receive greedily, without examination, whatever sooths superstition, and promotes wonder.

How many stories of this nature have, in all ages, been detected and exploded in their infancy? How many more have been celebrated for a time, and have afterwards sunk into neglect and oblivion? Where such reports, therefore, fly about, the solution of the phenomenon is obvious; and we judge in conformity to regular experience and observation, when we account for it by the known and natural principles of credulity and delusion. And shall we, rather than have a recourse to so natural a solution, allow of a miraculous violation of the most established laws of nature?

I need not mention the difficulty of detecting a falsehood in any private or even public history, at the place, where it is said to happen; much more when the scene is removed to ever so small a distance. Even a court of judicature, with all the authority, accuracy, and judgement, which they can employ, find themselves often at a loss to distinguish between truth and falsehood in the most recent actions. But the matter never comes to any issue, if trusted to the common method of altercations and debate and flying rumours; especially when men's passions have taken part on either side.

In the infancy of new religions, the wise and learned commonly esteem the matter too inconsiderable to deserve their attention or regard. And when afterwards they would willingly detect the cheat, in order to undeceive the deluded multitude, the season is now past, and the records and witnesses, which might clear up the matter, have perished beyond recovery.

No means of detection remain, but those which must be drawn from the very testimony itself of the reporters: and these, though always sufficient with the judicious and knowing, are commonly too fine to fall under the comprehension of the vulgar.

98. Upon the whole, then, it appears, that no testimony for any kind of miracle has ever amounted to a probability, much less to a proof; and that, even supposing it amounted to a proof, it would be opposed by another proof, derived from the very nature of the fact, which it would endeavour to establish. It is experience only, which gives authority to human testimony; and it is the same experience, which assures us of the laws of nature. When, therefore, these two kinds of experience are contrary, we have nothing to do but substract the one from the other, and embrace an opinion, either on one side or the other, with that assurance which arises from the remainder. But according to the principle here explained, this substraction, with regard to all popular religions, amounts to an entire annihilation; and therefore we may establish it as a maxim, that no human testimony can have such force as to prove a miracle, and make it a just foundation for any such system of religion.

99. I beg the limitations here made may be remarked, when I say, that a miracle can never be proved, so as to be the foundation of a system of religion. For I own, that otherwise, there may possibly be miracles, or violations of the usual course of nature, of such a kind as to admit of proof from human testimony; though, perhaps, it will be impossible to find any such in all the records of history. Thus, suppose, all authors, in all languages, agree, that, from the first of January 1600, there was a total darkness over the whole earth for eight days: suppose that the tradition of this extraordinary event is still strong and lively among the people: that all travellers, who return from foreign countries, bring us accounts of the same tradition, without the least variation or contradiction: it is evident, that our present philosophers, instead of doubting the fact, ought to receive it as certain, and ought to search for the causes whence it might be derived. The decay, corruption, and dissolution of nature, is an event rendered probable by so many analogies, that any phenomenon, which seems to have a tendency towards that catastrophe, comes within the reach of human testimony, if that testimony be very extensive and uniform.

But suppose, that all the historians who treat of England, should agree, that, on the first of January 1600, Queen Elizabeth died; that both before and after her death she was seen by her physicians and the whole court, as is usual with persons of her rank; that her successor was acknowledged and proclaimed by the parliament; and that, after being interred a month, she again appeared, resumed the throne, and governed England for three years: I must confess that I should be surprised at the concurrence of so many odd circumstances, but should not have the least inclination to believe so miraculous an event. I should not doubt of her pretended death, and of those other public circumstances that followed it: I should only assert it to have been pretended, and that it neither was, nor possibly could be real. You would in vain object to me the difficulty, and almost impossibility of deceiving the world in an affair of such consequence; the wisdom and solid judgement of that renowned queen; with the little or no advantage which she could reap from so poor an artifice: All this might astonish me; but I would still reply, that the knavery and folly of men are such common phenomena, that I should rather believe the most extraordinary events to arise from their concurrence, than admit of so signal a violation of the laws of nature.

But should this miracle be ascribed to any new system of religion; men, in all ages, have been so much imposed on by ridiculous stories of that kind, that this very circumstance would be a full proof of a cheat, and sufficient, with all men of sense, not only to make them reject the fact, but even reject it without farther examination. Though the Being to whom the miracle is ascribed, be, in this case, Almighty, it does not, upon that account, become a whit more probable; since it is impossible for us to know the attributes or actions of such a Being, otherwise than from the experience which we have of his productions, in the usual course of nature. This still reduces us to past observation, and obliges us to compare the instances of the violation of truth in the testimony of men, with those of the violation of the laws of nature by miracles, in order to judge which of them is most likely and probable. As the violations of truth are more common in the testimony concerning religious miracles, than in that concerning any other matter of fact; this must diminish very much the authority of the former testimony, and make us form a general resolution, never to lend any attention to it, with whatever specious pretence it may be covered.

Lord Bacon seems to have embraced the same principles of reasoning. "We ought," says he, "to make a collection or particular history of all monsters and prodigious births or productions, and in a word of every thing new, rare, and extraordinary in nature. But this must be done with the most severe scrutiny, lest we depart from truth. Above all, every relation must be considered as suspicious, which depends in any degree upon religion, as the prodigies of Livy: And no less so, every thing that is to be found in the writers of natural magic or alchimy, or such authors, who seem, all of them, to have an unconquerable appetite for falsehood and fable" [*Novum Organum*, book 2, aphorism 29].

100. I am the better pleased with the method of reasoning here delivered, as I think it may serve to confound those dangerous friends or disguised enemies to the *Christian Religion*, who have undertaken to defend it by the principles of human reason. Our most holy religion is founded on *Faith*, not on reason; and it is a sure method of exposing it to put it to such a trial as it is, by no means, fitted to endure. To make this more evident, let us examine those miracles, related in scripture; and not to lose ourselves in too wide a field, let us confine ourselves to such as we find in the *Pentateuch*, which we shall examine, according to the principles of these pretended Christians, not as the word or testimony of God himself, but as the production of a mere human writer and historian. Here then we are first to consider a book, presented to us by a barbarous and ignorant people, written in an age when they were still more barbarous, and in all probability long after the facts which it relates, corroborated by no concurring testimony, and resembling those fabulous accounts, which every nation gives of its origin. Upon reading this book, we find it full of prodigies and miracles. It gives an account of a state of the world and of human nature entirely different from the present: Of our fall from that state: Of the age of man, extended to near a thousand years: Of the destruction of the world by a deluge: Of the arbitrary choice of one people, as the favourites of heaven; and that people the countrymen of the author: Of their deliverance from bondage by prodigies the most astonishing imaginable: I desire anyone to lay his hand upon his heart, and after a serious consideration declare, whether he thinks that the falsehood of such a book, supported by such a testimony, would be more extraordinary and miraculous than all the miracles it relates; which is, however, necessary to make it be received, according to the measures of probability above established.

101. What we have said of miracles may be applied, without any variation, to prophecies; and indeed, all prophecies are real miracles, and as such only, can be admitted as proofs of any revelation. If it did not exceed the capacity of human nature to foretell future events, it would be absurd to employ any prophecy as an argument for a divine mission or authority from heaven. So that, upon the whole, we may conclude, that the *Christian Religion* not only was at first attended with miracles, but even at this day cannot be believed by any reasonable person without one. Mere reason is insufficient to convince us of its veracity: And whoever is moved by *Faith* to assent to it, is conscious of a continued miracle in his own person, which subverts all the principles of his understanding, and gives him a determination to believe what is most contrary to custom and experience.

Hume was not the first major philosopher to take a strong stand against the possibility of miracles. His attack is just the best known and among the most eloquent. But a century earlier, in 1670, Spinoza published anonymously the *Tractatus Theologico-Politicus*, which contains severe criticisms of many aspects of organized religion. The sixth chapter, "Of Miracles," defines miracle as whatever cannot be explained by natural causes and makes three main points: (1) the order of nature is fixed and eternal, so the very concept of miracle, as a deviation from nature, is absurd; (2) God's reality, attributes, and providence are knowable through nature but not through miracles; and (3) whatever God does *is* the order of nature, and even those astonishing events reported in scripture can be interpreted as natural rather than miraculous.

If the religious perspective is that which sees the content of consciousness as revelation, rather than as purely mundane phenomena or ordinary ideas, then belief or disbelief in miracles would make no difference to that perspective. The natural world would be just as much a mark of God as any miracle would be. The reality of God can be proved by Anselm or Aquinas, felt by Pascal or Schleiermacher, intuited by Merton or the mystics, known by Whitehead in his solitariness, and experienced in many profound and genuinely religious ways which do not involve any deviation from nature. The experience of the greater-than-greatest God would be cheapened by the co-presence of miracles. The sublimity of the *mysterium tremendum et fascinans* does not need the admixture of parlor tricks.

If God were evil or cruel, then miracles could not be ruled out, but a truly benevolent God would not toy with us in such a way. The God who is greater than any we can conceive would at the very least respect both the regularity of God's own given clues (*vestigia*), or indications of the divine in the natural world, and the human reason whose manifest and divinely ordained purpose — from the religious perspective — is to attract creatures back to God, i.e., to support *epistrophê* or *conversio*. This point is quite simple conceptually and ought not to be as controversial as it is in the actual world.

If superstition is defined as belief in that which is not understood, then belief in miracles is a form of superstition. The more prudent course would be to suspend belief until understanding is achieved, either empirically or speculatively, and to spare no effort in trying to understand. However, even though actively seeking something worthy of rational belief may be more pragmatic than believing in order to understand, neither attitude is more or less "religious" than the other. Each could be a version of the religious perspective, since each is the attitude of a sincere truth-seeker. Both seek to integrate faith and reason, the one seeking reason by means of faith, the other seeking faith by means of reason.

10

What is Evil and Why Does it Exist?

The purpose of this and the next chapter is to put evil in perspective, to describe and compare some traditional theories of evil, suffering, and death, and to promote inquiry into what kind of spirit is likely to derive comfort from each of these theories.

The two strongest types of evidence for the reality of God are (1) the various formal philosophical arguments or proofs and (2) the various kinds of spontaneous religious experience, such as mystical awareness, ecstasy, communion, felt response to prayer or piety, etc. But some of the strongest counterevidence, i.e., evidence against accepting the reality of God, is the existence of evil. Defenders of theism are always obliged to explain away the obvious fact that there is evil in the world.

Philosophers traditionally distinguish two basic types of evil: (2) natural evil, such as pain, earthquakes, heartbreak, mosquitoes, etc., i.e., that which we suffer; and (2) moral evil, such as sin, crime, dishonesty, etc., i.e., that which we do. The demarcation between the two types is often blurry and they are often closely related. For example, the moral evil of the Nazis inflicted natural evil on the Jews. Apart from these two general categories are at least twelve standard conceptions of evil:

1. The free will defense, or the *ad maiorem gloriam Dei* ("to the greater glory of God") argument — Augustine argued that God is greater by saving sinners than by creating automatons incapable of sin. God did not create moral evil; humans created it by exercising their God-given free will. This theory cannot explain natural evil.

2. The absurdist theory of evil — Evil is a permanent mystery, impossible to understand. This position is favored by fideists for whom philosophy is impious or blasphemous if it questions the received word of God. As Tertullian wrote, "What does Athens have to do with Jerusalem?" American personalist philosopher Edgar Sheffield Brightman (1884-1953), who did not himself believe

in any meaningless evil that has no purpose and cannot be explained rationally, called such evil the "dysteleological surd." Fideists counsel just to accept the dysteleological surd and to have faith that God's grace will save us from it.

3. Rational skepticism — This theory is the other side of the absurdist coin, i.e., such skeptics believe in the dysteleological surd but do not have faith in God to deliver them from it, or indeed, to control it at all. Evil manifestly exists, such as the 1755 Lisbon earthquake, in Voltaire's famous example; therefore the Judeo-Christian God certainly does not exist, and perhaps no God exists. This theory often has recourse to the "Epicurean trilemma," which attacks the omnipotence and omnibenevolence of God: If evil exists, then, either (1) God is willing but not able to eliminate it, or (2) God is able but not willing to eliminate it, or (3) God is neither willing nor able to eliminate it. Evil exists, therefore God is either (1) omnipotent but not omnibenevolent, (2) omnibenevolent but not omnipotent, or (3) neither omnipotent nor omnibenevolent.

4. The "life-is-a-trial" theory — God tests creatures to see if they are worthy of salvation, or to see what each will choose. The Hebrew Bible contains many examples of such trials, such as the ordeals of Job, Jeremiah, Adam in the Garden of Eden before the fall, Moses, and Ezekiel. This theory can easily run afoul of doctrines of divine foreknowledge, omnibenevolence, and omnipotence. Rabbi Harold S. Kushner's popular 1981 exploration of these topics, *When Bad Things Happen to Good People*, showed that he coped with the premature death of his son by believing in the dysteleological surd, denying God's omnipotence, but trusting in God's omnibenevolence.

5. The "suffering-builds-character" theory — Evil provides the opportunity for some to gain moral strength or to grow spiritually, so that those who suffer much can take small ills in stride, while for those who suffer few real hardships, small ills seem great. This theory seems to have originated in Paul's Epistle to the Philippians, 1:14,29, but it also has a Hegelian-Marxist corollary, insofar as lack of suffering diminishes character: The children of oppressed or working classes grow strong, while the children of the rich, whose everyday tasks are done for them, grow weak.

6. Privative theory of evil — Evil has no independent reality, but is only the absence of good. In Platonic and neo-Platonic cosmology, degrees of goodness, beauty, and value are equivalent to degrees of being, and degrees of evil are proportionately equivalent to non-being. God is the fullness of being. Typical Christian theo-

logy includes a privative theory of evil, consistent with Augustine's *ad maiorem gloriam Dei* argument and with his terminology of *aversio*, turning away from being toward non-being, and *conversio*, turning toward being away from non-being.

7. Substantive theory of evil, or ethical dualism — In Zoroastrianism and Manichaeanism, the primeval cosmic good principle (God, or light) co-exists with the primeval cosmic evil principle (the devil, or darkness). The two are equally real, of roughly equal strength, and are at war. Our duty is to choose sides in this war. Any religion that hypostatizes, reifies, or personifies any kind of devil espouses to that extent a substantive or even anthropomorphic theory of evil.

8. Metaphysical optimism, or the perspectival, perceptual, aesthetic, or totality theory of evil — Evil is only evil from some particular, finite standpoints, but from God's universal, infinite standpoint, there is no natural evil at all and moral evil is put to a better use. In perspectival theory, from the point of view of the host, a parasitic disease is certainly a natural evil, but from the point of view of the parasite, it is not. In his *Philosophical Dictionary* and especially in *Candide*, Voltaire ridiculed the idea that there is no such thing as natural evil.

9. The naturalistic fallacy — According to British philosopher George Edward Moore (1873-1858) in *Principia Ethica*, goodness and evilness are not objective properties of things as are, for example, yellowness or hardness. Rather, to claim that anything is either "good" or "evil" is only to express subjective approval or disapproval.

10. Metaphysical pessimism — For Schopenhauer and in ancient Buddhism, the world is evil by nature, simply because some evil exists, however little. There is no real difference between moral and natural evil, since all is suffering. For Schopenhauer, all this suffering and evil, and in fact, the whole universe itself, are caused by the will. There is no hope except to extinguish the will, which is to extinguish life and existence. Buddhism's four noble truths are that (1) life is suffering, or natural evil; (2) the cause of suffering is desire, or the root of moral evil; (3) Relief from suffering can only be achieved by eliminating desire; and (4) To eliminate desire, follow the noble eightfold path of right understanding, right intention, right speech, right action, right livelihood, right effort, right mindfulness, and right concentration. The path leads through various stages of enlightenment to nirvana, which is not heaven, but ex-

tinction, nothingness, or escape from the wheel of rebirth. For the Buddha, any kind of existence, even heavenly existence, would entail evil and suffering. The only way to eliminate evil and suffering is to eliminate existence itself.

11. Evil as obstruction — For Whitehead, evil is whatever prevents or destroys spiritual or moral progress. The fact that God is in every creature does not mean that God is in any way evil, even penultimately. God is essentially creative and stable; evil is destructive and unstable. Because of God's omnipresence, any evil that is manifested in the world is immediately juxtaposed with a reciprocal manifestation bent on eliminating that evil. This continuous challenge to evil is what Whitehead calls "moral order."

12. Evil as guilty conscience — For Heidegger, moral evil exists only if someone feels guilty. This feeling is primordial, may be unconscious, and is tantamount to being guilty, or to falling short of realizing the potential of one's own being. Heidegger's assessment of evil as the content of the experience of moral conflict is a variant on the privative theory, insofar as guilt is a kind of deficiency, but Heidegger makes clear that the concept of privation is not enough to explain either guilt or the genesis of conscience or moral awareness.

Leibniz, the leading metaphysical optimist, coined the term "theodicy" from the two Greek words for "God" and "justice," *theos* and *diké* (δίκη). It means "divine justice" or "the justness of God" and refers to any defense of God in the face of evil, or, more loosely, any theistic apology for evil. At the request of his readers, he appended to his 1710 *Theodicy* a summary of its general argument in syllogistic form. It appears here slightly revised from the 1908 second edition of George Martin Duncan's 1890 translation:

Some intelligent persons have desired that this supplement be made, and I have the more readily yielded to their wishes as in this way I have an opportunity to again remove certain difficulties and to make some observations which were not sufficiently emphasized in the work itself.

First Objection. Whoever does not choose the best is lacking in power, or in knowledge, or in goodness.

God did not choose the best in creating this world.

Therefore, God lacks in power, or in knowledge, or in goodness.

Answer. I deny the minor, that is, the second premise of this syllogism; and our opponent proves it by this:

Prosyllogism.[1] Whoever makes things in which there is evil, which could have been made without any evil, or the making of which could have been omitted, does not choose the best.

God has made a world in which there is evil, a world, I say, which could have been made without any evil, or the making of which could have been omitted altogether.

Therefore, God has not chosen the best.

Answer. I grant the minor of this prosyllogism; for it must be confessed that there is evil in this world which God has made, and that it was possible to make a world without evil, or even not to create a world at all, for its creation has depended on the free will of God; but I deny the major, that is, the first of the two premises of the prosyllogism, and I might content myself with simply demanding its proof; but in order to make the matter clearer, I have wished to justify this denial by showing that the best plan is not always that which seeks to avoid evil, since it may happen that *the evil is accompanied by a greater good.* For example, a general of an army will prefer a great victory with a slight wound to a condition without wound and without victory. We have proved this more fully in the large work by making it clear, by instances taken from mathematics and elsewhere, that an imperfection in the part may be required for a greater perfection in the whole. In this I have followed the opinion of St. Augustine, who has said a hundred times, that God has permitted evil in order to bring about good, that is, a greater good; and that of Thomas Aquinas ... that the permitting of evil tends to the good of the universe. I have shown that the ancients called Adam's fall *felix culpa*, a happy sin, because it had been retrieved with immense advantage by the incarnation of the Son of God, who has given to the universe something nobler than anything that ever would have been among creatures except for it. For the sake of a clearer understanding, I have added, following many good authors, that it was in accordance with order and the general good that God allowed to certain creatures the opportunity of exercising their liberty, even when he foresaw that they would turn to evil, but which he could so well rectify; because it was not fitting that, in order to hinder sin, God should always act in an extraordinary manner. To overthrow this objection, therefore, it is sufficient to show that a world with evil might be better than a world without evil; but I have gone even farther, in the work, and have even proved that this universe must be in reality better than every other possible universe.

Second Objection. If there is more evil than good in intelligent creatures, then there is more evil than good in the whole work of God.

---

[1] [A "prosyllogism" is a syllogism whose conclusion forms either the major or minor premise of another; in this case, the minor premise of the First Objection.]

Now, there is more evil than good in intelligent creatures.

Therefore, there is more evil than good in the whole work of God.

Answer. I deny the major and the minor of this conditional syllogism. As to the major, I do not admit it at all, because this pretended deduction from a part to the whole, from intelligent creatures to all creatures, supposes tacitly and without proof that creatures destitute of reason cannot enter into comparison nor into account with those which possess it. But why may it not be that the surplus of good in the nonintelligent creatures which fill the world, compensates for, and even incomparably surpasses, the surplus of evil in the rational creatures? It is true that the value of the latter is greater; but, in compensation, the others are beyond comparison the more numerous, and it may be that the proportion of number and quantity surpasses that of value and of quality.

As to the minor, that is no more to be admitted; that is, it is not at all to be admitted that there is more evil than good in the intelligent creatures. There is no need even of granting that there is more evil than good in the human race, because it is possible, and in fact very probable, that the glory and the perfection of the blessed are incomparably greater than the misery and the imperfection of the damned, and that here the excellence of the total good in the smaller number exceeds the total evil in the greater number. The blessed approach the Divinity, by means of a Divine Mediator, as near as may suit these creatures, and make such progress in good as is impossible for the damned to make in evil, approach as nearly as they may to the nature of demons. God is infinite, and the devil is limited; the good may and does go to infinity, while evil has its bounds. It is therefore possible, and is credible, that in the comparison of the blessed and the damned, the contrary of that which I have said might happen in the comparison of intelligent and nonintelligent creatures, takes place; namely, it is possible that in the comparison of the happy and the unhappy, the proportion of degree exceeds that of number, and that in the comparison of intelligent and nonintelligent creatures, the proportion of number is greater than that of value. I have the right to suppose that a thing is possible so long as its impossibility is not proved; and indeed that which I have here advanced is more than a supposition.

But in the second place, if I should admit that there is more evil than good in the human race, I have still good grounds for not admitting that there is more evil than good in all intelligent creatures. For there is an inconceivable number of genii, and perhaps of other rational creatures. And an opponent could not prove that in all the City of God, composed as well of genii as of rational animals without number and of an infinity of kinds, evil exceeds good. And although in order to answer an objection, there is no need of proving that a thing is, when its mere possibility suffices; yet, in this work, I have not omitted to show that it is a consequence of the supreme perfection of the Sovereign of the universe, that the kingdom of God is the most perfect of all possible states or governments, and that consequently the little evil there is, is required for the consummation of the immense good which is found there.

Third Objection. If it is always impossible not to sin, it is always unjust to punish.

Now, it is always impossible not to sin; or, in other words, every sin is necessary.

Therefore, it is always unjust to punish.

The minor of this is proved thus:

First Prosyllogism. All that is predetermined is necessary.

Every event is predetermined.

Therefore, every event (and consequently sin also) is necessary.

Again this second minor is proved thus:

Second Prosyllogism. That which is future, that which is foreseen, that which is involved in the causes, is predetermined.

Every event is such.

Therefore, every event is predetermined.

Answer. I admit in a certain sense the conclusion of the second prosyllogism, which is the minor of the first; but I shall deny the major of the first prosyllogism, namely, that every thing predetermined is necessary; understanding by the necessity of sinning, for example, or by the impossibility of not sinning, or of not performing any action, the necessity with which we are here concerned, that is, that which is essential and absolute, and which destroys the morality of an action and the justice of punishments. For if anyone understood another necessity or impossibility, namely, a necessity which should be only moral, or which was only hypothetical (as will be explained shortly); it is clear that I should deny the major of the objection itself. I might content myself with this answer and demand the proof of the proposition denied; but I have again desired to explain my procedure in this work, in order to better elucidate the matter and to throw more light on the whole subject, by explaining the necessity which ought to be rejected and the determination which must take place. That *necessity* which is contrary to morality and which ought to be rejected, and which would render punishment unjust, is an insurmountable necessity which would make all opposition useless, even if we should wish with all our heart to avoid the necessary action, and should make all possible efforts to that end. Now, it is manifest that this is not applicable to voluntary actions, because we would not perform them if we did not choose to. Also their prevision and predetermination are not absolute, but presuppose the will: if it is certain that we shall perform them, it is not less certain that we shall choose to perform them. These voluntary actions and their consequences will not take place no matter what we do or whether we wish them or not; but, *through* that which we shall do and through that which we shall wish to do, which leads to them. And this is involved in prevision and in predetermination, and even constitutes their ground. And the necessity of such an event is called conditional or hypothetical, or the necessity of consequence, because it supposes the will, and the other *requisites*; whereas the necessity which destroys morality and renders punishment unjust and reward useless, exists in things which will be whatever we may do or whatever we may wish to do, and, in a word, is in that which is essential; and this is what is called an absolute necessity. Thus it is to no purpose, as regards what is absolutely necessary, to make prohibitions or commands, to propose penalties or prizes, to praise or to blame; it will be none the less. On the other hand, in voluntary actions and in that which depends upon them, precepts armed with power to punish and to recompense are very often of use and are included in the order of causes which make an action exist. And it is for this reason that not only cares and labors but also prayers are useful; God having had these prayers in view before he regulated things and having had that consideration for them which was proper. This is why the precept which says *ora et labora* (pray and work), holds altogether good; and not only those who (under the vain pretext of the necessity of events) pretend that the care which business demands may be neglected, but also those who reason against prayer, fall into what the ancients even then called the *lazy sophism*. Thus the predetermination of events by causes is just what contributes to morality instead of destroying it, and causes incline the will, without compelling it. This is why the *determination* in question is not a necessitation — it is certain (to him who knows all) that the effect will follow this inclination; but this effect does not follow by a necessary consequence, that is, one the contrary of which implies contradiction. It is also by an internal inclination such as this that the will is determined, without there being any necessity. Suppose that one has the greatest passion in the world (a great thirst, for example), you will admit to me that the soul can find some reason for resisting it, if it were only that of showing its power. Thus, although one may never be in a perfect indifference of equilibrium and there may be always a preponderance of inclination for the side taken, it, nevertheless, never renders the resolution taken absolutely necessary.

Fourth Objection. Whoever can prevent the sin of another and does not do so, but rather contributes to it, although he is well informed of it, is accessory to it.

God can prevent the sin of intelligent creatures; but he does not do so, and rather contributes to it by his concurrence and by the opportunities which he brings about, although he has a perfect knowledge of it.

Hence, etc.

Answer. I deny the major of this syllogism. For it is possible that one could prevent sin, but ought not, because he could not do it without himself committing a sin, or (when God is in question) without performing an unreasonable action. Examples have been given and the application to God himself has been made. It is possible also that we contribute to evil and that sometimes we even open the road to it, in doing things which we are obliged to do; and, when we do our duty or (in speaking of God) when, after thorough consideration, we do that which reason demands, we are not responsible for the results, even when we foresee them. We do not desire these evils; but we are willing to permit them for the sake of a greater good which we cannot reasonably help preferring to other considerations. And this is a *consequent* will, which results from *antecedent* wills by which we will the good. I know that some persons, in speaking of the antecedent and consequent will of God, have understood by the *antecedent* that which wills that all men should be saved; and by the *consequent*, that which wills, in consequence of persistent sin, that some should be damned. But these are merely illustrations of a more general idea, and it may be said for the same reason that God, by his antecedent will, wills that men should not sin; and by his consequent or final and decreeing will (that which is always followed by its effect), he wills to permit them to sin, this permission being the result of superior reasons. And we have the right to say in general that the antecedent will of God tends to the production of good and the prevention of evil, each taken in itself and as if alone (*particulariter et secundum quid* [in a partial way and according to some thing], Thom[as Aquinas, *Summa Theologiae*, Part] I, question 19, article 6), according to the measure of the degree of each good and of each evil; but that the divine consequent or final or total will tends toward the production of as many goods as may be put together, the combination of which becomes in this way determined, and includes also the permission of some evils and the exclusion of some goods, as the best possible plan for the universe demands. [Jacobus] Arminius, in his *Anti-Perkinsus* [i.e., *An Examination of a Treatise Concerning the Order and Mode of Predestination and the Amplitude of Divine Grace, by Rev. William Perkins*], has very well explained that the will of God may be called consequent, not only in relation to the action of the creature considered beforehand in the divine understanding, but also in relation to other anterior divine acts of will. But this consideration of the passage cited from Thomas Aquinas, and one from [John Duns] Scotus ... is enough to show that they make this distinction as I have done here. Nevertheless, if anyone objects to this use of terms let him substitute *deliberating* will, in place of antecedent, and *final* or decreeing will, in place of consequent. For I do not wish to dispute over words.

Fifth Objection. Whoever produces all that is real in a thing, is its cause.

God produces all that is real in sin.

Hence, God is the cause of sin.

Answer. I might content myself with denying the major or the minor, since the term real admits of interpretations which would render these propositions false. But in order to explain more clearly, I will make a distinction. *Real* signifies either that which is positive only, or, it includes also privative beings. In the first case, I deny the major and admit the minor; in the second case, I do the contrary. I might have limited myself to this, but I have chosen to proceed still farther and give the reason for this distinction. I have been very glad therefore to draw attention to the fact that every reality purely positive or absolute is a perfection; and that imperfection comes from limitation, that is, from the privative: for to limit is to refuse progress, or the greatest possible progress. Now God is the cause of all perfections and consequently of all realities considered as purely positive. But limitations or privations result from the original imperfection of creatures, which limits their receptivity. And it is with them as with a loaded vessel, which the river causes to move more or less slowly according to the weight which it carries: thus its speed depends upon the river, but the retardation which limits this speed comes from the load. Thus in the *Theodicy*, we have shown how the creature, in causing sin, is a defective cause; how errors and evil inclinations are born of privation; and how privation is accidentally efficient; and I have justified the opinion of St. Augustine (*Ad Simplicianum*, Book I, Question 2), who explains, for example, how God makes the soul obdurate, not by giving it something evil, but because the effect of his good impression is limited by the soul's resistance and by the circumstances which contribute to this resistance, so that he does not give it all the good which would overcome its evil. *Nec (inquit) ab illo erogatur aliquid quo homo fit deterior, sed tantum quo fit melior non erogatur.*[2] But if God had wished to do more, he would have had to make either other natures for creatures or other miracles to change their natures, things which the best plan could not admit. It is as if the current of the river must be more rapid than its fall admitted or that the boats should be loaded more lightly, if it were necessary to make them move more quickly. And the original limitation or imperfection of creatures requires that even the best plan of the universe could not receive more good, and could not be exempt from certain evils, which, however, are to result in a greater good. There are certain disorders in the parts which marvelously enhance the beauty of the whole; just as certain dissonances, when properly used, render harmony more beautiful. But this depends on what has already been said in answer to the first objection.

Sixth Objection. Whoever punishes those who have done as well as it was in their power to do, is unjust.

God does so.

Hence, etc.

Answer. I deny the minor of this argument. And I believe that God always gives sufficient aid and grace to those who have a good will, that is, to those who

---

[2] [Leibniz misquoted Augustine. The actual Latin is: *ut non ab illo irrogetur aliquid quo sit homo deterior, sed tantum quo sit melior non erogetur.* "... that is not to provide something to make matters worse, but just not to grant that which could make matters better."]

do not reject this grace by new sin. Thus I do not admit the damnation of infants who have died without baptism or outside of the church; nor the damnation of adults who have acted according to the light which God has given them. And I believe that *if any one has followed the light which has been given him*, he will undoubtedly receive greater light when he has need of it, as the late M. [Johann] Hülsemann, a profound and celebrated theologian at Leipzig, has somewhere remarked; and if such a man has failed to receive it during his lifetime he will at least receive it when at the point of death.

Seventh Objection. Whoever gives only to some, and not to all, the means which produces in them effectively a good will and salutary final faith, has not sufficient goodness.

God does this.

Hence, etc.

Answer. I deny the major of this. It is true that God could overcome the greatest resistance of the human heart; and does it, too, sometimes, either by internal grace, or by external circumstances which have a great effect on souls; but he does not always do this. Whence comes this distinction, it may be asked, and why does his goodness seem limited? It is because, as I have already said in answering the first objection, it would not have been in order always to act in an extraordinary manner, and to reverse the connection of things. The reasons of this connection, by means of which one is placed in more favorable circumstances than another, are hidden in the depths of the wisdom of God: they depend upon the universal harmony. The best plan of the universe, which God could not fail to choose, made it so. We judge from the event itself; since God has made it, it was not possible to do better. Far from being true that this conduct is contrary to goodness, it is supreme goodness which led him to it. This objection with its solution might have been drawn from what was said in regard to the first objection; but it seemed useful to touch upon it separately.

Eighth Objection. Whoever cannot fail to choose the best, is not free.

God cannot fail to choose the best.

Hence, God is not free.

Answer. I deny the major of this argument; it is rather true liberty, and the most perfect, to be able to use one's free will for the best, and to always exercise this power, without ever being turned aside either by external force or by internal passions, the first of which causes slavery of the body, the second, slavery of the soul. There is nothing less servile, and nothing more in accordance with the highest degree of freedom, than to be always led toward the good, and always by one's own inclination, without any constraint and without any displeasure. And to object therefore that God had need of external things, is only a sophism. He created them freely; but having proposed to himself an end, which is to exercise his goodness, wisdom has determined him to choose the means best fitted to attain this end. To call this a need, is to take that term in an unusual sense which frees it from all imperfection, just as when we speak of the wrath of God.

Seneca has somewhere said that God commanded just once, but that he obeys always, because he obeys laws which he willed to prescribe to himself: *semel jussit, semper paret* [once commanded, always obeys]. But he might better have said that God always commands and is always obeyed; for in willing, he always follows the inclination of his own nature, and all other things always follow his will. And as this will is always the same, it cannot be said that he obeys only that will which he formerly had. Nevertheless, although his will is always infallible and always tends toward the best, the evil, or the lesser good, which he rejects, does not cease to be possible in itself; otherwise the necessity of the good would be geometrical (so to speak), or metaphysical, and altogether absolute; the contingency of things would be destroyed, and there would be no choice. But this sort of necessity, which does not destroy the possibility of the contrary, has this name only by analogy; it becomes effective, not by the pure essence of things, but by that which is outside of them, above them, namely, by the will of God. This necessity is called moral, because, to the sage, *necessity* and *what ought to be* are equivalent things; and when it always has its effect, as it really has in the perfect sage, that is, in God, it may be said to be a happy necessity. The nearer creatures approach to it, the nearer they approach to perfect happiness. Also this kind of necessity is not that which we try to avoid and which destroys morality, rewards and praise. For that which it brings does not happen whatever we may do or will, but because we will it so. And a will to which it is natural to choose well, merits praise so much more; also it carries its reward with it, which is sovereign happiness. And as this constitution of the divine nature gives entire satisfaction to him who possesses it, it is also the best and the most desirable for the creatures who are all dependent on God. If the will of God did not have for a rule the principle of the best, it would either tend toward evil, which would be the worst; or it would be in some way indifferent to good and to evil, and would be guided by chance; but a will which would allow itself always to act by chance, would not be worth more for the government of the universe than the fortuitous concourse of atoms, without there being any divinity therein. And even if God should abandon himself to chance only in some cases and in a certain way (as he would do, if he did not always work entirely for the best and were capable of preferring a lesser work to a greater, that is, an evil to a good, since that which prevents a greater good is an evil), he would be imperfect, as well as the object of his choice; he would not merit entire confidence; he would act without reason in such a case, and the government of the universe would be like certain games, equally divided between reason and chance. All this proves that this objection which is made against the choice of the best, perverts the notions of the free and of the necessary, and represents to us the best even as evil, which is either malicious or ridiculous.

11

What Happens After Death?

Few issues provoke such intense and general speculation as the sometimes worrisome, sometimes comforting fact that we are all bound to die. We may each deny it, we may each be frightened, but we would each like to know what, if anything, awaits us after death.

There are at least eight major conceptions of death and its aftermath, seven of which involve some form of immortality and only one that regards death as extinction. The idea of immortality, especially personal immortality, is an important component of most Western and many Eastern cultures and a driving force behind much religious thought and faith worldwide. Yet the idea is vague at best. For Kant, three concepts were ultimately inexplicable: God, freedom, and immortality. When he asked how knowledge of God, freedom, or immortality could be possible, he had to admit that such knowledge is not possible, because there is no rational or empirical standpoint from which we finite beings could apprehend any reliable information according to which we might consider any of these three. Any ideas that we have of God, freedom, or immortality can only be believed, not known, and are always matters of faith.

The eight ways of thinking about the aftermath of death are:

1. All souls are blessed, and each one will go to a comfortable place after death, regardless of what they each did in their respective lives, because life itself, with all its intrinsic suffering or natural evil, is punishment enough for any moral evil. Examples include the ancient Greek concept of the "Elysian Fields"; the doctrine of Dutch reformer Jacobus Arminius (1560-1609), Arminianism, which arose in opposition to the Calvinist tenet that all souls are in bondage to sin with some souls predestined to hell, and asserted instead that all souls are free to do good works and thus to save themselves from hell just by each exercising their individual free will to accept God's grace; and the various forms of universalism, including most types of Christian Unitarianism.

2. The afterlife exists, but only in this world, not in some

other world, so dead souls either wander as ghosts on earth or haunt certain locations. This idea is mostly the stuff of fairy tales rather than serious religion.

3. God will judge all departed souls, rewarding the good, penitent, and faithful with eternal bliss in heaven but condemning the sinful to eternal punishment or even torment in hell. This theory is a central focus of both Christianity and Islam.

4. The afterlife consists of a vague, indifferent, shadowy existence, offering neither reward nor punishment, neither happiness nor misery. It is simply a place where people go when they die, and little more is said of it. Examples include the ancient Greek Hades and the Hebrew Sheol.

5. The very process of physical rotting is a natural act of spiritual regeneration. Cultures that believe that the physical world is essentially spiritual treat corpses reverently, in such a way to ease their transition back to the natural order of spirit. The final resting place of a corpse, particularly the corpse of an ancestor or a chief, thereby becomes exceptionally sacred ground because the dead person's spirit inhabits it. Examples include the burial customs of many Native American tribes and the "going-into-the-mountain" concept of the medieval Icelanders, which involved arranging the dead body in whatever position the person had specified before death and then covering it with a very large mound of stones. This belief and practice was quite distinct from the popular notion of Viking funerals as leading the deceased hero to Valhalla.

6. Reincarnation is the belief that when one body dies, its soul must instantly reappear in another, new body, not necessarily human. Souls transmigrate because they cannot exist without bodies and because they cannot die. The way we each live determines our respective karma or "fate," which then determines the body in which each soul returns. This is the basic Hindu and Buddhist idea of the wheel of rebirth, from which souls strive to escape, because the world is essentially evil, full of suffering, illusion, betrayal, and disappointment.

7. The souls of the dead return to the Universal Soul. This is different from the universal salvation described above in (1) because it does not involve personal immortality, but only a melting, as it were, of souls into an immortal and universal (eternal and infinite) spiritual energy force. This is typical of the Hindu concept of escape from the wheel of rebirth, but has also found its way into much so-called "New Age" theology in the West. Yoko Ono Len-

non famously told their five-year-old son Sean that, by being murdered, John Lennon had become "part of God."

8. There is no afterlife at all, but only non-existence, extinction, nothing. One example is the physicalist, materialist, or reductionist position that denies the duality of mortal body and immortal soul, claims that physical processes are all there is to life, and believes that once any organism's life is over, that organism no longer persists in any way except perhaps in the memories of certain other organisms. Some, like French atheist and existentialist philosopher Jean-Paul Sartre (1905-1980), believe that the total extinction of life after death underscores the absurdity and meaninglessness of human existence, which is never free and to which no cosmic secrets are ever revealed; but others, notably the Roman Stoics, derive comfort from believing that we did not exist at all before birth and we will not exist at all after death, so all the trials, evils, sufferings, and injustices of life will soon no longer trouble us. The Stoics approved of suicide as escape from unbearable life, and constantly reminded their readers and hearers that "the door is always open" by which one may run away from life by voluntary death. But the best example of this eighth theory is the orthodox Buddhist escape from the wheel of rebirth, nirvana, which literally means "extinguishing" and which is often represented by the metaphor of the flame, which has travelled to billions of new candles as each candle has burned down, and finally goes out, not illuminating any more candles. After animating billions of bodies, the tortured soul is finally allowed to fade into nothing. For Schopenhauer, this nothingness is the annihilation of the will; for Buddhists, nirvana is the stopping of desire.

Plato's *Phaedo*,[*] in the slightly revised classic translation of Benjamin Jowett (1817-1893), master of Balliol College, Oxford University, describes the renowned death of Socrates and in so doing addresses several theories of death and offers several arguments for immortality:

{57} *Echecrates:* Were you yourself, Phaedo, in the prison with Socrates on the day when he drank the poison?

---

[*] Numbers in {braces} in the text are Stephanus numbers, the standard method of citing Plato, i.e., references to the pagination of the 1578 Geneva edition of Plato's works printed by Henri Estienne or "Henricus Stephanus" (1531-1598), three volumes with Greek and Latin in parallel columns.

Phaedo: Yes, Echecrates, I was.

Echecrates: I wish that you would tell me about his death. What did he say in his last hours? We were informed that he died by taking poison, but no one knew anything more; for no Phliasian ever goes to Athens now, and a long time has elapsed since any Athenian found his way to Phlius, and therefore we had no clear account.

{58}   *Phaedo:* Did you not hear of the proceedings at the trial?

Echecrates: Yes; someone told us about the trial, and we could not understand why, having been condemned, he was put to death, not at the time, but long afterwards. What was the reason for this?

Phaedo: An accident, Echecrates. The reason was that the stern of the ship which the Athenians send to Delos happened to have been crowned on the day before he was tried.

Echecrates: What is this ship?

Phaedo: This is the ship in which, as the Athenians say, Theseus went to Crete when he took with him the fourteen youths, and was the savior of them and of himself. And they are said to have vowed to Apollo at the time, that if they were saved they would send a yearly mission to Delos. Now this custom still continues, and the whole period of the voyage to and from Delos, beginning when the priest of Apollo crowns the stern of the ship, is a holy season, during which the city is not allowed to be polluted by public executions; and when the vessel is detained by adverse winds, there may be a very considerable delay. As I was saying, the ship was crowned on the day before the trial, and this was the reason why Socrates lay in prison and was not put to death until long after he was condemned.

Echecrates: What was the manner of his death, Phaedo? What was said or done? And which of his friends had he with him? Or were they not allowed by the authorities to be present? And did he die alone?

Phaedo: No; there were several of his friends with him.

Echecrates: If you have nothing to do, I wish that you would tell me what passed, as exactly as you can.

Phaedo: I have nothing to do, and will try to gratify your wish. For to be reminded of Socrates is always one of my greatest delights, whether I speak myself or hear another speak of him.

Echecrates: You will have listeners who are of the same mind with you, and I hope that you will be as exact as you can.

Phaedo: I remember the strange feeling which came over me at being with him. For I could hardly believe that I was present at the death of a friend, and therefore I did not pity him, Echecrates; his manner and his language were so noble and fearless in the hour of death that to me he appeared blessed. I thought {59} that in going to the other world he could not be without a divine call, and that he would be happy, if any man ever was, when he arrived there, and therefore I did not pity him as might seem natural at such a time. But neither could I feel the pleasure which I usually felt in philosophical discourse (for philosophy was the theme of which we spoke). I was pleased, and I was also pained, because I knew that he was soon to die, and this strange mixture of feeling was shared by us all; we were laughing and weeping by turns, especially the excitable Apollodorus — you know the sort of man?

Echecrates: Yes.

Phaedo: He was quite beside himself; and I and all of us were greatly moved.

Echecrates: Who were present?

Phaedo: Of native Athenians there were, besides Apollodorus, Critobulus and his father Crito, Hermogenes, Epigenes, Aeschines, and Antisthenes; likewise Ctesippus of the deme of Paeania, Menexenus, and some others; but Plato, if I am not mistaken, was ill.

Echecrates: Were there any strangers?

Phaedo: Yes, there were; Simmias the Theban, and Cebes, and Phaedondes; Euclid and Terpsion, who came from Megara.

Echecrates: And was Aristippus there, and Cleombrotus?

Phaedo: No, they were said to be in Aegina.

Echecrates: Anyone else?

Phaedo: I think that these were about all.

Echecrates: And what was the discourse of which you spoke?

Phaedo: I will begin at the beginning, and endeavor to repeat the entire conversation. You must understand that we had been previously in the habit of assembling early in the morning at the court in which the trial was held, and which is not far from the prison. There we remained talking with one another until the opening of the prison doors (for they were not opened very early); then we went in and generally passed the day with Socrates. On the last morning the meeting was earlier than usual; this was owing to our having heard on the previous evening that the sacred ship had arrived from Delos, and therefore we agreed to meet very early at the accustomed place. On our going to the prison, the jailer who answered the door, instead of admitting us, came out and told us to wait until he called us. "For the Eleven," he said, "are now with Socrates; they are taking off his chains, and giving orders that he is to die today." He soon returned and said that {60} we might come in. On entering we found Socrates just released from chains, and [his wife] Xanthippe, whom you know, sitting by him, and holding his child in her arms. When she saw us she uttered a cry and said, as women will: "O Socrates, this is the last time that either you will converse with your friends, or they with you." Socrates turned to Crito and said: "Crito, let someone take her home." Some of Crito's people accordingly led her away, crying out and beating herself. And when she was gone, Socrates, sitting up on the couch, began to bend and rub his leg, saying, as he rubbed: "How singular is the thing called pleasure, and how curiously related to pain, which might be thought to be the opposite of it; for they never come to a man together, and yet he who pursues either of them is generally compelled to take the other. They are two, and yet they grow together out of one head or stem; and I cannot help thinking that if Aesop had noticed them, he would have made a fable about God trying to reconcile their strife, and how, when he could not, he fastened their heads together; and this is the reason why when one comes the other follows, as I find in my own case that pleasure comes following after the pain in my leg, which was caused by the chain."

Upon this Cebes said: I am very glad indeed, Socrates, that you mentioned the name of Aesop. For that reminds me of a question which has been asked by many, and was asked of me only the day before yesterday by Evenus the poet, and as he will be sure to ask again, you may as well tell me what I should say to him, if you would like him to have an answer. He wanted to know why you, who never before wrote a line of poetry, now that you are in prison are putting Aesop into verse, and also composing that hymn in honor of Apollo.

Tell him, Cebes, he replied, that I had no idea of rivalling him or his poems; which is the truth, for I knew that I could not do that. But I wanted to see whether I could purge away a scruple which I felt about the meaning of certain dreams. In the course of my life I have often had intimations in dreams "that I should make music." The same dream came to me sometimes in one form, and sometimes in another, but always saying the same or nearly the same words: "Make and cultivate music," said the dream. And hitherto I had imagined that this was only intended to exhort and encourage me in the study of philosophy, which {61} has always been the pursuit of my life, and is the noblest and best of music. The dream was bidding me to do what I was already doing, in the same way that the competitor in a race is bidden by the spectators to run when he is already running. But I was not certain of this, as the dream might have meant music in the popular sense of the word, and being under sentence of death, and the festival giving me a respite, I thought that I should be safer if I satisfied the scruple, and, in obedience to the dream, composed a few verses before I departed. And first I made a hymn in honor of the god of the festival, and then considering that a poet, if he is really to be a poet ("maker"), should not only put words together but make stories, and as I have no invention, I took some fables of Aesop, which I had ready at hand and knew, and turned them into verse. Tell Evenus this, Cebes, and bid him be of good cheer; say that I would have him come after me if he be a wise man, and not tarry; and that today I am likely to be going, for the Athenians say that I must.

Simmias said: What a message for such a man! Having been a frequent companion of his, I should say that, as far as I know him, he will never take your advice unless he is obliged.

Why, said Socrates, — is not Evenus a philosopher?

I think that he is, said Simmias.

Then he, or any man who has the spirit of philosophy, will be willing to die, though he will not take his own life, for that is held not to be right.

Here he changed his position, and put his legs off the couch on to the ground, and during the rest of the conversation he remained sitting.

Why do you say, inquired Cebes, that a man ought not to take his own life, but that the philosopher will be ready to follow the dying?

Socrates replied: And have you, Cebes and Simmias, who are acquainted with Philolaus, never heard him speak of this?

Yes, but I never understood him, Socrates.

My words, too, are only an echo; but I am very willing to say what I have heard, and indeed, as I am going to another place, I ought to be thinking and talking of the nature of the pilgrimage which I am about to make. What can I do better in the interval between this and the setting of the sun?

Then tell me, Socrates, why is killing oneself held not to be right, as I have certainly heard Philolaus affirm when he was staying with us at Thebes? And there are others who say the same, although I never understood any of them.

{62}   But do your best, replied Socrates, and the day may come when you will understand. I suppose that you wonder why, as most evil things may sometimes or accidentally be good, death, which may be better than life in some cases, is to be the only exception; and why, when a man is better dead, he is not permitted to be his own benefactor, but must wait for the hand of another.

Yes, indeed, said Cebes, laughing, and speaking in his native Doric.

I admit the appearance of inconsistency, replied Socrates, but there may not be any real inconsistency in this after all. There is a doctrine whispered in secret that man is a prisoner who has no right to open the door of his prison and run away; this is a great mystery which I do not quite understand. Yet I, too, believe that the gods are our guardians, and that we are a possession of theirs. Do you not agree?

Yes, I agree to that, said Cebes.

And if one of your own possessions, an ox or an ass, for example, took the liberty of putting himself out of the way when you had given no intimation of your wish that he should die, would you not be angry with him, and would you not punish him if you could?

Certainly, replied Cebes.

Then, if we look at it this way, there may be reason in saying that a man should wait, and not take his own life until God summons him, as he is now summoning me.

Yes, Socrates, said Cebes, there is surely reason in that. And yet how can you reconcile this seemingly true belief that God is our guardian and we his possessions, with that willingness to die which we were attributing to the philosopher? That the wisest of men should be willing to leave this service in which they are ruled by the gods, who are the best of rulers, is not reasonable, for surely no wise man thinks that when set at liberty he can take better care of himself than the gods take of him. A fool may perhaps think this — he may argue that he had better run away from his master, not considering that his duty is to remain to the end and not to run away from the good and that there is no sense in his running away. But the wise man will want to be ever with him who is better than himself. Now this, Socrates, is the reverse of what was just now said; for upon this view the wise man should sorrow and the fool rejoice at passing out of life.

{63}   The earnestness of Cebes seemed to please Socrates. Here, said he, turning to us, is a man who is always inquiring, and is not to be easily convinced by the first argument he hears.

And in this case, added Simmias, his objection does appear to me to have some force. For what can be the meaning of a truly wise man wanting to fly away and lightly leave a master who is better than himself? And I rather imagine that Cebes is referring to you; he thinks that you are too ready to leave us, and too ready to leave the gods who, as you acknowledge, are our good rulers.

Yes, replied Socrates; there is reason in that. And you think that I ought to answer this indictment as if I were in court?

That is what we should like, said Simmias.

Then I must try to make a better impression upon you than I did when defending myself before the judges. For I am quite ready to admit, Simmias and Cebes, that I ought to be grieved at death, if I were not persuaded that I am going to other gods who are wise and good (and of this I am as certain as I can be of anything of the sort) and to men departed (though I am not so certain of this), who are better than those whom I leave behind; and therefore I do not grieve as I might have done, for I have good hope that there is yet something remaining for the dead, and, as has been said of old, some far better thing for the good than for the evil.

But do you mean to take away your thoughts with you, Socrates? said Simmias. Will you not communicate them to us? — for their benefit is one in which we too may hope to share. Moreover, if you succeed in convincing us, that will be an answer to the charge against yourself.

I will do my best, replied Socrates. But you must first let me hear what Crito wants; he has long been waiting to say something to me.

Only this, Socrates, replied Crito, the attendant who is to give you the poison has been telling me that you are not to talk much, and he wants me to let you know this; for by talking heat is increased, and this interferes with the action of the poison; those who excite themselves are sometimes obliged to drink the poison two or three times.

Then, said Socrates, let him mind his business and be prepared to give me the poison two or three times, if necessary; that is all.

I was almost certain that you would say that, replied Crito; but I was obliged to satisfy him.

Never mind him, he said.

And now I will make answer to you, my judges, and show that he who has lived as a true philosopher has reason to be of good cheer when he is about to {64} die, and that after death he may hope to receive the greatest good in the other world. And how this may be, Simmias and Cebes, I will endeavor to explain. For I deem that the true disciple of philosophy is likely to be misunderstood by other men. They do not perceive that he is always pursuing death and dying; and if this is true, why should he be dejected, having had the desire of death all his life long, when that which he has been always pursuing and desiring arrives?

Simmias laughed and said, I swear that I cannot help laughing, though I am not in a laughing humor, when I think what the many will say when they hear this. They will say that this is very true, and our people at home will agree with them in saying that the life which philosophers desire is truly death, and that they have found them out to be deserving of the death which they desire.

And they are right, Simmias, in saying this, with the exception of the words "they have found them out"; for they have not found out either what is the nature of this death which the true philosopher desires or how he deserves or desires death. But let us forget them and have a word with ourselves. Do we believe that there is such a thing as death?

To be sure, replied Simmias.

And is it anything but the separation of soul and body? And is being dead the attainment of this separation; when the soul exists in itself and is parted from the body as the body is parted from the soul — is that death?

Exactly that and nothing else, he replied.

And there is another question, my friend, about which I should like to have your opinion, for the answer to it will probably throw light on our present inquiry: Do you think that the philosopher ought to care about the pleasures — if they are to be called pleasures — of eating and drinking?

Certainly not, answered Simmias.

And what do you say of the pleasures of love — should he care about them?

By no means.

And will he think much of the other ways of indulging the body — for example, the acquisition of costly raiment, or sandals, or other adornments of the body? Instead of caring about them, does he not rather despise anything more than nature needs? What do you say?

I should say that the true philosopher would despise them.

Would you not say that he is entirely concerned with the soul and not with the body? He would like, as far as he can, to get away from the body and turn to the soul.

That is true.

{65}   In matters of this sort philosophers, above all other men, may be observed in every sort of way to sever the soul from communion with the body.

That is true.

On that account, Simmias, the rest of the world are of the opinion that a life which has no bodily pleasures and no part in them is not worth having; and that he who thinks nothing of bodily pleasures is almost as if dead.

That is quite true.

What again shall we say of the actual acquirement of knowledge? — Is the body, if invited to share in the inquiry, a hinderer or a helper? I mean to say, have sight and hearing any truth in them? Are they not, as the poets are always telling us, inaccurate witnesses? And yet, if even they are inaccurate and indistinct, what is to be said of the other senses — for you will allow that these two are the best of them?

Certainly, he replied.

Then when does the soul attain truth? — for in attempting to consider anything in company with the body it is obviously deceived.

Yes, that is true.

Then must not true existence be revealed to it in thought, if at all?

Yes.

And thought is best when the mind is gathered into itself and none of these things trouble it — neither sounds nor sights nor pain nor any pleasure — when it has as little as possible to do with the body, and has no bodily sense or feeling, but is aspiring after being?

Certainly.

And in this the philosopher dishonors the body; his soul runs away from the body and desires to be alone and by itself?

That is true.

Well, but there is another thing, Simmias: Is there or is there not absolute justice?

Assuredly there is.

And absolute beauty and absolute good?

Of course.

But did you ever behold any of them with your eyes?

Certainly not.

Or did you ever reach them with any other bodily sense? — and I speak not of these alone, but of absolute greatness, and health, and strength, and of the essence or true nature of everything. Has the reality of them ever been perceived by you through the bodily organs, or rather, is not the nearest approach to the knowledge of their several natures made by him who so orders his intellectual vision as to have the most exact conception of the essence of that which he considers?

Certainly.

And he attains to the purest knowledge of them who goes to each of them with the mind alone, not allowing, when in the act of thought, the intrusion or introduction of sight or any other sense in the company of reason, but penetrates, {66} with the very light of the mind in its clearness, the very light of truth in each. He has gotten rid, as far as he can, of eyes and ears and of the whole body, which he conceives only as a distracting element, hindering the soul from the acquisition of knowledge when they are in company with it. — Is not this the sort of man who, if ever man did, is likely to attain the knowledge of existence?

There is admirable truth in that, Socrates, replied Simmias.

And when real philosophers consider all this, must not they make a reflection, of which they will speak to one another in such words as these: We have found, they will say, a path of speculation which seems to bring us and our argument to the conclusion that, while we are in the body and while the soul is mingled with this mass of evil, our desire will not be satisfied, and our desire is for the truth. For the body is a source of endless trouble to us by reason of the mere requirement of food; and also is liable to diseases which overtake and impede us in the search after truth; and by filling us so full of loves, and lusts, and fears, and fancies, and idols, and every sort of folly, prevents our ever having, as people say, so much as a thought. For where do wars, and fights, and factions come from? From where but the body and the lusts of the body? Wars are occasioned by the love of money, and money has to be acquired for the sake and in the service of the body; and in consequence of all these impediments the time which ought to be given to philosophy is lost. Moreover, if there is time and an inclination toward philosophy, yet the body introduces a turmoil and confusion and fear into the course of speculation, and hinders us from seeing the truth; and all experience shows that if we would have pure knowledge of anything we must be quit of the body, and the soul in itself must behold all things in themselves. Then I suppose that we shall attain that which we desire, and of which we say that we are lovers, and that is wisdom, not while we live, but after death, as the argument shows; for if while in company with the body the soul cannot have pure knowledge, one of two things seems to follow — either knowledge is not to be attained at all, or, if at {67} all, after death. For then, and not till then, the soul will be in itself alone and without the body. In this present life, I reckon that we make the nearest approach to knowledge when we have the least possible concern or interest in the body, and are not saturated with the bodily nature, but remain pure until the hour when God himself is pleased to release us. And then the foolishness of the body will be cleared away and we shall be pure and hold converse with other pure souls, and know of ourselves the clear light everywhere; and this is surely the light of truth. For no impure thing is allowed to approach the pure. These are the sort of words, Simmias, which the true lovers of wisdom cannot help saying to one another, and thinking. Will you agree with me in that?

Certainly, Socrates.

But if this is true, my friend, then there is great hope that, going where I go, I shall there be satisfied with that which has been the chief concern of you and me in our past lives. And now that the hour of departure is appointed to me, this is the hope with which I depart, and not I only, but every man who believes that he has his mind purified.

Certainly, replied Simmias.

And what is purification but the separation of the soul from the body, as I was saying before; the habit of the soul gathering and collecting itself into itself, out of all the courses of the body; the dwelling in its own place alone, as in another life, so also in this, as far as it can; the release of the soul from the chains of the body?

Very true, he said.

And is that which is termed death only this very separation and release of the soul from the body?

To be sure, he said.

And the true philosophers, and they only, study and are eager to release the soul. Is not the separation and release of the soul from the body their special study?

That is true.

And as I was saying at first, there would be a ridiculous contradiction in men studying to live as nearly as they can in a state of death, and yet lamenting when death comes.

Certainly.

Then, Simmias, as the true philosophers are ever studying death, to them, of all men, death is the least terrible. Look at the matter in this way: How inconsistent of them it would be to have been always enemies of the body, and wanting to have the soul alone, and when this is granted to them, to be trembling and lamenting instead of rejoicing at their departing to that place where, when {68} they arrive, they hope to gain that which in life they loved — and this was wisdom — and at the same time to be rid of the company of their enemy. Many a man has been willing to go to the world below in the hope of seeing there an earthly love, or wife, or son, and conversing with them. And will he who is a true lover of wisdom, and is persuaded in like manner that only in the world below he can worthily enjoy it, still lament at death? Will he not depart with joy? Surely he will, my friend, if he be a true philosopher. For he will have a firm conviction that there only, and nowhere else, he can find wisdom in its purity. And if this be true, he would be very absurd, as I was saying, if he were to fear death.

He would, indeed, replied Simmias.

And when you see a man who is lamenting at the approach of death, is not his reluctance a sufficient proof that he is not a lover of wisdom, but a lover of the body, and probably at the same time a lover of either money or power, or both?

That is very true, he replied.

There is a virtue, Simmias, which is named courage. Is not that a special attribute of the philosopher?

Certainly.

Again, there is temperance. Is not the calm, and control, and disdain of the passions, which even the many call temperance, a quality belonging only to those who despise the body and live in philosophy?

That is not to be denied.

For the courage and temperance of other men, if you will consider them, are really a contradiction.

How is that, Socrates?

Well, he said, you are aware that death is regarded by men in general as a great evil.

That is true, he said.

And do not courageous men endure death because they are afraid of yet greater evils?

That is true.

Then all but the philosophers are courageous only from fear, and because they are afraid; and yet that a man should be courageous from fear, and because he is a coward, is surely a strange thing.

Very true.

And are not the temperate exactly in the same case? They are temperate because they are intemperate — which may seem to be a contradiction, but is nevertheless the sort of thing which happens with this foolish temperance. For there are pleasures which they are afraid of losing, and therefore they abstain {69} from one class of pleasures because they are overcome by another; and while intemperance is defined as "being under the dominion of pleasure," they overcome pleasure only because they are overcome by pleasure. And that is what I mean by saying that they are temperate through intemperance.

That appears to be true.

Yet the exchange of one fear or pleasure or pain for another fear or pleasure or pain, which are measured like coins, the greater for the less, is not the exchange of virtue. My dear Simmias, is there not one true coin for which all things ought to be exchanged? — And that is wisdom; and only in exchange for this, and in company with this, is anything truly bought or sold, whether courage or temperance or justice. And is not all true virtue the companion of wisdom, no matter what fears or pleasures or other similar goods or evils may or may not attend it? But the virtue which is made up of these goods, when they are severed from wisdom and exchanged with one another, is a shadow of virtue only, nor is there any freedom or health or truth in it; but in the true exchange there is a purging away of all these things; and temperance, and justice, and courage, and wisdom itself are a purgation of them. And I conceive that the founders of the mysteries had a real meaning and were not mere triflers when they intimated in a figure long ago that he who passes unsanctified and uninitiated into the world below will live in a slough, but that he who arrives there after initiation and purification will dwell with the gods. For "many," as they say in the mysteries, "are the thyrsus-bearers, but few are the mystics" — meaning, as I interpret the words, "the true philosophers." Among them my whole life I have been seeking, according to my ability, to find a place; whether I have sought in a right way or not, and whether I have succeeded or not, I shall truly know in a little while, if God will, when I myself arrive in the other world — that is my belief. And now, Simmias and Cebes, I have answered those who charge me with not grieving or lamenting at parting from you and my masters in this world; and I am right in not lamenting, for I believe that I shall find other masters and friends who are as good in the world below. But most men do not believe this, and I shall be glad if my words have any more success with you than with the judges of the Athenians.

Cebes answered: I agree, Socrates, in the greater part of what you say. {70} But in what concerns the soul, men are apt to be incredulous; they fear that when it leaves the body its place may be nowhere, and that on the very day of death it may be destroyed and perish — immediately on its release from the body, issuing forth like smoke or air and vanishing away into nothingness. For if it could only hold together and be itself after it was released from the evils of the body, there would be good reason to hope, Socrates, that what you say is true. But much persuasion and many arguments are required in order to prove that when the man is dead the soul yet exists, and has any power or intelligence.

True, Cebes, said Socrates; and shall I suggest that we talk a little of the probabilities of these things?

I am sure, said Cebes, that I should greatly like to know your opinion about them.

I reckon, said Socrates, that no one who heard me now, not even if he were one of my old enemies, the comic poets, could accuse me of idle talking about matters in which I have no concern. Let us, then, if you please, proceed with the inquiry.

Whether the souls of men after death are or are not in the world below, is a question which may be argued in this manner: The ancient doctrine of which I have been speaking affirms that they go from this into the other world, and return here, and are born again from the dead. Now if this be true, and the living come from the dead, then our souls must be in the other world, for if not, how could they be reincarnated? And this would be conclusive, if there were any real evidence that the living are only born from the dead; but if there is no evidence of this, then other arguments will have to be adduced.

That is very true, replied Cebes.

Then let us consider this whole question, not in relation to man only, but in relation to animals generally, and to plants, and to everything of which there is generation, and the proof will be easier. Are not all things which have opposites generated out of their opposites? I mean such things as good and evil, justice and unjustness — and there are innumerable other opposites which are generated out of opposites. And I want to show that this holds universally of all opposites; I mean to say, for example, that anything which becomes greater must become greater after being less.

True.

{71}   And that which becomes less must have been once greater and then become less.

Yes.

And the weaker is generated from the stronger, and the swifter from the slower.

Very true.

And the worse is from the better, and the more just is from the more unjust.

Of course.

And is this true of all opposites? Are we convinced that all of them are generated out of opposites?

Yes.

And in this universal opposition of all things, are there not also two intermediate processes which are ever going on, from one opposite to the other, and back again; where there is a greater and a less there is also an intermediate process of increase and diminution, and that which grows is said to wax, and that which decays to wane?

Yes, he said.

And there are many other processes, such as division and composition, cooling and heating, which equally involve a passage into and out of one another. And this necessarily holds of all opposites, even though not always expressed in words — they are generated out of one another, and there is a passing or process from one to the other of them?

Very true, he replied.

Well, and is there not an opposite of life, as sleep is the opposite of waking?

Yes, he said.

And what is that?

Death, he answered.

And these, then, are generated, if they are opposites, the one from the other, and have there their two intermediate processes also?

Of course.

Now, said Socrates, I will analyze one of the two pairs of opposites which I have mentioned to you, and also its intermediate processes, and you shall analyze the other to me. The state of sleep is opposed to the state of waking, and out of sleeping waking is generated, and out of waking, sleeping, and the process of generation is in the one case falling asleep, and in the other waking up. Are you agreed about that?

Quite agreed.

Then suppose that you analyze life and death to me in the same manner. Is not death opposed to life?

Yes.

And are they generated one from the other?

Yes.

What is generated from life?

Death.

And what from death?

I can only say in answer — life.

Then the living, whether things or persons, Cebes, are generated from the dead?

That is clear, he replied.

Then the inference is, that our souls are in the world below?

That is true.

And one of the two processes or generations is visible — for surely the act of dying is visible?

Surely, he said.

What then is the result? Shall we exclude the opposite process, and suppose nature to go on one leg only? And if not, must not a corresponding process of generation in death also be assigned to death?

Certainly, he replied.

And what is that process?

Revival.

{72}   And revival, if there be such a thing, is the birth of the dead into the world of the living?

Quite true.

Then there is a new way in which we arrive at the inference that the living come from the dead, just as the dead come from the living; and if this is true, then the souls of the dead must be in some place out of which they come again. And this, I think, has been satisfactorily proved.

Yes, Socrates, he said; all this seems to flow necessarily out of our previous admissions.

And that these admissions are not unfair, Cebes, he said, may be shown, I think, in this way: If generation were in a straight line only, and there were no compensation or circle in nature, no turn or return of elemental opposites into one another, then you know that all things would at last have the same form and pass into the same state, and there would be no more generation of them.

I do not see what you mean, Cebes said.

A simple thing enough, which I will illustrate by the case of sleep, he replied. You know that if there were no alternation of sleeping and waking, then the story of the sleeping Endymion would in the end have no meaning, because all other things would be asleep too, and he would not be thought of. Or if there were composition only, and no division of substances, then the chaos of Anaxagoras would come again. And in like manner, my dear Cebes, if all things which partook of life were to die, and after they were dead remained in the form of death, and did not come to life again, all would at last die, and nothing would be alive — how could this be otherwise? For if the living spring from any other things except the dead, and they die, must not all things at last be swallowed up in death?

There is no escape from that, Socrates, said Cebes; and I think that what you say is absolutely true.

Yes, he said, Cebes, I entirely think so, too; and we are not victims of a vain delusion; but I am confident in believing that there truly is such a thing as living again, and that the living spring from the dead, and that the souls of the dead are in existence, and that the good souls have a better portion than the evil.

Cebes added: Your favorite doctrine, Socrates, that knowledge is simply recollection, if true, also necessarily implies a previous time in which we learned {73} that which we now recollect. But this would be impossible unless our soul was in some place before existing in the human form; here, then, is another argument of the soul's immortality.

But tell me, Cebes, said Simmias, interposing, what proofs are given of this doctrine of recollection? I am not very sure at this moment that I remember them.

One excellent proof, said Cebes, is afforded by questions. If you put a question to a person in the right way, he will give a true answer from within himself; but how could he do this unless there were knowledge and right reason already in him? And this is most clearly shown when he is taken to a diagram or to anything of that sort.

But if, said Socrates, you are still incredulous, Simmias, I would ask you whether you may not agree with me when you look at the matter in another way. I mean, if you are still incredulous as to whether knowledge is recollection.

Incredulous, I am not, said Simmias; but I want to have this doctrine of recollection brought to my own recollection, and, from what Cebes has said, I am beginning to recollect and to be convinced; but I should still like to hear what more you have to say.

This is what I would say, he replied: We should agree, if I am not mistaken, that what a man recollects he must have known at some previous time.

Very true.

And what is the nature of this knowledge or recollection? And, in asking this, I mean to ask whether, when a person has already seen or heard or in any way perceived anything, and he knows not only that, but something else of which he has not the same, but another kind of knowledge, we may not fairly say that he recollects that which comes into his mind. Are we agreed about that?

What do you mean?

I mean what I may illustrate by the following instance: The knowledge of a lyre is not the same as the knowledge of a man?

True.

And yet what is the feeling of lovers when they recognize a lyre, or a garment, or anything else which the beloved has been in the habit of using? Do not they, from knowing the lyre, form in the mind's eye an image of the youth to whom the lyre belongs? And this is recollection; and in the same way anyone who sees Simmias may remember Cebes; and there are endless other things of the same nature.

Yes, indeed, there are — endless, replied Simmias.

And this sort of thing, he said, is recollection, and is most commonly a process of recovering that which has been forgotten through time and inattention.

Very true, he said.

Well; and may you not also from seeing the picture of a horse or a lyre remember a man? And from the picture of Simmias, may you be led to remember Cebes?

True.

Or you may also be led to the recollection of Simmias himself?

{74}   True, he said.

And in all these cases, the recollection may be derived from things either like or unlike?

That is true.

And when the recollection is derived from like things, then there is sure to be another question, which is, whether the likeness of that which is recollected is in any way defective or not.

Very true, he said.

And shall we proceed a step further, and affirm that there is such a thing as equality, not of wood with wood, or of stone with stone, but that, over and above this, there is absolute equality? Shall we affirm this?

Affirm, yes, and swear to it, replied Simmias, with all possible confidence.

And do we know the nature of this absolute essence?

To be sure, he said.

And from where did we obtain this knowledge? Did we not see equalities of material things, such as pieces of wood and stones, and gather from them the idea of an equality which is different from them? — Will you admit that? Or look at the matter again in this way: Do not the same pieces of wood or stone appear at one time equal, and at another time unequal?

That is certain.

But are real equals ever unequal? Or is the idea of equality ever the idea of inequality?

That surely was never yet known, Socrates.

Then these so-called equals are not the same with the idea of equality?

I should say, clearly not, Socrates.

And yet from these equals, although differing from the idea of equality, you conceived and attained that idea?

Very true, he said.

Which might be like, or might be unlike them?

Yes.

But that makes no difference; whenever from seeing one thing you conceived another, whether like or unlike, there must surely have been an act of recollection?

Very true.

But what would you say of equal portions of wood and stone, or other material equals? And what is the impression produced by them? Are they equals in the same sense as absolute equality? Or do they fall short of this absolute equality in some measure?

Yes, he said, in a very great measure, too.

And must we not allow that when I or anyone look at any object, and perceive that the object aims at being some other thing, but falls short, and cannot attain to it — he who makes this observation must have had previous knowledge of that to which, as he says, the other, although similar, was inferior?

Certainly.

And has not this been our case in the matter of equals and of absolute equality?

Precisely.

Then we must have known absolute equality prior to the time when we {75} first saw the material equals, and reflected that all these apparent equals aim at this absolute equality, but fall short of it?

That is true.

And do we recognize also that this absolute equality has only been known, and can only be known, through the medium of sight or touch, or of some other sense, for they are really all the same?

Yes, Socrates, as far as the argument is concerned, one of them is the same as the other.

And from the senses, then, is derived the knowledge that all sensible things aim at an idea of equality of which they fall short — is not that true?

Yes.

Then before we began to see or hear or perceive in any way, we must have had a knowledge of absolute equality, or we could not have referred the equals which are derived from the senses to that standard — for to that they all aspire, and of that they fall short?

That, Socrates, is certainly to be inferred from the previous statements.

And did we not see and hear and acquire our other senses as soon as we were born?

Certainly.

Then we must have acquired the knowledge of the idea of equality at some time previous to this?

Yes.

That is to say, before we were born, I suppose?

True.

And if we acquired this knowledge before we were born, and were born having it, then we also knew before we were born and at the instant of birth not only equal or the greater or the less, but all other ideas; for we are speaking not only of absolute equality, but also of absolute beauty, goodness, justice, holiness, and of all which we stamp with the name of essence in the dialectical process, when we ask and answer questions. Of all this we may certainly affirm that we acquired the knowledge before birth?

That is true.

But if, after having acquired it, we have not forgotten that which we acquired, then we must always have been born with knowledge, and shall always continue to know as long as life lasts — for knowing is the acquiring and retaining of knowledge and not forgetting. Is not forgetting, Simmias, just the losing of knowledge?

Quite true, Socrates.

But if the knowledge which we acquired before birth was lost by us at birth, and afterwards by the use of the senses we recovered that which we previously knew, will not that which we call learning be a process of recovering our knowledge, and may not this be rightly termed recollection by us?

Very true.

{76}   For this is clear, that when we perceived something, either by the help of sight or hearing, or some other sense, there was no difficulty in receiving from this a conception of some other thing like or unlike which had been forgotten and which was associated with this; and therefore, as I was saying, one of two alternatives follows: either we had this knowledge at birth and continued to know through life, or, after birth, those who are said to learn only remember, and learning is recollection only.

Yes, that is quite true, Socrates.

And which alternative, Simmias, do you prefer? Had we the knowledge at our birth, or did we remember afterwards the things which we knew previously to our birth?

I cannot decide at the moment.

At any rate you can decide whether he who has knowledge ought or ought not to be able to give a reason for what he knows.

Certainly, he ought.

But do you think that every man is able to give a reason about these very matters of which we are speaking?

I wish that they could, Socrates, but I greatly fear that tomorrow at this time there will be no one able to give a reason worth having.

Then you are not of the opinion, Simmias, that all men know these things?

Certainly not.

Then they are in the process of recollecting what they learned before.

Certainly.

But when did our souls acquire this knowledge? — Not since we were born as men?

Certainly not.

And therefore previously?

Yes.

Then, Simmias, our souls must have existed before they were in the form of man — without bodies, and must have had intelligence.

Unless indeed you suppose, Socrates, that these notions were given us at the moment of birth; for this is the only time that remains.

Yes, my friend, but if so, then when did we lose them? For they are not in us when we are born — that is admitted. Did we lose them at the moment of receiving them, or at some other time?

No, Socrates, I perceive that I was unconsciously talking nonsense.

Then may we not say, Simmias, that if, as we are always repeating, there is an absolute beauty, and goodness, and essence in general, and to this, which is now discovered to be a previous condition of our being, we refer all our sensations, and with this compare them — assuming this to have a prior existence, then our souls must have had a prior existence, but if not, there would be no force in the argument? There can be no doubt that if these absolute ideas existed before we were born, then our souls must have existed before we were born, and if not the ideas, then not the souls.

Yes, Socrates, I am convinced that there is precisely the same necessity for the existence of the soul before birth, and of the essence of which you are {77} speaking, and of the inseparability of this soul from this essence; and the argument arrives at a result which happily agrees with my own opinion. For there is nothing which to my mind is so evident as that beauty, goodness, and other ideas of which you were just now speaking have a most real and absolute existence; and I am satisfied with the proof.

Well, but is Cebes equally satisfied? For I must convince him too.

I think, said Simmias, that Cebes is satisfied; although he is the most incredulous of mortals, yet I believe that he is sufficiently convinced of the existence of the soul before birth. But that after death the soul will continue to exist is not yet proven even to my own satisfaction. I cannot get rid of the feeling of the many to which Cebes was referring — the feeling that when the man dies the soul may be scattered, and that this may be the end of it. For admitting that it may be generated and created in some other place, and may have existed before entering the human body, why after having entered in and gone out again may it not itself be destroyed and come to an end?

Very true, Simmias, said Cebes; that our soul existed before we were born was the first half of the argument, and this appears to have been proven; but that the soul will exist after death as well as before birth is the other half, of which the proof is still wanting, and has to be supplied.

But that proof, Simmias and Cebes, has been already given, said Socrates, if you put the two arguments together — I mean this and the former one, in which we admitted that everything living is born of the dead. For if the soul existed before birth, and in coming to life and being born can be born only from death and dying, must it not after death continue to exist, since it has to be born again? Surely the proof which you desire has been already furnished. Still I suspect that you and Simmias would be glad to probe the argument further. Like children, you are haunted with a fear that when the soul leaves the body, the wind may really blow it away and scatter it; especially if a man should happen to die in stormy weather and not when the sky is calm.

Cebes answered with a smile: Then, Socrates, you must argue us out of our fears — and yet, strictly speaking, they are not our fears, but there is a child within us to whom death is a sort of hobgoblin; him too we must persuade not to be afraid when he is alone with us in the dark.

Socrates said: Let the voice of the charmer be applied daily until you have charmed him away.

{78}   And where shall we find a good charmer of our fears, Socrates, when you are gone?

Greece, he replied, is a large place, Cebes, and has many good men, and there are barbarous races not a few. Seek for him among them all, far and wide, sparing neither pains nor money; for there is no better way of using your money. And you must not forget to seek for him among yourselves too; for he is nowhere more likely to be found.

The search, replied Cebes, shall certainly be made. And now, if you please, let us return to the point of the argument at which we digressed.

By all means, replied Socrates; what else should I please?

Very good, he said.

Must we not, said Socrates, ask ourselves some question of this sort? — What is that which, as we imagine, is liable to be scattered away, and about which we fear? And what again is that about which we have no fear? And then we may proceed to inquire whether that which suffers dispersion is or is not of the nature of the soul — our hopes and fears as to our own souls will turn upon that.

That is true, he said.

Now whatever is compounded or composite may be supposed to be naturally capable of being dissolved in like manner as of being compounded; but that which is uncompounded, and that only, must be, if anything is, indissoluble.

Yes; that is what I should imagine, said Cebes.

And the uncompounded may be assumed to be the same and unchanging, where the compound is always changing and never the same?

That I also think, he said.

Then now let us return to the previous discussion. Is that idea or essence, which in the dialectical process we define as essence or true existence — whether essence of equality, beauty, or anything else — are these essences, I say, liable at times to some degree of change? Or are they, each of them, always what they are, having the same simple, self-existent, and unchanging forms, and not admitting of variation at all, or in any way, or at any time?

They must be always the same, Socrates, replied Cebes.

And what would you say of the many beautiful — whether men or horses or garments or any other things which may be called equal or beautiful — are they all unchanging and the same always, or quite the reverse? May they not rather be described as almost always changing and hardly ever the same either with themselves or with one another?

The latter, replied Cebes; they are always in a state of change.

{79}   And these you can touch and see and perceive with the senses, but the unchanging things you can perceive only with the mind — they are invisible and are not seen?

That is very true, he said.

Well, then, he added, let us suppose that there are two sorts of existences, one seen, the other unseen.

Let us suppose them.

The seen is the changing, and the unseen is the unchanging.

That may be also supposed.

And, further, is not one part of us body, and the rest of us soul?

To be sure.

And to which class may we say that the body is more alike and akin?

Clearly to the seen: no one can doubt that.

And is the soul seen or not seen?

Not by man, Socrates.

And by "seen" and "not seen" do we mean that which is or is not visible
to the eye of man?

Yes, to the eye of man.

And what do we say of the soul? Is that seen or not seen?

Not seen.

Unseen then?

Yes.

Then the soul more resembles the unseen, and the body the seen?

That is most certain, Socrates.

And were we not saying long ago that the soul, when using the body as
an instrument of perception, that is to say, when using the sense of sight or hearing or some other sense (for the meaning of perceiving through the body is perceiving through the senses) — were we not saying that the soul too is then
dragged by the body into the region of the changeable, and wanders, and is confused; the world spins round it, and it is like a drunkard under their influence?

Very true.

But when returning into itself it reflects; then it passes into the other
world, the realm of purity, and eternity, and immortality, and unchangeableness,
which are its kindred, and with them it ever lives, when it is by itself and is not
limited or hindered; then it ceases from its erring ways, and being in communion
with the unchanging is unchanging. And this state of the soul is called wisdom?

That is well and truly said, Socrates, he replied.

And to which class is the soul more nearly alike and akin, as far as may
be inferred from this argument, as well as from the preceding one?

I think, Socrates, that, in the opinion of everyone who follows the argument, the soul will be infinitely more like the unchangeable. Even the most stupid
person will not deny that.

And is the body more like the changing?

Yes.

Yet once more consider the matter in this light: When the soul and the

{80} body are united, then nature orders the soul to rule and govern, and the body to obey and serve. Now which of these two functions is akin to the divine? And which to the mortal? Does not the divine appear to you to be that which naturally orders and rules, and the mortal that which is subject and servant?

True.

And which does the soul resemble?

The soul resembles the divine, and the body the mortal — there can be no doubt of that, Socrates.

Then reflect, Cebes, is not the conclusion of the whole matter this — that the soul is in the very likeness of the divine, and immortal, and intelligible, and uniform, and indissoluble, and unchangeable; and that the body is in the very likeness of the human, and mortal, and unintelligible, and multiform, and dissoluble, and changeable? Can this, my dear Cebes, be denied?

No, indeed.

But if this be true, then is not the body liable to speedy dissolution, and is not the soul almost or altogether indissoluble?

Certainly.

And do you further observe, that after a man is dead, the body, which is the visible part of man, and has a visible framework, which is called a corpse, and which would naturally be dissolved and decomposed and dissipated, is not dissolved or decomposed at once, but may remain for a good while, if the constitution be sound at the time of death, and the season of the year favorable? For the body when shrunk and embalmed, as is the custom in Egypt, may remain almost entire through infinite ages; and even in decay, still there are some portions, such as the bones and ligaments, which are practically indestructible. You allow that?

Yes.

And are we to suppose that the soul, which is invisible, in passing to the true Hades, which like it is invisible, and pure, and noble, and on its way to the good and wise God, where, if God will, my soul is also soon to go — that the soul, I repeat, if this be its nature and origin, will be blown away and perish immediately on quitting the body, as the many say? That can never be, my dear Simmias and Cebes. The truth rather is that the soul, which is pure at departing, draws after it no bodily taint, having never voluntarily had connection with the body, which it is ever avoiding, itself gathered into itself (for such abstraction has been the study {81} of its life). And what does this mean but that it has been a true disciple of philosophy and has practiced how to die easily? And is not philosophy the study of death?

Certainly.

That soul, I say, itself invisible, departs to the invisible world, to the divine and immortal and rational. Upon arriving there, it lives in bliss and is released from the error and folly of men, their fears and wild passions, and all other human ills, and forever dwells, as they say of the initiated, in company with the gods. Is not this true, Cebes?

Yes, said Cebes, beyond a doubt.

But the soul which has been polluted, and is impure at the time of its departure, and is the companion and servant of the body always, and is in love with and fascinated by the body and by the desires and pleasures of the body, until it is led to believe that the truth only exists in a bodily form, which a man may touch and see and taste and use for the purposes of his lusts — the soul, I mean, which has become accustomed to hating and fearing and avoiding the intellectual principle, which to the bodily eye is dark and invisible, and can be attained only by philosophy — do you suppose that such a soul as this will depart pure and unalloyed?

That is impossible, he replied.

It is engrossed by the corporeal, which the continual association and constant care of the body have made natural to it.

Very true.

And this corporeal aspect, my friend, may be conceived to be that heavy, weighty, earthy element of sight by which such a soul is depressed and dragged down again into the visible world, because it is afraid of the invisible and of the world below — prowling about tombs and sepulchres, in the neighborhood of which, as they tell us, are seen certain ghostly apparitions of souls which have not departed pure, but are cloyed with sight and therefore visible.

That is very likely, Socrates.

Yes, that is very likely, Cebes; and these must be the souls, not of the good, but of the evil, who are compelled to wander about such places in payment of the penalty of their former evil way of life; and they continue to wander until the desire which haunts them is satisfied and they are imprisoned in another body. And they may be supposed to be fixed in the same natures which they had in their former life.

What natures do you mean, Socrates?

I mean to say that men who have followed after gluttony, and wantonness, and drunkenness, and have had no thought of avoiding them, would pass {82} into asses and animals of that sort. What do you think?

I think that exceedingly probable.

And those who have chosen the portion of injustice, and tyranny, and violence, will pass into wolves, or into hawks and kites; where else can we suppose them to go?

Yes, said Cebes; that is doubtless the place of natures such as theirs.

And there is no difficulty, he said, in assigning to all of them places answering to their several natures and propensities?

There is not, he said.

Even among them, some are happier than others; and the happiest both in themselves and their place of abode are those who have practiced the civil and social virtues which are called temperance and justice and are acquired by habit and attention, without philosophy and reason.

Why are they the happiest?

Because they may be expected to pass into some gentle, social nature which is like their own, such as that of bees or ants, or even back again into the form of man, and just and moderate men may spring from them.

That is not impossible.

But he who is a philosopher, or a lover of learning, and is entirely pure at departing, is alone permitted to reach the gods. And this is the reason, Simmias and Cebes, why the true votaries of philosophy abstain from all fleshly lusts, and endure and refuse to give themselves up to them — not because they fear poverty or the ruin of their families, like the lovers of money, and the world in general; nor like the lovers of power and honor, because they dread the dishonor or disgrace of evil deeds.

No, Socrates, that would not become them, said Cebes.

No, indeed, he replied; and therefore they who have a care of their souls, and do not merely live in the fashions of the body, say farewell to all this; they will not walk in the ways of the blind; and when philosophy offers them purification and release from evil, they feel that they ought not to resist its influence, and to it they incline, and wherever it leads, they follow it.

What do you mean, Socrates?

I will tell you, he said. The lovers of knowledge are conscious that their souls, when philosophy receives them, are simply fastened and glued to their bodies; the soul is only able to view existence through the bars of a prison, and not in its own nature. The soul wallows in the mire of all ignorance, and philosophy sees the terrible nature of its confinement, and that the captive of desire is led to {83} conspire in its own captivity. For the lovers of knowledge are aware that this was the original state of the soul, and that when it was in this state philosophy received and gently counseled it, and wanted to release it, pointing out to it that the eye is full of deceit, and also the ear and the other senses, and persuading it to retire from them in all but the necessary use of them and to be gathered up and collected into itself, and to trust only itself and its own intuitions of absolute existence, and mistrust that which comes to it through others and is subject to vicissitude — philosophy shows it that this is visible and tangible, but that what the soul sees in its own nature is intelligible and invisible. And the soul of the true philosopher thinks that it ought not to resist this deliverance, and therefore abstains from pleasures and desires and pains and fears, as far as it is able; reflecting that when a man has great joys or sorrows or fears or desires, he suffers from them, not the sort of evil which might be anticipated — as, for example, the loss of his health or property, which he has sacrificed to his lusts — but he has suffered an evil greater far, which is the greatest and worst of all evils, and one of which he never thinks.

And what is that, Socrates? asked Cebes.

Why, this: When the feeling of pleasure or pain in the soul is most intense, all of us naturally suppose that the object of this intense feeling is then plainest and truest: but this is not the case.

Very true.

And this is the state in which the soul is most enthralled by the body.

How is that?

Why, because each pleasure and pain is a sort of nail which nails and rivets the soul to the body, and engrosses it, and makes it believe that what the body affirms to be true, is true; and from agreeing with the body and having the same delights, the soul is obliged to have the same habits and ways, and is not likely ever to be pure at its departure to the world below, but is always saturated with the body, so that it soon sinks into another body and there germinates and grows, and therefore has no part in the communion of the divine and pure and simple.

That is most true, Socrates, answered Cebes.

And this, Cebes, is the reason why the true lovers of knowledge are temperate and brave; and not for the reason which the world gives.

{84}   Certainly not.

Certainly not! For not in that way does the soul of a philosopher reason; it will not ask philosophy to release it in order that when released it may deliver itself up again to the thraldom of pleasures and pains, doing work that will only be undone again, weaving instead of unweaving its Penelope's web. But it will make itself a calm of passion and follow reason, and dwell in reason, beholding the true and divine (which is not matter of opinion), and derive nourishment therefrom. Thus it seeks to live while it lives, and after death it hopes to go to its own kindred and to be freed from human ills. Never fear, Simmias and Cebes, that a soul which has been thus nurtured and has had these pursuits, will at its departure from the body be scattered and blown away by the winds and be nowhere and nothing.

When Socrates had done speaking, for a considerable time there was silence; he himself and most of us appeared to be meditating on what had been said; only Cebes and Simmias spoke a few words to one another. And Socrates observing this asked them what they thought of the argument, and whether there was anything wanting. For, said he, much is still open to suspicion and attack, if anyone were disposed to sift the matter thoroughly. If you are talking of something else I would rather not interrupt you, but if you are still doubtful about the argument do not hesitate to say exactly what you think, and let us have anything better which you can suggest; and if I am likely to be of any use, allow me to help you.

Simmias said, I must confess, Socrates, that doubts did arise in our minds, and each of us was urging and inciting the other to put the question which he wanted to have answered but which neither of us liked to ask, fearing that our importunity might be troublesome under present circumstances.

Socrates smiled and said, Simmias, how strange that is; I am not very likely to persuade other men that I do not regard my present situation as a misfortune, if I cannot even persuade you, and you will keep fancying that I am at all more troubled now than at any other time. Will you not allow that I have as much of the spirit of prophecy in me as the swans? For they, when they perceive that they must die, having sung all their life long, do then sing more loudly than ever, {85} rejoicing in the thought that they are about to go away to the God whose ministers they are. But men, because they are themselves afraid of death, slanderously affirm of the swans that they sing a lament at the last, not considering that no bird sings when cold, or hungry, or in pain, not even the nightingale, nor the swallow, nor yet the hoopoe; which are said indeed to tune a lay of sorrow, although I do not believe this to be true of them any more than of the swans. But because they are sacred to Apollo and have the gift of prophecy and anticipate the good things of another world, therefore they sing and rejoice in that day more than they ever did before. And I too, believing myself to be a consecrated servant of the same God, and the fellow servant of the swans, and thinking that I have received from my master gifts of prophecy which are not inferior to theirs, would not go out of life less merrily than the swans. Never mind then about this, but speak and ask anything which you like, while the eleven magistrates of Athens allow.

Well, Socrates, said Simmias, then I will tell you my difficulty, and Cebes will tell you his. For I dare say that you, Socrates, feel, as I do, how very hard or almost impossible is the attainment of any certainty about questions such as these in the present life. And yet I should deem him a coward who did not try to prove what is said about them to the uttermost, or whose heart failed him before he had examined them on every side. For he should persevere until he has attained one of two things: Either he should discover or learn the truth about them; or, if this be impossible, I would have him take the best and most irrefutable of human notions, and let this be the raft upon which he sails through life — not without risk, as I admit, if he cannot find some word of God which will more surely and safely carry him. And now, as you bid me, I will venture to question you, as I should not like to reproach myself hereafter with not having said at this time what I think. For when I consider the matter either alone or with Cebes, the argument does certainly appear to me, Socrates, to be insufficient.

Socrates answered, I dare say, my friend, that you may be right, but I should like to know in what respect the argument is not sufficient.

In this respect, replied Simmias, might not a person use the same argument about harmony and the lyre — might he not say that harmony is a thing {86} invisible, incorporeal, perfect, divine, abiding in the lyre which is harmonized, but that the lyre and the strings are matter and material, composite, earthy, and akin to mortality? And when someone breaks the lyre, or cuts and rends the strings, then he who takes this view would argue as you do, and on the same analogy, that the harmony survives and has not perished — for you cannot imagine, as he would say, that the lyre without the strings and the mortal broken strings themselves remain, and yet that the harmony, which is of heavenly and immortal nature and kindred, has perished — and perished before the mortal. The harmony, he would say, certainly exists somewhere, and the wood and strings will decay before the harmony decays. For I suspect, Socrates, that the notion of the soul which we are all of us inclined to entertain, would also be yours, and that you too would conceive the body to be strung, and held together, by the elements of hot and cold, wet and dry, and the like, and that the soul is the harmony or due proportionate admixture of them. And, if this is true, the inference clearly is that when the strings of the body are unduly loosened or overstrained through disease or other injury, then the soul, though most divine, like other harmonies of music or of the works of art, of course perishes at once, although the material remainder of the body may last for a considerable time, until they are either decayed or burned. Now if anyone maintains that the soul, being the harmony of the elements of the body, is first to perish in that which is called death, how shall we answer him?

Socrates looked fixedly at us, as his manner was, and said with a smile, Simmias has reason on his side; and why does not some one of you who is abler than myself answer him? For there is force in his attack upon me. But perhaps, before we answer him, we had better also hear what Cebes has to say against the argument — this will give us time for reflection, and when both of them have spoken, we may either assent to them if their words appear to be in consonance with the truth, or if not, we may take up the other side, and argue with them. Please to tell me then, Cebes, he said, what was the difficulty which troubled you?

Cebes said, I will tell you. My feeling is that the argument is still in the same position, and open to the same objections which were urged before; for I {87} am ready to admit that the existence of the soul before entering into the bodily form has been very ingeniously, and, if I may be allowed to say so, quite sufficiently proven; but the existence of the soul after death is still, in my judgment, unproven. Now my objection is not the same as that of Simmias; for I am not disposed to deny that the soul is stronger and more lasting than the body, being of the opinion that in all such respects the soul very far excels the body. Well, then, says the argument to me, why do you remain unconvinced? When you see that the weaker is still in existence after the man is dead, will you not admit that the more lasting must also survive during the same period of time? Now I, like

Simmias, will employ a figure; and I shall ask you to consider whether the objection is to the point. The analogy which I propose is that of an old weaver, who dies, and after his death somebody says: He is not dead, he must be alive; for there is the coat which he himself wove and wore, and which is still whole and undecayed. And then he proceeds to ask of someone who is incredulous, whether a man lasts longer, or the coat which is in use and wear; and when he is answered that a man lasts far longer, thinks that he has thus certainly demonstrated the survival of the man, who is the more lasting, because the less lasting remains. But that, Simmias, as I would beg you to observe, is not the truth; everyone sees that he who talks thus is talking nonsense. For the truth is that this weaver, having worn and woven many such coats, though he outlived several of them, was himself outlived by the last; but this is surely very far from proving that a man is slighter and weaker than a coat. Now the relation of the body to the soul may be expressed in a similar figure; for you may say with reason that the soul is lasting, and the body weak and short-lived in comparison. And every soul may be said to wear out many bodies, especially in the course of a long life. For if while the man is alive the body deliquesces and decays, and yet the soul always weaves its garment anew and repairs the waste, then of course, when the soul perishes, it must have on its last garment, and this only will survive it; but then again when the soul is dead the body will at last show its native weakness, and soon pass into decay. Therefore this is an argument on which I would rather not rely as proving that the {88} soul exists after death. For suppose that we grant even more than you affirm as within the range of possibility and, besides acknowledging that the soul existed before birth, admit also that after death the souls of some continue to exist, and will exist, and will be born and die again and again, and that there is a natural strength in the soul which will hold out and be born many times — for all this, we may be still inclined to think that it will weary in the labors of successive births, and may at last succumb in one of its deaths and utterly perish; and this death and dissolution of the body which brings destruction to the soul may be unknown to any of us, for no one of us can have had any experience of it; and if this be true, then I say that he who is confident in death has but a foolish confidence, unless he is able to prove that the soul is altogether immortal and imperishable. But if he is not able to prove the soul's immortality, he who is about to die will always have reason to fear that when the body is disunited, the soul also may utterly perish.

All of us, as we afterwards remarked to one another, had an unpleasant feeling at hearing them say this. When we had been so firmly convinced before, now to have our faith shaken seemed to introduce a confusion and uncertainty, not only into the previous argument, but into any future one. Either we were not good judges, or there were no real grounds of belief.

Echecrates: There I feel with you — indeed I do, Phaedo, and when you were speaking, I was beginning to ask myself the same question: What argument can I ever trust again? For what could be more convincing than the argument of Socrates, which has now fallen into discredit? That the soul is a harmony is a doctrine which has always had a wonderful attraction for me, and, when mentioned, came back to me at once, as my own original conviction. And now I must begin again and find another argument which will assure me that when the man is dead the soul survives. Tell me, I beg, how did Socrates proceed? Did he appear to share the unpleasant feeling which you mention? Or did he receive the interruption calmly and give a sufficient answer? Tell, as exactly as you can, what passed.

Phaedo: Often, Echecrates, I have admired Socrates, but never more {89} than at that moment. That he should be able to answer was nothing, but what astonished me was, first, the gentle and pleasant and approving manner in which he regarded the words of the young men, and then his quick sense of the wound which had been inflicted by the argument, and his ready application of the healing art. He might be compared to a general rallying his defeated and broken army, urging them to follow him and return to the field of engagement.

Echecrates: How was that?

· *Phaedo:* You shall hear, for I was close to him on his right hand, seated on a sort of stool, and he on a couch which was a good deal higher. Now he had a way of playing with my hair, and then he stroked my head, and pressed the hair upon my neck, and said: Tomorrow, Phaedo, I suppose that these fair locks of yours will be severed.

Yes, Socrates, I suppose that they will, I replied.

Not so, if you will take my advice.

What shall I do with them? I said.

Today, he replied, and not tomorrow, if this argument dies and we cannot bring it to life again, you and I will both shave our locks; and if I were you, and could not maintain my ground against Simmias and Cebes, I would myself take an oath, like the Argives, not to wear hair any more until I had renewed the conflict and defeated them.

Yes, I said, but Heracles himself is said not to be a match for two.

Summon me then, he said, and I will be your Iolaus until the sun goes down.

I summon you rather, I said, not as Heracles summoning Iolaus, but as Iolaus might summon Heracles.

That will be all the same, he said. But first let us take care that we avoid a danger.

And what is that? I said.

The danger of becoming misologists, he replied, which is one of the very worst things that can happen to us. For as there are misanthropists or haters of men, there are also misologists or haters of ideas, and both spring from the same cause, which is ignorance of the world. Misanthropy arises from the too great confidence of inexperience; you trust a man and think him altogether true and good and faithful, and then in a little while he turns out to be false and knavish; and then another and another, and when this has happened several times to a man, especially within the circle of his most trusted friends, as he deems them, and he has often quarreled with them, he at last hates all men, and believes that no one has any good in him at all. I dare say that you must have observed this.

Yes, I said.

And is not this feeling discreditable? The reason is that a man, having to deal with other men, has no knowledge of them; for if he had knowledge he would {90} have known the true state of the case, that few are the good and few the evil, and that the great majority are in the interval between them.

How do you mean? I said.

I mean, he replied, as you might say of the very large and very small, that nothing is more uncommon than a very large or a very small man; and this applies generally to all extremes, whether of great and small, or swift and slow, or fair and foul, or black and white; and whether the instances you select be men or dogs or anything else, few are the extremes, but many are in the mean between them. Did you ever observe this?

Yes, I said, I have.

And do you not imagine, he said, that if there were a competition in evil, the first in evil would be found to be very few?

Yes, that is very likely, I said.

Yes, that is very likely, he replied; not that in this respect arguments are like men — there I was led on by you to say more than I had intended; but the point of comparison was that when a simple man who has no skill in dialectics believes an argument to be true which he afterwards imagines to be false, whether really false or not, and then another and another, he has no longer any faith left, and great disputers, as you know, come to think at last that they have grown to be the wisest of mankind; for they alone perceive the utter unsoundness and instability of all arguments, or indeed of all things which, like the currents in the Euripus, go up and down in never ceasing ebb and flow.

That is quite true, I said.

Yes, Phaedo, he replied, and very melancholy too, if there be such a thing as truth or certainty or possibility of knowledge at all, that a man should have lighted upon some argument or other which at first seemed true and then turned out to be false, and instead of blaming himself and his own want of wit, because he is annoyed, should at last be too glad to transfer the blame from himself to arguments in general; and forever afterwards should hate and revile them, and lose the truth and knowledge of existence.

Yes, indeed, I said; that is very melancholy.

Let us, then, in the first place, he said, be careful of admitting into our

souls the notion that there is no truth or health or soundness in any arguments at
all; but let us rather say that there is as yet no health in us, and that we must
acquit ourselves like men and do our best to gain intellectual health — you and
all other men with a view to the whole of your future life, and I myself with a view to
{91} death. For at this moment I am sensible that I have not the temper of a philosopher; like the vulgar, I am only a partisan. Now the partisan, when he is engaged in a dispute, cares nothing about the rights of the question, but is anxious
only to convince his hearers of his own assertions. And the difference between
him and me at the present moment is only this — that whereas he seeks to convince his hearers that what he says is true, I am rather seeking to convince myself;
to convince my hearers is a secondary matter with me. And just see how much I
gain by this argumentation. For if what I say is true, then I do well to be persuaded
of the truth, but if there be nothing after death, still, during the short time that remains, I shall not worry my friends with lamentations, and my ignorance will not
last, but will die with me, and therefore no harm will be done. This is the state of
mind, Simmias and Cebes, in which I approach the argument. And I would ask you
to be thinking of truth and not of Socrates. Agree with me if I seem to you to be
speaking the truth; or if not, then withstand me might and main, that I may not deceive you as well as myself in my enthusiasm, and, like the bee, leave my sting in
you before I die.

And now let us proceed, he said. And first of all let me be sure that I have
in my mind what you were saying. Simmias, if I remember rightly, has fears and
misgivings whether the soul, being in the form of harmony, although a fairer and
diviner thing than the body, may not perish first. On the other hand, Cebes appeared to grant that the soul was more lasting than the body, but he said that no
one could know whether the soul, after having worn out many bodies, might not
perish itself and leave its last body behind it; and that this is death, which is the
destruction not of the body but of the soul, for in the body the work of destruction
is ever going on. Are not these, Simmias and Cebes, the points which we have to
consider?

They both agreed to this statement of them.

He proceeded: And did you deny the force of the whole preceding
argument, or of a part only?

Of a part only, they replied.

And what did you think, he said, of that part of the argument in which we
{92} said that knowledge was recollection only, and inferred from this that the
soul must have previously existed somewhere else before it was enclosed in the
body?

Cebes said that he had been wonderfully impressed by that part of the
argument, and that his conviction remained unshaken. Simmias agreed, adding
that he himself could hardly imagine the possibility of his ever thinking differently

about that.

But, rejoined Socrates, you will have to think differently, my Theban friend, if you still maintain that harmony is a compound, and that the soul is a harmony which is made out of strings set in the frame of the body; for you will surely never allow yourself to say that a harmony is prior to the elements which compose the harmony.

No, Socrates, that is impossible.

But do you not see that this is what you imply when you say that the soul existed before it took the form and body of a man, and was made up of elements which as yet had no existence? For harmony is not like the soul, as you suppose; but first the lyre, and the strings, and the sounds exist in a state of discord, and then harmony is made last of all, and perishes first. And how can such a notion of the soul as this agree with the other?

Not at all, replied Simmias.

And yet, he said, there surely ought to be harmony when harmony is the theme of discourse.

There ought, replied Simmias.

But there is no harmony, he said, in the two propositions that knowledge is recollection and that the soul is a harmony. Which of them, then, will you retain?

I think, Simmias replied, that I have a much stronger faith, Socrates, in the first of the two, which has been fully demonstrated to me, than in the latter, which has not been demonstrated at all, but rests only on probable and plausible grounds, and is therefore believed by the many; and I know too well that these arguments from probabilities are impostors and, unless great caution is observed in the use of them, they are apt to be deceptive — in geometry, and in other things too. But the doctrine of knowledge and recollection has been proven to me on trustworthy grounds; and the proof was that the soul must have existed before it came into the body, because to it belongs the essence of which the very name implies existence. Having, as I am convinced, rightly accepted this conclusion, and on sufficient grounds, I must, as I suppose, cease to argue or allow others to argue that the soul is a harmony.

Let me, Simmias, Socrates said, put the matter in another point of view: {93} Do you imagine that a harmony or any other composition can be in a state other than that of the elements out of which it is compounded?

Certainly not.

Or do or suffer anything other than they do or suffer?

He agreed.

Then, properly speaking, a harmony does not lead the parts or elements which make up the harmony, but only follows them.

He assented.

For harmony cannot possibly have any motion, or sound, or other quality which is opposed to the parts.

That would be impossible, he replied.

And does not every harmony depend upon the manner in which the elements are harmonized?

I do not understand you, he said.

I mean to say that a harmony admits of degrees, and is more of a harmony, and more completely a harmony, when more completely harmonized, if that be possible; and less of a harmony, and less completely a harmony, when less harmonized.

True.

But does the soul admit of degrees? Or is one soul in the very least degree more or less, or more or less completely, a soul than another?

Not in the least.

Yet surely one soul is said to have intelligence and virtue, and to be good, and another soul is said to have folly and vice, and to be an evil soul — and this is said truly?

Yes, truly.

But what will those who maintain the soul to be a harmony say of this presence of virtue and vice in the soul? — Will they say that there is another harmony, and another discord, and that the virtuous soul is harmonized and, itself being a harmony, has another harmony within it, and that the vicious soul is disharmonious and has no harmony within it?

I cannot say, replied Simmias, but I suppose that something of that kind would be asserted by those who say that the soul is a harmony.

And we have already admitted that no soul is more a soul than another; and this is equivalent to admitting that harmony is not more or less harmony, or more or less completely a harmony?

Quite so.

And that which is not more or less a harmony is not more or less harmonized?

True.

And that which is not more or less harmonized cannot have more or less of harmony, but only an equal harmony?

Yes, an equal harmony.

Then one soul not being more or less absolutely a soul than another, is not more or less harmonized?

Exactly.

And therefore has neither more nor less of harmony or of discord?

It has not.

And having neither more nor less of harmony or of discord, one soul has no more vice or virtue than another, if vice be discord and virtue harmony?

Not at all more.

{94}   Or speaking more correctly, Simmias, the soul, if it is a harmony, will never have any vice; because a harmony, being absolutely a harmony, has no part in the disharmonious?

No.

And therefore a soul which is absolutely a soul has no vice?

How can it have, consistently with the preceding argument?

Then, according to this, if the souls of all animals are equally and absolutely souls, they will be equally good?

I agree with you, Socrates, he said.

And can all this be true, think you, he said; and are all these consequences admissible — which nevertheless seem to follow from the assumption that the soul is a harmony?

Certainly not, he said.

Once more, he said, what ruling principle is there of human matters other than the soul, and especially the wise soul? Do you know of any?

Indeed, I do not.

And is the soul in agreement with the affections of the body? Or is it at variance with them? For example, when the body is hot and thirsty, does not the soul incline us against drinking? And when the body is hungry, against eating? And these are only two instances out of ten thousand of the opposition of the soul to the things of the body.

Very true.

But we have already acknowledged that the soul, being a harmony, can never utter a note at variance with the tensions and relaxations and vibrations and other affections of the strings out of which it is composed; it can only follow, it cannot lead them?

Yes, he said, we acknowledged that, certainly.

And yet do we not now discover the soul to be doing the exact opposite — leading the elements of which it is believed to be composed; almost always opposing and coercing them in all sorts of ways throughout life, sometimes more violently with the pains of medicine and gymnastic; then again more gently; now, threatening, now reprimanding the desires, passions, fears, as if talking to a thing which is not itself, as Homer in the *Odyssey* [Book 20, lines 17-18] represents Odysseus doing in the words:

> He beat his breast, and thus reproached his heart:
> Endure, my heart; far worse hast thou endured!

Do you think that Homer could have written this under the idea that the soul is a harmony capable of being led by the affections of the body, and not rather of a nature which leads and masters them; and itself a far diviner thing than any harmony?

Yes, Socrates, I quite agree to that.

{95}   Then, my friend, we can never be right in saying that the soul is a harmony, for that would clearly contradict the divine Homer as well as ourselves.

True, he said.

Thus, said Socrates, we have mollified Harmonia, your Theban goddess, Cebes, who has not been ungracious to us, I think; but what shall I say to the Theban Cadmus, and how shall I propitiate him?

I think that you will discover a way of propitiating him, said Cebes; I am sure that you have answered the argument about harmony in a manner that I could never have expected. For when Simmias mentioned his objection, I quite imagined that no answer could be given to him, and therefore I was surprised at finding that his argument could not withstand even your first onset; and not impossibly the other, whom you call Cadmus, may share a similar fate.

No, my good friend, said Socrates, let us not boast, lest some evil eye should put to flight the word which I am about to speak. That, however, may be left in the hands of those above, while I draw near in Homeric fashion, and try the mettle of your words. Briefly, the sum of your objection is as follows: You want to have proven to you that the soul is imperishable and immortal, and you think that the philosopher who is confident in death has but a vain and foolish confidence, if he thinks that he will fare better in the world below than one who has led another sort of life, unless he can prove this; and you say that the demonstration of the strength and divinity of the soul, and of its existence prior to our becoming men, does not necessarily imply its immortality. Granting that the soul is long-lived, and has known and done much in a former state, still it is not on that account immortal; and its entrance into the human form may be a sort of disease which is the beginning of dissolution, and may at last, after the toils of life are over, end in what is called death. And whether the soul enters into the body once only or many times, that, as you would say, makes no difference in the fears of individuals. For any man, who is not devoid of natural feeling, has reason to fear, if he has no knowledge or proof of the soul's immortality. That is what I suppose you to say, Cebes, which I designedly repeat, in order that nothing may escape us, and that you may, if you wish, add or subtract anything.

But, said Cebes, as far as I can see at present, I have nothing to add or subtract; you have expressed my meaning.

Socrates paused awhile, and seemed to be absorbed in reflection. At {96} length he said: This is a very serious inquiry which you are raising, Cebes, involving the whole question of generation and corruption, about which I will, if you like, give you my own experience; and you can apply this, if you think that anything which I say will avail towards the solution of your difficulty.

I should very much like, said Cebes, to hear what you have to say.

Then I will tell you, said Socrates. When I was young, Cebes, I had a pro-digious desire to know that branch of philosophy which is called natural science, which appeared to me to have lofty aims, as being the science which has to do with the causes of things, and which teaches why a thing is, and how it is created and destroyed; and I was always agitating myself with the consideration of such questions as these: Is the growth of animals the result of some decay which the hot and cold principle contracts, as some have said? Is the blood the element with which we think, or the air, or fire, or perhaps nothing of this sort — but the brain may be the originating power of the perceptions of hearing and sight and smell, and memory and opinion may come from them, and science may be based on memory and opinion when no longer in motion, but at rest? And then I went on to examine their decay, and then to the things of heaven and earth, and at last I con-cluded that I was wholly incapable of these inquiries, as I will satisfactorily prove to you. For I was fascinated by them to such a degree that my eyes grew blind to things that I had seemed to myself, and also to others, to know quite well; and I forgot what I had previously thought to be self-evident, that the growth of man is the result of eating and drinking; for when by the digestion of food flesh is added to flesh and bone to bone, and whenever there is an aggregation of congenial elements, the lesser bulk becomes larger and the small man greater. Was not that a reasonable notion?

Yes, said Cebes, I think so.

Well; but let me tell you something more. There was a time when I thought that I understood pretty well the meaning of greater and lesser; and when I saw a large man standing by a little one I fancied that one was taller than the other by a head; or one horse would appear to be greater than another horse; and still more clearly did I seem to perceive that ten is two more than eight, and that two cubits are more than one, because two is twice one.

And what is now your notion of such matters? said Cebes.

I should be far enough from imagining, he replied, that I knew the cause of any of them, indeed I should, for I cannot satisfy myself that when one is added {97} to one, the one to which the addition is made becomes two, or that the two units added together make two by reason of the addition. For I cannot under-stand how, when separated from the other, each of them was one and not two, and now, when they are brought together, the mere juxtaposition or meeting of them can be the cause of their becoming two; nor can I understand how the divi-sion of one is the way to make two; for then a different cause would produce the same effect — as in the former instance the addition and juxtaposition of one to one was the cause of two, in this the separation and subtraction of one from the other would be the cause. Nor am I any longer satisfied that I understand the reason why one or anything else either is generated or destroyed or exists at all, but I have in my mind some confused notion of another method, and can never fathom this.

Then I heard someone reading from a book of Anaxagoras, as he said, saying that mind was the disposer and cause of all, and I was quite delighted at the notion of this, which appeared quite admirable, and I said to myself: If mind is the disposer, mind will dispose all for the best, and put each particular in the best place; and I argued that if anyone desired to find out the cause of the generation or destruction or existence of anything, he must find out what state of being or suffering or doing was best for that thing, and therefore a man had only to consider the best for himself and others, and then he would also know the worst, since that the same science comprised both. And I rejoiced to think that I had found in Anaxagoras a teacher of the causes of existence such as I desired, and I imagined that he would tell me first whether the earth is flat or round, and then he would further explain the cause and the necessity of this; and then he would teach me the nature of the best and show that this was best; and if he said that the earth was in the center, he would explain why this position was the best, and I should be satisfied if this were shown to me, and not want any other sort of cause. And I {98} thought that I would then go and ask him about the sun and moon and stars, and that he would explain to me their comparative swiftness, and their returnings and various states, and how their several affections, active and passive, were all for the best. For I could not imagine that when he spoke of mind as the disposer of them, he would give any other account of their being as they are, except that this was best; and I thought when he had explained to me in detail the cause of each and the cause of all, he would then go on to explain to me what was best for each and what was good for all. I had hopes which I would not have sold for any amount of money, and I seized the books and read them as fast as I could in my eagerness to know the better and the worse.

What hopes I had formed, and how grievously was I disappointed! As I proceeded, I found my philosopher altogether forsaking mind or any other principle of order, but having recourse to air, and ether, and water, and other eccentricities. I might compare him to a person who began by maintaining generally that mind is the cause of the actions of Socrates, but who, when he endeavored to explain the causes of my several actions in detail, went on to show that I sit here because my body is made up of bones and muscles; and the bones, as he would say, are hard and have ligaments which divide them, and the muscles are elastic, and they cover the bones, which have also a covering or environment of flesh and skin which contains them; and as the bones are lifted at their joints by the contraction or relaxation of the muscles, I am able to bend my limbs, and this is why I am sitting here in a curved posture — that is what he would say, and he would have a similar explanation of my talking to you, which he would attribute to sound, and air, and hearing, and he would assign ten thousand other causes of the same sort, forgetting to mention the true cause, which is that the Athenians have thought fit to condemn me, and accordingly I have thought it better and more right to remain here and undergo my sentence; for I am inclined to think that {99} these muscles and bones of mine would have run off to Megara or Boeotia — by the dog of Egypt they would, if they had been guided only by their own idea of what was best, and if I had not chosen as the better and nobler part, instead of playing truant and running away, to endure any punishment that the State inflicts. There is surely a strange confusion of causes and conditions in all this. It may be said, indeed, that without bones and muscles and the other parts of the body I cannot execute my purposes. But to say that I do as I do because of them, and that this is the way in which mind acts, and not from the choice of the best, is a very careless and idle mode of speaking. I wonder that they cannot distinguish the cause from the condition, which the many, feeling about in the dark, are always mistaking and misnaming. And thus one man makes a vortex all round and steadies the earth by the heavens; another claims that the air is the support of the earth, which is a sort of broad trough. Any power which, in disposing them as they are, disposes them for the best never enters into their minds, nor do they imagine that there is any superhuman strength in that. They rather expect to find holding the world another Atlas, who is stronger and more everlasting and more binding than the good is; and they are clearly of the opinion that the obligatory and binding power of the good is as nothing; and yet this is the principle which I want to learn, if anyone would teach me. But as I have failed either to discover the nature of the best myself or to learn it from anyone else, I will exhibit to you, if you like, what I have found to be the second best mode of inquiring into the cause.

I should very much like to hear that, he replied.

Socrates proceeded: I thought that as I had failed in the contemplation of true existence, I ought to be careful that I did not lose the eye of my soul; as people may injure their bodily eye by observing and gazing on the sun during an eclipse, unless they take the precaution of only looking at the image reflected in the water, or in some similar medium. So in my own case, and I was afraid that my soul might be blinded altogether if I looked at things with my eyes or tried by the help of the senses to apprehend them. And I thought that I had better recourse {100} to ideas, and to seek in them the truth of existence. I dare say that the simile is not perfect — for I am very far from admitting that he who contemplates existence through the medium of ideas, sees them only as "images," any more than he who sees them in their working and effects. However, this was the method that I adopted: I first assumed some principle which I judged to be the strongest, and then I affirmed as true whatever seemed to agree with this, whether relating to the cause or to anything else; and that which disagreed I regarded as untrue. But I should like to explain my meaning clearly, as I do not think that you understand me.

No, indeed, replied Cebes, not very well.

There is nothing new, he said, in what I am about to tell you; but only what I have been always and everywhere repeating in the previous discussion and on other occasions: I want to show you the nature of that cause which has occupied my thoughts, and I shall have to go back to those familiar words which are in the mouth of everyone, and first of all assume that there is an absolute beauty and goodness and greatness, and the like. Grant me this, and I hope to be able to show you the nature of the cause, and to prove the immortality of the soul.

Cebes said: You may proceed at once with the proof, as I readily grant you this.

Well, he said, then I should like to know whether you agree with me in the next step; for I cannot help thinking that, if there be anything beautiful other than absolute beauty, it can only be beautiful insofar as it partakes of absolute beauty — and this I should say of everything. Do you agree with this notion of the cause?

Yes, he said, I agree.

He proceeded: I know nothing and can understand nothing of any other of those wise causes which are alleged; and if a person says to me that the bloom of color, or form, or anything else of that sort is a source of beauty, I leave all that, which is only confusing to me, and believe simply and singly, and perhaps foolishly, and am assured in my own mind that nothing makes a thing beautiful but the presence of beauty and the participation of the thing in it in whatever way or manner obtained; for as to the manner I am uncertain, but I stoutly contend that by beauty all beautiful things become beautiful. This appears to me to be the only safe answer that I can give, either to myself or to anyone else, and to this I cling, in the persuasion that this principle will never be overthrown, and that I may safely reply to myself or anyone else that by beauty beautiful things become beautiful. Do you not agree with that?

Yes, I agree.

And that only by greatness do great things become great and greater things greater, and by smallness the lesser become lesser.

True.

Then if a person remarks that A is taller by a head than B, and B less {101} by a head than A, you would refuse to admit this, and would stoutly contend that what you mean is only that the greater is greater by, and by reason of, greatness, and the lesser is lesser only by, or by reason of, smallness; and thus you would avoid the danger of saying that the greater is greater and the lesser is lesser by the measure of the head, which is the same in both, and would also avoid the monstrous absurdity of supposing that the greater man is greater by reason of the head, which is small. Would you not be afraid of that?

Indeed, I should, said Cebes, laughing.

In like manner would you be afraid to say that ten exceeded eight by, and by reason of, two; but would you say by, and by reason of, number; or that two cubits exceed one cubit not by a half, but by magnitude — is that what you would say, for there is the same danger of error in all these cases?

Very true, he said.

Again, would you not be cautious of affirming that the addition of one to one, or the division of one, is the cause of two? And you would earnestly and loudly affirm that you know of no way in which anything comes into existence except by participation in its own proper essence, and consequently, as far as you know, the only cause of two is its participation in duality; that is the way to make two, and the participation in one is the way to make one. You would say: I will let alone puzzles of division and addition — wiser heads than mine may answer them; inexperienced as I am, and ready to start, as the proverb says, at my own shadow, I cannot afford to give up the sure ground of a principle. And if anyone assails you there, you would not mind him, or answer him until you had seen whether the consequences which follow agree with one another or not, and when you are further required to give an explanation of this principle, you would go on to assume a higher principle, and even a higher, until you found a resting place in the highest; but you would not confuse the principle and the consequences in your reasoning like the destructive Eristic critics — at least not if you wanted to discover real existence. Not that this confusion signifies to them who never care {102} or think about the matter at all, for they have the wit to be well pleased with themselves, however great may be the turmoil of their ideas. But you, if you are a philosopher, will, I believe, do as I say.

What you say is most true, said Simmias and Cebes, both speaking at once.

Echecrates: Yes, Phaedo; and I do not wonder at their assenting. Anyone who has the least sense will acknowledge the wonderful clarity of Socrates's reasoning.

Phaedo: Certainly, Echecrates; and that was the feeling of the whole company at the time.

Echecrates: Yes, and equally of ourselves, who were not of the company, and are now listening to your recital. But what followed?

Phaedo: After all this was admitted, and they had agreed about the existence of ideas and the participation in them of the other things which derive their names from them, Socrates, if I remember rightly, said:

This is your way of speaking; and yet when you say that Simmias is greater than Socrates and less than Phaedo, do you not predicate of Simmias both greatness and smallness?

Yes, I do.

But still you allow that Simmias does not really exceed Socrates, as the words may seem to imply, because he is Simmias, but by reason of the size which he has; just as Simmias does not exceed Socrates because he is Simmias, any more than because Socrates is Socrates, but because he has smallness when compared with the greatness of Simmias?

True.

And if Phaedo exceeds him in size, that is not because Phaedo is Phaedo, but because Phaedo has greatness relatively to Simmias, who is comparatively smaller?

That is true.

And therefore Simmias is said to be great, and is also said to be small, because he is in a mean between them, exceeding the smallness of the one by his greatness, and allowing the greatness of the other to exceed his smallness. He added, laughing, I am speaking like a book, but I believe that what I am now saying is true.

Simmias assented to this.

I say this because I want you to agree with me in thinking, not only that absolute greatness will never be great and also small, but that greatness in us or in the concrete will never admit the small or admit to being exceeded. Instead of this, one of two things will happen: Either the greater will fly or retire before the opposite, which is the lesser, or, at the advance of the lesser, will cease to exist; but it will not, if allowing or admitting smallness, be changed by that; even as I, having received and admitted smallness when compared with Simmias, remain just as I was, and am the same small person. And as the idea of greatness cannot condescend ever to be or to become small, in like manner the smallness in us cannot be or become great; nor can any other opposite which remains the same {103} ever be or become its own opposite, but either passes away or perishes in the change.

That, replied Cebes, is quite my notion.

One of the company, though I do not exactly remember which of them, on hearing this, said: By heaven, is not this the direct contrary of what was admitted before — that out of the greater came the lesser and out of the lesser the greater, and that opposites are simply generated from opposites; but now this principle seems to be utterly denied.

Socrates inclined his head to the speaker and listened. I like your courage, he said, in reminding us of this. But you do not observe that there is a difference between the two cases. For then we were speaking of opposites in the concrete, and now of the essential opposite, which, as is affirmed, neither in us nor in nature can ever be at variance with itself. Then, my friend, we were speaking of things in which opposites are inherent and which are called after them, but now about the opposites which are inherent in them and which give their name to them; these essential opposites will never, as we maintain, admit of generation into or out of one another. At the same time, turning to Cebes, he said: Were you at all disconcerted, Cebes, at our friend's objection?

That was not my feeling, said Cebes; and yet I cannot deny that I am often apt to be disconcerted.

Then we are agreed after all, said Socrates, that the opposite will never in any case be opposed to itself?

To that we are quite agreed, he replied.

Yet once more let me ask you to consider the question from another point of view, and see whether you agree with me: There is a thing which you term heat, and another thing which you term cold?

Certainly.

But are they the same as fire and snow?

Most assuredly not.

Heat is not the same as fire, nor is cold the same as snow?

That's right.

And yet you will surely admit that when snow, as was said before, is under the influence of heat, they will not remain snow and heat; but, at the advance of the heat, the snow will either retire or perish?

Very true, he replied.

And the fire too at the advance of the cold will either retire or perish; and when the fire is under the influence of the cold, they will not remain, as before, fire and cold.

That is true, he said.

And in some cases the name of the idea is not confined to the idea; but anything else which, not being the idea, exists only in the form of the idea, may also lay claim to it. I will try to make this clearer by an example: The odd number is always called by the name of odd?

Very true.

But is this the only thing which is called odd? Are there not other things {104} which have their own name, and yet are called odd, because, although not the same as oddness, they are never without oddness? — That is what I mean to ask — whether numbers such as the number three are not of the class of odd. And there are many other examples: Would you not say, for example, that three may be called by its proper name, and also be called odd, which is not the same as three? And this may be said not only of three but also of five, and every alternate number — each of them without being oddness is odd, and in the same way two and four, and the other whole series of alternate numbers, has every number even, without being evenness. Do you admit that?

Yes, he said, how can I deny that?

Then now mark the point at which I am aiming: Not only do essential opposites exclude one another, but also concrete things, which, although not in themselves opposed, contain opposites; these, I say, also reject the idea which is opposed to that which is contained in them, and when it approaches them they either perish or withdraw. There is the number three for example; will it not endure annihilation or anything sooner than be converted into an even number, while remaining three?

Very true, said Cebes.

And yet, he said, the number two is certainly not opposed to the number three?

It is not.

Then not only do opposite ideas repel the advance of one another, but also there are other things which repel the approach of opposites.

That is quite true, he said.

Suppose, he said, that we endeavor, if possible, to determine what these are.

By all means.

Are they not, Cebes, such as compel the things of which they have possession, not only to take their own form, but also the form of some opposite?

What do you mean?

I mean, as I was just now saying, and have no need to repeat to you, that those things which are possessed by the number three must not only be three in number, but must also be odd.

Quite true.

And on this oddness, of which the number three has the impress, the opposite idea will never intrude?

No.

And this impress was given by the odd principle?

Yes.

And to the odd is opposed the even?

True.

Then the idea of the even number will never arrive at three?

No.

Then three has no part in the even?

None.

Then the triad or number three is uneven?

Very true.

To return then to my distinction of natures which are not opposites, and yet do not admit opposites, as, in this instance, three, although not opposed to the even, does not any the more admit of the even, but always brings the opposite {105} into play on the other side; or as two does not receive the odd, or fire the cold — from these examples (and there are many more of them) perhaps you may be able to arrive at the general conclusion that not only opposites will not receive opposites, but also that nothing which brings the opposite will admit the opposite of that which it brings in that to which it is brought. And here let me recapitulate — for there is no harm in repetition. The number five will not admit the nature of the even, any more than ten, which is the double of five, will admit the nature of the odd. The double, though not strictly opposed to the odd, rejects the odd altogether. Nor again will parts in the ratio of 3:2, nor any fraction in which there is a half, nor again in which there is a third, admit the notion of the whole, although they are not opposed to the whole. You will agree to that?

Yes, he said, I entirely agree and go along with you in that.

And now, he said, I think that I may begin again; and to the question which I am about to ask I will beg you to give not the old safe answer, but another, of which I will offer you an example; and I hope that you will find in what has been just said another foundation which is as safe. I mean that if anyone asks you "What is that, the inherence of which makes the body hot?" you will reply not heat (this is what I call the safe and stupid answer), but fire, a far better answer, which we are now in a condition to give. Or if anyone asks you "Why is a body diseased?" you will not say from disease, but from fever; and instead of saying that oddness is the cause of odd numbers, you will say that the monad is the cause of them; and so of things in general, as I dare say that you will understand sufficiently without my adducing any further examples.

Yes, he said, I quite understand you.

Tell me, then, what is that, the inherence of which will render the body alive?

The soul, he replied.

And is this always the case?

Yes, he said, of course.

Then whatever the soul possesses, to that it comes bearing life?

Yes, certainly.

And is there any opposite to life?

There is, he said.

And what is that?

Death.

Then the soul, as has been acknowledged, will never receive the opposite of what it brings.

Impossible, replied Cebes.

And now, he said, what did we call that principle which repels the even?

The odd.

And that principle which repels the musical, or the just?

The unmusical, he said, and the unjust.

And what do we call the principle which does not admit of death?

The immortal, he said.

And does the soul admit of death?

No.

Then the soul is immortal?

Yes, he said.

And may we say that this is proven?

Yes, abundantly proven, Socrates, he replied.

{106}   And supposing that the odd were imperishable, must not three be imperishable?

Of course.

And if that which is cold were imperishable, when the warm principle came attacking the snow, must not the snow have retired whole and unmelted — for it could never have perished, nor could it have remained and admitted the heat?

True, he said.

Again, if the uncooling or warm principle were imperishable, the fire when assailed by cold would not have perished or have been extinguished, but would have gone away unaffected?

Certainly, he said.

And the same may be said of the immortal. If the immortal is also imperishable, the soul when attacked by death cannot perish; for the preceding argument shows that the soul will not admit of death, or ever be dead, any more than three or the odd number will admit of the even, or fire or the heat in the fire, of the cold. Yet a person may say, "But although the odd will not become even at the approach of the even, why may not the odd perish and the even take the place of the odd?" Now to him who makes this objection, we cannot answer that the odd principle is imperishable; for this has not been acknowledged, but if this had been acknowledged, there would have been no difficulty in contending that, at the approach of the even, the odd principle and the number three took their departure; and the same argument would have held good of fire and heat and any other thing.

Very true.

And the same may be said of the immortal. If the immortal is also imperishable, then the soul will be imperishable as well as immortal; but if not, some other proof of its imperishableness will have to be given.

No other proof is needed, he said; for if the immortal, being eternal, is liable to perish, then nothing is imperishable.

Yes, replied Socrates, and yet all men will agree that God, and the essential form of life, and the immortal in general, will never perish.

Yes, all men, he said — that is true; and what is more, gods, if I am not mistaken, as well as men.

Seeing then that the immortal is indestructible, must not the soul, if it is immortal, be also imperishable?

Most certainly.

Then when death attacks a man, the mortal portion of him may be supposed to die, but the immortal goes out of the way of death and is preserved safe and sound?

True.

Then, Cebes, beyond question the soul is immortal and imperishable, {107} and our souls will truly exist in another world!

I am convinced, Socrates, said Cebes, and have nothing more to object; but if my friend Simmias, or anyone else, has any further objection, he had better speak out, and not keep silence, since I do not know how there can ever be a more fitting time to which he can defer the discussion, if there is anything which he wants to say or have said.

But I have nothing more to say, replied Simmias; nor do I see any room for uncertainty, except that which arises necessarily out of the greatness of the subject and the feebleness of man, and which I cannot help feeling.

Yes, Simmias, replied Socrates, that is well said, and may I add that first principles, even if they appear certain, should be carefully considered; and when they are satisfactorily ascertained, then, with a sort of hesitating confidence in human reason, you may, I think, follow the course of the argument; and if this is clear, there will be no need for any further inquiry.

That, he said, is true.

But then, my friends, he said, if the soul is really immortal, what care should be taken of it, not only in respect of the portion of time which is called life, but of eternity! And the danger of neglecting the soul from this point of view does indeed appear to be awful. If death had only been the end of all, the wicked would have had a good bargain in dying, for they would have been happily quit not only of their body, but of their own evil together with their souls. But now, as the soul plainly appears to be immortal, there is no release or salvation from evil except the attainment of the highest virtue and wisdom. For the soul when on its progress to the world below takes nothing with it but nurture and education, which are indeed said greatly to benefit or greatly to injure the departed, at the very beginning of its pilgrimage in the other world.

For after death, as they say, the genius of each individual, to whom each belonged in life, leads him to a certain place in which the dead are gathered together for judgment, from where they go into the world below, following the guide who is appointed to conduct them from this world to the other; and when they have there received their due and remained for their time, another guide brings them back again after many revolutions of ages. Now this journey to the other {108} world is not, as Aeschylus says in the *Telephus*, a single and straight path — no guide would be wanted for that, and no one could miss a single path; but there are many partings of the road, and windings, as I must infer from the rites and sacrifices which are offered to the gods below in places where three ways meet on earth. The wise and orderly soul is conscious of its situation and follows in the straight path; but the soul which desires the body, and which, as I was relating before, has long been fluttering about the lifeless frame and the world of sight, is after many struggles and many sufferings carried away with difficulty and violence by its attendant genius, and when it arrives at the place where the other souls are gathered, if it is impure and has done impure deeds, or has been concerned in foul murders or other crimes which are the brothers of these, and the works of brothers in crime — from that soul everyone flees and turns away; no one will be its companion, no one its guide, but alone it wanders in extremity of evil until certain times are fulfilled, and when they are fulfilled, it is borne irresistibly to its own fitting habitation; as every pure and just soul which has passed through life in the company and under the guidance of the gods has also its own proper home.

Now the earth has divers wonderful regions, and is indeed in nature and extent very unlike the notions of geographers, as I believe on the authority of one who shall be nameless.

What do you mean, Socrates? said Simmias. I have myself heard many descriptions of the earth, but I do not know in what you are putting your faith, and I should like to know.

Well, Simmias, replied Socrates, the recital of this tale does not, I think, require the art of Glaucus; and I know not that the art of Glaucus could prove the truth of my tale, which I myself should never be able to prove, and even if I could, I fear, Simmias, that my life would come to an end before the argument was completed. I may describe to you, however, the form and regions of the earth according to my conception of them.

That, said Simmias, will be enough.

Well, then, he said, my conviction is that the earth is a round body in the center of the heavens, and therefore has no need of air or any similar force as a {109} support, but is kept there and hindered from falling or inclining any way by the steady uniformity of the surrounding heaven and by its own equipoise. For that which, being in equipoise, is in the center of that which is equably diffused, will not incline in any way to any degree, but will always remain in the same state and not deviate. And this is my first notion.

Which is surely a correct one, said Simmias.

Also I believe that the earth is very vast, and that we who dwell in the region extending from the river Phasis to the Pillars of Heracles, along the borders of the sea, are just like ants or frogs about a marsh, and inhabit a small portion only, and that many others dwell in many similar places. For I should say that in all parts of the earth there are hollows of various forms and sizes, in which the water and the mist and the lower air collect. But the true earth is pure and in the pure heaven, in which also are the stars — that is the heaven which is commonly spoken of as the ether, of which this earth is but the sediment collecting in the hollows beneath. But we who live in these hollows are deceived into the notion that we are dwelling above on the surface of the earth; which is just as if a creature who was at the bottom of the sea were to fancy that he was on the surface of the water, and that the sea was the heaven through which he saw the sun and the other stars — he having never come to the surface by reason of his feebleness and sluggishness, and having never lifted up his head and seen, nor ever heard from one who had seen, how much purer and fairer the world above is than his own. Now this is exactly our case, for we are dwelling in a hollow of the earth, and fancy that we are on the surface; and the air we call heaven, and in this we imagine that the stars move. But this fancy is also due to our feebleness and sluggishness, which prevent our reaching the surface of the air; for if any man could arrive at the exterior limit, or take the wings of a bird and fly upward, like a fish who puts his head out of the water and sees this world, he would see a world beyond; and, if the nature of man could sustain the sight, he would acknowledge that this other world was the place of the true heaven and the true light and {110} the true earth. For this earth, and the stones, and the entire region which surrounds us, are spoiled and corroded, like the things in the sea which are corroded by the brine; for in the sea too there is hardly any noble or perfect growth, but only caverns, and sand, and an endless slough of mud; and even the shore is not to be compared to the fairer sights of this world. And greater by far is the superiority of the other world. Now of that earth which is under heaven, I can tell you a charming tale, Simmias, which is well worth hearing.

And we, Socrates, replied Simmias, shall be charmed to listen.

The tale, my friend, he said, is as follows: In the first place, the earth, when looked at from above, seems streaked like one of those balls which have leather coverings in twelve pieces, and is of divers colors, of which the colors which painters use on earth are only a sample. But there the whole earth is made up of them, and they are brighter far and clearer than ours; there is a purple of wonderful luster, also the radiance of gold, and the white which is in the earth is whiter than any chalk or snow. Of these and other colors the earth is made up, and they are more in number and fairer than the eye of man has ever seen; and the very hollows (of which I was speaking) filled with air and water are seen like light flashing amid the other colors, and have a color of their own, which gives a sort of unity to the variety of earth. And in this fair region everything that grows — trees, and flowers, and fruits — is in a like degree fairer than any here; and there are hills, and stones in them in a like degree smoother, and more transparent, and fairer in color than our highly valued emeralds and sardonyxes and jaspers, and other gems, which are but minute fragments of them; for there all the stones are like our precious stones, and fairer still. The reason of this is that they are pure, and not, like our precious stones, infected or corroded by the corrupt briny elements which coagulate among us, and which breed foulness and disease both in earth and stones, as well as in animals and plants. They are the jewels of the upper earth, which also shines with gold and silver and the like, and they are {111} visible to sight and large and abundant and found in every region of the earth, and blessed is he who sees them. And upon the earth are animals and men, some in a middle region, others dwelling about the air as we dwell about the sea; others in islands which the air flows round, near the continent; and in short, the air is used by them as the water and the sea are by us, and the ether is to them what the air is to us. Moreover, the temperament of their seasons is such that they have no disease, and live much longer than we do, and have sight and hearing and smell, and all the other senses, in far greater perfection, in the same degree that air is purer than water or the ether than air. Also they have temples and sacred places in which the gods really dwell, and they hear their voices and receive their answers, and are conscious of them and hold converse with them, and they see the sun, moon, and stars as they really are, and their other blessedness is of a piece with this.

Such is the nature of the whole earth, and of the things which are around the earth; and there are divers regions in the hollows on the face of the globe everywhere, some of them deeper and also wider than that which we inhabit, others deeper and with a narrower opening than ours, and some are shallower and wider. All have numerous perforations, and passages broad and narrow in the interior of the earth, connecting them with one another; and there flows into and out of them, as into basins, a vast tide of water, and huge subterranean streams of perennial rivers, and springs hot and cold, and a great fire, and great rivers of fire, and streams of liquid mud, thin or thick (like the rivers of mud in Sicily, and the lava streams which follow them), and the regions about which they happen to flow are filled up with them. And there is a swinging or seesawing in the interior of the earth which moves all this up and down. Now the swinging is due to this cause: There is a chasm which is the vastest of them all, and pierces right {112} through the whole earth; this is that which Homer describes in these words [from the *Iliad*, Book 8, line 14]:

Far off, where is the inmost depth beneath the earth.

And this he elsewhere, and many other poets, have called Tartarus. And the seesawing is caused by the streams flowing into and out of this chasm, and they each have the nature of the soil through which they flow. And the reason why the streams are always flowing in and out is that the watery element has no bed or bottom, but surges and swings up and down, and the surrounding wind and air do the same; they follow the water up and down, here and there, over the earth — just as in the act of respiration the air is always in process of inhalation and exhalation; and the wind swinging with the water in and out produces fearful and irresistible blasts. When the waters retire with a rush into the lower parts of the earth, as they are called, they flow through the earth into those regions, and fill them up as with the alternating motion of a pump, and then when they leave those regions and rush back here, they again fill the hollows here, and when these are filled, flow through subterranean channels and find their way to their several places, forming seas, and lakes, and rivers, and springs. From there they again enter the earth, some of them making a long circuit into many lands, others going to few places and those not distant, and again fall into Tartarus, some at a point a good deal lower than that at which they rose, and others not much lower, but all in some degree lower than the point of issue. And some burst forth again on the opposite side, and some on the same side, and some wind round the earth with one or many folds, like the coils of a serpent, and descend as far as they can, but always return and fall into the chasm. The rivers on either side can descend only to the center and no further, for to the rivers on both sides the opposite side is a precipice.

Now these rivers are many, and mighty, and diverse, and there are four principal ones, of which the greatest and outermost is that called Oceanus, which flows round the earth in a circle; and in the opposite direction flows Acheron, {113} which passes under the earth through desert places, into the Acherusian Lake. This is the lake to the shores of which the souls of the many go when they are dead, and after waiting an appointed time, which is to some a longer and to some a shorter time, they are sent back again to be born as animals. The third river rises between the two, and near the place of rising pours into a vast region of fire, and forms a lake larger than the Mediterranean Sea, boiling with water and mud; and proceeding muddy and turbid, and winding about the earth, comes, among other places, to the extremities of the Acherusian Lake, but mingles not with the waters of the lake, and, after making many coils about the earth, plunges into Tartarus at a deeper level. This is that Pyriphlegethon, as the stream is called, which throws up jets of fire in various parts of the earth. The fourth river goes out on the opposite side, and falls first of all into a wild and savage region, which is all of a dark blue color, like lapis lazuli; and this is that river which is called the Stygian River, and falls into and forms Lake Styx, and after falling into that lake and receiving strange powers in the waters, passes under the earth, winding round in the opposite direction to Pyriphlegethon, and meeting near the Acherusian Lake from the opposite side. And the water of this river too mingles with no other, but flows round in a circle and falls into Tartarus over against Pyriphlegethon, and the name of this river, as the poet says, is Cocytus.

Such is the nature of the other world; and when the dead arrive at the place to which the genius of each respectively conveys them, first of all they have sentence passed upon them, as they have lived well and piously or not. And those who appear to have lived neither well nor ill, go to the river Acheron, and mount such conveyances as they can get, and are carried in them to the lake, and there they dwell and are purified of their evil deeds, and having suffered the penalty of the wrongs which they have done to others, they are absolved, and receive the rewards of their good deeds according to their several deserts. But those who appear to be incurable by reason of the greatness of their crimes — who have committed many and terrible deeds of sacrilege, murders foul and violent, or the like — such are hurled into Tartarus, which is their suitable destiny, and they never come out. Those again who have committed crimes, which, although great, are not unpardonable — who in a moment of anger, for example, have done violence {114} to a father or mother, and have repented for the remainder of their lives, or who have taken the life of another under some extenuating circumstances — these are plunged into Tartarus, the pains of which they are compelled to undergo for a year, but at the end of the year the wave casts them forth — mere homicides by way of Cocytus, parricides and matricides by Pyriphlegethon — and they are borne to the Acherusian Lake, and there they lift up their voices and call upon the victims whom they have slain or wronged, to have pity on them, and to receive them, and to let them come out of the river into the lake. And if they prevail, then they come forth and cease from their troubles; but if not, they are carried back again into Tartarus and from there into the rivers unceasingly, until they obtain mercy from those whom they have wronged; for that is the sentence inflicted upon them by their judges. Those also who are remarkable for having led holy lives are released from this earthly prison, and go to their pure home which is above, and dwell in the purer earth; and those who have duly purified themselves with philosophy live thereafter altogether without the body, in mansions fairer still, which may not be described, and of which the time would fail me to tell.

Therefore, Simmias, seeing all these things, what ought not we to do in order to obtain virtue and wisdom in this life? Fair is the prize, and the hope great!

I do not mean to affirm that the description which I have given of the soul and its mansions is exactly true — a man of sense ought not to say so. But I do say that, inasmuch as the soul is shown to be immortal, he may venture to think, not improperly or unworthily, that something of the kind is true. The venture is a glorious one, and he ought to comfort himself with words like these, which is the reason why I lengthen out the tale. On this account, I say, let a man be of good cheer about his soul, if he has cast away the pleasures and ornaments of the body as alien to him and as working harm rather than good, and has followed after the pleasures of knowledge in this life, and has adorned the soul in its own proper jewels, which are temperance, and justice, and courage, and nobility, and {115} truth — adorned in these the soul is ready to go on its journey to the world below, when its time comes. You, Simmias and Cebes, and all other men, will depart at some time or other. Me already, as the tragic poet would say, the voice of fate calls. Soon I must drink the poison; and I think that I had better repair to the bath first, in order that the women may not have the trouble of washing my body after I am dead.

When he had done speaking, Crito said:, Have you any commands for us, Socrates — anything to say about your children, or any other matter in which we can serve you?

Nothing particular, Crito, he said, but only, as I have always told you, I would have you look after yourselves; that is a service which you may always do for me and mine as well as for yourselves. And you need not make professions; for if you take no thought for yourselves, and walk not according to the precepts which I have given you, not now for the first time, then the warmth of your professions will be of no avail.

We will do our best, said Crito. But in what way would you have us bury you?

In any way that you like; only you must get hold of me, and take care that I do not run away from you. Then he turned to us, and added with a smile: I cannot make Crito believe that I am the same Socrates who has been talking and conducting the argument; he fancies that I am the other Socrates whom he will soon see, a dead body, and he asks how he shall bury me. And though I have spoken many words in the endeavor to show that when I have drunk the poison I shall leave you and go to the joys of the blessed — these words of mine, with which I comforted you and myself, have had, I perceive, no effect upon Crito. And therefore I want you to be surety for me now, as he was surety for me at the trial; but let the promise be of another sort; for he was my surety to the judges that I would remain, but you must be my surety to him that I shall not remain, but go away and depart; and then he will suffer less at my death, and not be grieved when he sees my body being burned or buried. I would not have him sorrow at my hard lot or say at the burial, "Thus we lay out Socrates" or "Thus we follow him to the grave" or "Thus we bury him"; for false words are not only evil in themselves, but they {116} infect the soul with evil. Be of good cheer, then, my dear Crito, and say that you are burying my body only, and do with that as is usual, and as you think best.

When he had spoken these words, he arose and went into the bathing chamber with Crito, who asked us to wait; and we waited, talking and thinking of the subject of discourse, and also of the greatness of our sorrow; he was like a father of whom we were being bereaved, and we were about to pass the rest of our lives as orphans. When he had taken his bath his children were brought to him — (he had two young sons and an elder one); and the women of his family also came, and he talked to them and gave them a few directions in the presence of Crito; and he then dismissed them and returned to us.

Now the hour of sunset was near, for a good deal of time had passed while he was within. When he came out, he sat down with us again after his bath, but not much was said. Soon the jailer, who was the servant of the Eleven, entered and stood by him, saying: To you, Socrates, whom I know to be the noblest and gentlest and best of all who ever came to this place, I will not impute the angry feelings of other men, who rage and swear at me when, in obedience to the authorities, I bid them drink the poison — indeed, I am sure that you will not be angry with me; for others, as you are aware, and not I, are to blame. And so fare you well, and try to bear lightly what must needs be; you know my errand. Then bursting into tears he turned away and went out.

Socrates looked at him and said: I return your good wishes, and will do as you bid. Then, turning to us, he said, How charming the man is. Since I have been in prison he has always been coming to see me, and at times he would talk to me, and was as good as could be to me, and now see how generously he sorrows for me. But we must do as he says, Crito; let the cup be brought, if the poison is prepared: if not, let the attendant prepare some.

Yet, said Crito, the sun is still upon the hilltops, and I know that many a one has taken the poison late; and after the announcement has been made to him, he has eaten and drunk, and even enjoyed sexual relations with his beloved. Do not hasten then, there is still time.

Socrates said: Yes, Crito, and they of whom you speak are right in doing thus, for they think that they will gain by the delay; but I am right in not doing thus, {117} for I do not think that I should gain anything by drinking the poison a little later; I should be sparing and saving a life which is already gone. I could only laugh at myself for this. Please then to do as I say, and do not refuse me.

Crito, when he heard this, made a sign to the servant, and the servant went out, and remained for some time, and then returned with the jailer carrying a cup of poison.

Socrates said, you, my good friend, who are experienced in these matters, shall give me directions how I am to proceed. The man answered, you have only to walk about until your legs are heavy, and then to lie down, and the poison will act. At the same time he handed the cup to Socrates, who in the easiest and gentlest manner, without the least fear or change of color or feature, looking at the man right in both eyes, Echecrates, as his manner was, took the cup and said, what do you say about making a libation out of this cup to some god? May I, or not? The man answered, we only prepare, Socrates, just as much as we deem enough. I understand, he said, yet I may and must pray to the gods to bless my journey from this to that other world — may this, then, which is my prayer, be granted to me. Then holding the cup to his lips, quite readily and cheerfully he drank off the poison. And up to that point, most of us had been able to control our sorrow; but now when we saw him drinking, and saw too that he had finished the draught, we could no longer hold back, and in spite of myself my own tears were flowing fast; so that I covered my face and wept for myself, for certainly I was not weeping for him, but at the thought of my own calamity in having lost such a companion. Nor was I the first, for Crito, when he found himself unable to restrain his tears, had got up and moved away, and I followed; and at that moment, Apollodorus, who had been weeping all the time, broke out in a loud cry which made cowards of us all. Socrates alone retained his calmness. What, he said, is this strange outcry? I sent the women away mainly in order that they might not offend us in this way, for I have heard that a man should die in peace. Be quiet, then, and have patience. When we heard these words, we were ashamed, and restrained our tears; and he walked about until, as he said, his legs began to fail, and then he lay on his back, according to the directions, and the man who gave him the poison now and then looked at his feet and legs; and after a while he pressed his foot hard and asked him if he could feel; and he said no; and then his leg, and so {118} upwards and upwards, and showed us that he was cold and stiff. And he felt them himself, and said, when the poison reaches the heart, that will be the end. He was beginning to grow cold about the groin, when he uncovered his face, for he had covered himself up, and said — these were his last words — he said, Crito, I owe a cock to Asclepius; will you remember to pay the debt? The debt shall be paid, said Crito; is there anything else? There was no answer to this question; but in a minute or two a movement was heard, and the attendants uncovered him; his eyes were set, and Crito closed his eyes and mouth.

Such was the end, Echecrates, of our friend, whom I may truly call the wisest, and most just, and best of all the men whom I have ever known.

Seldom in any culture has anyone personified serenity, equanimity, and courage in the face of certain death to the extent that Socrates did in Plato's *Crito* and *Phaedo*. He remained completely without fear of either God or death and preserved his self-respect above all else. Although cases might be made for including Socrates's view of death in either the first, third, fourth, or sixth of the eight categories of theories listed above, and although he minimized and perhaps discounted — note how he presented this part as myth rather than as discursive philosophical argument — the possibility that the afterlife might involve eternal torment or punishment, the manner and rationale of his death has had profound influence on Christianity and made him a hero to the Roman Stoics and even to atheists such as British utilitarian philosopher John Stuart Mill (1806-1873), who held that any adoration must be earned, not commanded.

Mill's untiring and outspoken opposition to the "muscular Christianity" of his day, which was grounded in the fear of hell and the terror of God, gained him a fierce and implacable adversary in the person of conservative British jurist James Fitzjames Stephen (1829-1894), who savaged Mill at every opportunity and collected these attacks in his 1873 book, *Liberty, Equality, Fraternity*. British literary critic Sir Leslie Stephen (1832-1904) recounted, in his 1895 biography of his brother, how Fitzjames was a bully and a fighter at school, never learned to find a place for forgiveness, and came at an early age to see the threat of punishment as the basis of all ethics and the threat of hell as the basis of all religion and morality: "Fitzjames thought meditation on hell more to the purpose [than on the goodness, happiness, and love of God, heaven, and Christ], and set about it deliberately. ... He refers to Mill's famous passage about [willingly] going to hell rather than worship a bad God [who would condemn anyone to eternal torment], and asks what Mill would say after an experience of a quarter of an hour [in hell]" (pp. 73-74).

The passage to which Fitzjames Stephen referred is in the following excerpt from Mill's 1865 book, *An Examination of Sir William Hamilton's Philosophy*, Chapter Seven, "The Philosophy of the Conditioned as Applied by Mr. [Henry Longueville] Mansel to the Limits of Religious Thought":

... it is necessary to suppose that the infinite goodness ascribed to God is not the goodness which we know and love in our fellow-creatures, distinguished only as infinite in degree; but is different in kind, and another quality altogether. Accordingly Mr Mansel combats as a heresy of his opponents, the opinion that infinite goodness differs only in degree from finite goodness. — Here, then, I take my stand upon the acknowledged principle of logic and of morality; that when we mean different things we have no right to call them by the same name, and to apply to them, the same predicates, moral and intellectual.

If, instead of the glad tidings that there exists a Being in whom all the excellences which the highest human form can conceive, exist in a degree inconceivable to us, I am informed that the world is ruled by a being whose attributes are infinite, but what they are we cannot learn, except that the highest human morality does not sanction them — convince me of this and I will hear my fate as I may. But when I am told that I must believe this, and at the same time call this being by the names which express and affirm the highest human morality, I say, in plain terms, that I will not. Whatever power such a being may have over me, there is one thing he shall not do; he shall not compel me to worship him. I will call no being good who is not what I mean when I apply that epithet to my fellow-creatures; and if such a being can sentence me to hell for not so calling him, to hell I will go.

12

What is Spirituality?

The feeling of oneness, either with God or with one's fellow living beings, is spirituality. Membership in a religious organization may sometimes promote spirituality, but it is not spirituality itself. Spirituality is always felt inwardly, though it may be expressed by outward signs such as rituals, sacraments, or good works.

Institutionalized religions may provide spiritual support based on doctrines ranging from the most conservative fundamentalism to the most liberal universalism, but they cannot create spirituality, and how that support is received and used to build spirituality is eventually determined by each individual believer. Thus spiritual religions emerge from the like-mindedness of fellow believers. Accordingly, for example, Christians may speak of the "visible church" on earth, their institutionalized religion, the finite worldly organization of mortal beings that only mirrors the "invisible church" in God's bosom, their spiritual religion, the infinite assembly or *ekklêsia* (ἐκκλησία) of immortal souls that constitutes heaven.

Spirituality often appears as piety, the topic of Plato's early dialogue, *Euthyphro*, here translated by Jowett:

{2} *Euthyphro:* Why have you left the Lyceum, Socrates? And what are you doing in the porch of the King Archon? Surely you cannot be concerned in a suit before the king, like myself?

Socrates: Not in a suit, Euthyphro; impeachment is the word which the Athenians use.

Eu: What! I suppose that some one has been prosecuting you, for I cannot believe that you are the prosecutor of another.

Soc: Certainly not.

Eu: Then some one else has been prosecuting you?

Soc: Yes.

Eu: And who is he?

Soc: A young man who is little known, Euthyphro; and I hardly know him. His name is Meletus, and he is of the deme of Pitthis. Perhaps you may remember his appearance; he has a beak, and long straight hair, and a beard which is ill grown.

Eu: No, I do not remember him, Socrates. But what is the charge which he brings against you?

Soc: What is the charge? Well, a very serious charge, which shows a good deal of character in the young man, and for which he is certainly not to be despised. He says he knows how the youth are corrupted and who are their corruptors. I fancy that he must be a wise man, and seeing that I am the reverse of a wise man, he has found me out, and is going to accuse me of corrupting his young friends. And of this our mother the state is to be the judge. Of all our political men he is the only one who seems to me to begin in the right way, with {3} the cultivation of virtue in youth; like a good husbandman, he makes the young shoots his first care, and clears away us who are the destroyers of them. This is only the first step; he will afterwards attend to the elder branches; and if he goes on as he has begun, he will be a very great public benefactor.

Eu: I hope that he may; but I rather fear, Socrates, that the opposite will turn out to be the truth. My opinion is that in attacking you he is simply aiming a blow at the foundation of the state. But in what way does he say that you corrupt the young?

Soc: He brings a wonderful accusation against me, which at first hearing excites surprise: he says that I am a poet or maker of gods, and that I invent new gods and deny the existence of old ones; this is the ground of his indictment.

Eu: I understand, Socrates; he means to attack you about the familiar sign which occasionally, as you say, comes to you. He thinks that you are a neologian, and he is going to have you up before the court for this. He knows that such a charge is readily received by the world, as I myself know too well; for when I speak in the assembly about divine things, and foretell the future to them, they laugh at me and think me a madman. Yet every word that I say is true. But they are jealous of us all; and we must be brave and go at them.

Soc: Their laughter, friend Euthyphro, is not a matter of much consequence. For a man may be thought wise; but the Athenians, I suspect, do not much trouble themselves about him until he begins to impart his wisdom to others, and then for some reason or other, perhaps, as you say, from jealousy, they are angry.

Eu: I am never likely to try their temper in this way.

Soc: I dare say not, for you are reserved in your behavior, and seldom impart your wisdom. But I have a benevolent habit of pouring out myself to everybody, and would even pay for a listener, and I am afraid that the Athenians may think me too talkative. Now if, as I was saying, they would only laugh at me, as you say that they laugh at you, the time might pass gaily enough in the court; but perhaps they may be in earnest, and then what the end will be you soothsayers only can predict.

Eu: I dare say that the affair will end in nothing, Socrates, and that you will win your cause; and I think that I shall win my own.

Soc: And what is your suit, Euthyphro? Are you the pursuer or the defendant?

Eu: I am the pursuer.

Soc: Of whom?

{4}   *Eu:* You will think me mad when I tell you.

Soc: Why, has the fugitive wings?

Eu: Nay, he is not very volatile at his time of life.

Soc: Who is he?

Eu: My father.

Soc: Your father! My good man?

Eu: Yes.

Soc: And of what is he accused?

Eu: Of murder, Socrates.

Soc: By the powers, Euthyphro! How little does the common herd know of the nature of right and truth. A man must be an extraordinary man, and have made great strides in wisdom, before he could have seen his way to bring such an action.

Eu: Indeed, Socrates, he must.

Soc: I suppose that the man whom your father murdered was one of your relatives — clearly he was; for if he had been a stranger you would never have thought of prosecuting him.

Eu: I am amused, Socrates, at your making a distinction between one who is a relation and one who is not a relation; for surely the pollution is the same in either case, if you knowingly associate with the murderer when you ought to clear yourself and him by proceeding against him. The real question is whether the murdered man has been justly slain. If justly, then your duty is to let the matter alone; but if unjustly, then even if the murderer lives under the same roof with you and eats at the same table, proceed against him. Now the man who is dead was a poor dependent of mine who worked for us as a field laborer on our farm in Naxos, and one day in a fit of drunken passion he got into a quarrel with one of our domestic servants and slew him. My father bound him hand and foot and threw him into a ditch, and then sent to Athens to ask of a diviner what he should do with him. Meanwhile he never attended to him and took no care about him, for he regarded him as a murderer; and thought that no great harm would be done even if he did die. Now this was just what happened. For such was the effect of cold and hunger and chains upon him, that before the messenger returned from the diviner, he was dead. And my father and family are angry with me for taking the part of the murderer and prosecuting my father. They say that he did not kill him, and that if he did, the dead man was but a murderer, and I ought not to take any notice, for that a son is impious who prosecutes a father. Which shows, Socrates, how little they know what the gods think about piety and impiety.

Soc: Good heavens, Euthyphro! And is your knowledge of religion and of things pious and impious so very exact, that, supposing the circumstances to be as you state them, you are not afraid lest you too may be doing an impious thing in bringing an action against your father?

Eu: The best of Euthyphro, and that which distinguishes him, Socrates, {5} from other men, is his exact knowledge of all such matters. What should I be good for without it?

Soc: Rare friend! I think that I cannot do better than be your disciple. Then before the trial with Meletus comes on I shall challenge him, and say that I have always had a great interest in religious questions, and now, as he charges me with rash imaginations and innovations in religion, I have become your disciple. You, Meletus, as I shall say to him, acknowledge Euthyphro to be a great theologian, and sound in his opinions; and if you approve of him you ought to approve of me, and not have me into court; but if you disapprove, you should begin by indicting him who is my teacher, and who will be the ruin, not of the young, but of the old; that is to say, of myself whom he instructs, and of his old father whom he admonishes and chastises. And if Meletus refuses to listen to me, but will go on, and will not shift the indictment from me to you, I cannot do better than repeat this challenge in the court.

Eu: Yes, indeed, Socrates; and if he attempts to indict me I am mistaken if I do not find a flaw in him; the court shall have a great deal more to say to him than to me.

Soc: And I, my dear friend, knowing this, am desirous of becoming your disciple. For I observe that no one appears to notice you — not even this Meletus; but his sharp eyes have found me out at once, and he has indicted me for impiety. And therefore, I adjure you to tell me the nature of piety and impiety, which you said that you knew so well, and of murder, and of other offences against the gods. What are they? Is not piety in every action always the same? And impiety, again — is it not always the opposite of piety, and also the same with itself, having, as impiety, one notion which includes whatever is impious?

Eu: To be sure, Socrates.

Soc: And what is piety, and what is impiety?

Eu: Piety is doing as I am doing; that is to say, prosecuting any one who is guilty of murder, sacrilege, or of any similar crime — whether he be your father or mother, or whoever he may be — that makes no difference; and not to prosecute them is impiety. And please to consider, Socrates, what a notable proof I will give you of the truth of my words, a proof which I have already given to others: — of the principle, I mean, that the impious, whoever he may be, ought not to go unpunished. For do not men regard Zeus as the best and most righteous of the

{6} gods? — And yet they admit that he bound his father (Cronos) because he wickedly devoured his sons, and that he too had punished his own father (Uranus) for a similar reason, in a nameless manner. And yet when I proceed against my father, they are angry with me. So inconsistent are they in their way of talking when the gods are concerned, and when I am concerned.

Soc: May not this be the reason, Euthyphro, why I am charged with impiety — that I cannot away with these stories about the gods? And therefore I suppose that people think me wrong. But, as you who are well informed about them approve of them, I cannot do better than assent to your superior wisdom. What else can I say, confessing as I do, that I know nothing about them? Tell me, for the love of Zeus, whether you really believe that they are true.

Eu: Yes, Socrates; and things more wonderful still, of which the world is in ignorance.

Soc: And do you really believe that the gods, fought with one another, and had dire quarrels, battles, and the like, as the poets say, and as you may see represented in the works of great artists? The temples are full of them; and notably the robe of Athene, which is carried up to the Acropolis at the great Panathenaea, is embroidered with them. Are all these tales of the gods true, Euthyphro?

Eu: Yes, Socrates; and, as I was saying, I can tell you, if you would like to hear them, many other things about the gods which would quite amaze you.

Soc: I dare say; and you shall tell me them at some other time when I have leisure. But just at present I would rather hear from you a more precise answer, which you have not as yet given, my friend, to the question, What is "piety"? When asked, you only replied, doing as you do, charging your father with murder.

Eu: And what I said was true, Socrates.

Soc: No doubt, Euthyphro; but you would admit that there are many other pious acts?

Eu: There are.

Soc: Remember that I did not ask you to give me two or three examples of piety, but to explain the general idea which makes all pious things to be pious. Do you not recollect that there was one idea which made the impious impious, and the pious pious?

Eu: I remember.

Soc: Tell me what is the nature of this idea, and then I shall have a standard to which I may look, and by which I may measure actions, whether yours or those of any one else, and then I shall be able to say that such and such an action is pious, such another impious.

Eu: I will tell you, if you like.

Soc: I should very much like.

Eu: Piety, then, is that which is dear to the gods, and impiety is that which is not dear to them.

{7}   *Soc:* Very good, Euthyphro; you have now given me the sort of answer which I wanted. But whether what you say is true or not I cannot as yet tell, although I make no doubt that you will prove the truth of your words.

Eu: Of course.

Soc: Come, then, and let us examine what we are saying. That thing or person which is dear to the gods is pious, and that thing or person which is hateful to the gods is impious, these two being the extreme opposites of one another. Was not that said?

Eu: It was.

Soc: And well said?

Eu: Yes, Socrates, I thought so; it was certainly said.

Soc: And further, Euthyphro, the gods were admitted to have enmities and hatreds and differences?

Eu: Yes, that was also said.

Soc: And what sort of difference creates enmity and anger? Suppose for example that you and I, my good friend, differ about a number; do differences of this sort make us enemies and set us at variance with one another? Do we not go at once to arithmetic, and put an end to them by a sum?

Eu: True.

Soc: Or suppose that we differ about magnitudes, do we not quickly end the differences by measuring?

Eu: Very true.

Soc: And we end a controversy about heavy and light by resorting to a weighing machine?

Eu: To be sure.

Soc: But what differences are there which cannot be thus decided, and which therefore make us angry and set us at enmity with one another? I dare say the answer does not occur to you at the moment, and therefore I will suggest that these enmities arise when the matters of difference are the just and unjust, good and evil, honorable and dishonorable. Are not these the points about which men differ, and about which when we are unable satisfactorily to decide our differences, you and I and all of us quarrel, when we do quarrel?

Eu: Yes, Socrates, the nature of the differences about which we quarrel is such as you describe.

Soc: And the quarrels of the gods, noble Euthyphro, when they occur, are of a like nature?

Eu: Certainly they are.

Soc: They have differences of opinion, as you say, about good and evil, just and unjust, honorable and dishonorable: there would have been no quarrels among them, if there had been no such differences — would there now?

Eu: You are quite right.

Soc: Does not every man love that which he deems noble and just and good, and hate the opposite of them?

Eu: Very true.

Soc: But, as you say, people regard the same things, some as just and others as unjust — about these they dispute; and so there arise wars and fightings among them.

{8}   *Eu:* Very true.

Soc: Then the same things are hated by the gods and loved by the gods, and are both hateful and dear to them?

Eu: True.

Soc: And upon this view the same things, Euthyphro, will be pious and also impious?

Eu: So I should suppose.

Soc: Then, my friend, I remark with surprise that you have not answered the question which I asked. For I certainly did not ask you to tell me what action is both pious and impious: but now it would seem that what is loved by the gods is also hated by them. And therefore, Euthyphro, in thus chastising your father you may very likely be doing what is agreeable to Zeus but disagreeable to Cronos or Uranus, and what is acceptable to Hephaestus but unacceptable to Here, and there may be other gods who have similar differences of opinion.

Eu: But I believe, Socrates, that all the gods would be agreed as to the propriety of punishing a murderer: there would be no difference of opinion about that.

Soc: Well, but speaking of men, Euthyphro, did you ever hear any one arguing that a murderer or any sort of evil-doer ought to be let off?

Eu: I should rather say that these are the questions which they are always arguing, especially in courts of law: they commit all sorts of crimes, and there is nothing which they will not do or say in their own defence.

Soc: But do they admit their guilt, Euthyphro, and yet say that they ought not to be punished?

Eu: No; they do not.

Soc: Then there are some things which they do not venture to say and do: for they do not venture to argue that the guilty are to be unpunished, but they deny their guilt, do they not?

Eu: Yes.

Soc: Then they do not argue that the evil-doer should not be punished, but they argue about the fact of who the evil-doer is, and what he did and when?

Eu: True.

Soc: And the gods are in the same case, if as you assert they quarrel about just and unjust, and some of them say while others deny that injustice is done among them. For surely neither God nor man will ever venture to say that the doer of injustice is not to be punished?

Eu: That is true, Socrates, in the main.

Soc: But they join issue about the particulars — gods and men alike; and, if they dispute at all, they dispute about some act which is called in question, and which by some is affirmed to be just, by others to be unjust. Is not that true?

Eu: Quite true.

{9}   *Soc:* Well then, my dear friend Euthyphro, do tell me, for my better instruction and information, what proof have you that in the opinion of all the gods a servant who is guilty of murder, and is put in chains by the master of the dead man, and dies because he is put in chains before he who bound him can learn from the interpreters of the gods what he ought to do with him, dies unjustly; and that on behalf of such an one a son ought to proceed against his father and accuse him of murder. How would you show that all the gods absolutely agree in approving of his act? Prove to me that they do, and I will applaud your wisdom as long as I live.

Eu: It will be a difficult task; but I could make the matter very clear indeed to you.

Soc: I understand; you mean to say that I am not so quick of apprehension as the judges: for to them you will be sure to prove that the act is unjust, and hateful to the gods.

Eu: Yes indeed, Socrates; at least if they will listen to me.

Soc: But they will be sure to listen if they find that you are a good speaker. There was a notion that came into my mind while you were speaking; I said to myself: "Well, and what if Euthyphro does prove to me that all the gods regarded the death of the serf as unjust, how do I know anything more of the nature of piety and impiety? For granting that this action may be hateful to the gods, still piety and impiety are not adequately defined by these distinctions, for that which is hateful to the gods has been shown to be also pleasing and dear to them." And therefore, Euthyphro, I do not ask you to prove this; I will suppose, if you like, that all the gods condemn and abominate such an action. But I will amend the definition so far as to say that what all the gods hate is impious, and what they love pious or holy; and what some of them love and others hate is both or neither. Shall this be our definition of piety and impiety?

Eu: Why not, Socrates?

Soc: Why not! certainly, as far as I am concerned, Euthyphro, there is no reason why not. But whether this admission will greatly assist you in the task of instructing me as you promised, is a matter for you to consider.

Eu: Yes, I should say that what all the gods love is pious and holy, and the opposite which they all hate, impious.

Soc: Ought we to enquire into the truth of this, Euthyphro, or simply to accept the mere statement on our own authority and that of others? What do you say?

Eu: We should enquire; and I believe that the statement will stand the test of enquiry.

Soc: We shall know better, my good friend, in a little while. The point which I should first wish to understand is whether the pious or holy is beloved by {10} the gods because it is holy, or holy because it is beloved of the gods.

Eu: I do not understand your meaning, Socrates.

Soc: I will endeavor to explain: We speak of carrying and we speak of being carried, of leading and being led, seeing and being seen. You know that in all such cases there is a difference, and you know also in what the difference lies?

Eu: I think that I understand.

Soc: And is not that which is beloved distinct from that which loves?

Eu: Certainly.

Soc: Well; and now tell me, is that which is carried in this state of carrying because it is carried, or for some other reason?

Eu: No; that is the reason.

Soc: And the same is true of what is led and of what is seen?

Eu: True.

Soc: And a thing is not seen because it is visible, but conversely, visible because it is seen; nor is a thing led because it is in the state of being led, or carried because it is in the state of being carried, but the converse of this. And now I think, Euthyphro, that my meaning will be intelligible; and my meaning is, that any state of action or passion implies previous action or passion. It does not become because it is becoming, but it is in a state of becoming because it becomes; neither does it suffer because it is in a state of suffering, but it is in a state of suffering because it suffers. Do you not agree?

Eu: Yes.

Soc: Is not that which is loved in some state either of becoming or suffering?

Eu: Yes.

Soc: And the same holds as in the previous instances; the state of being loved follows the act of being loved, and not the act the state.

Eu: Certainly.

Soc: And what do you say of piety, Euthyphro? Is not piety, according to your definition, loved by all the gods?

Eu: Yes.

Soc: Because it is pious or holy, or for some other reason?

Eu: No, that is the reason.

Soc: It is loved because it is holy, not holy because it is loved?

Eu: Yes.

Soc: And that which is dear to the gods is loved by them, and is in a state to be loved of them because it is loved of them?

Eu: Certainly.

Soc: Then that which is dear to the gods, Euthyphro, is not holy, nor is that which is holy loved of God, as you affirm; but they are two different things.

Eu: How do you mean, Socrates?

Soc: I mean to say that the holy has been acknowledged by us to be loved of God because it is holy, not to be holy because it is loved.

Eu: Yes.

Soc: But that which is dear to the gods is dear to them because it is loved by them, not loved by them because it is dear to them.

Eu: True.

Soc: But, friend Euthyphro, if that which is holy is the same with that which is dear to God, and is loved because it is holy, then that which is dear to {11} God would have been loved as being dear to God; but if that which is dear to God is dear to him because loved by him, then that which is holy would have been holy because loved by him. But now you see that the reverse is the case, and that they are quite different from one another. For one is of a kind to be loved cause it is loved, and the other is loved because it is of a kind to be loved. Thus you appear to me, Euthyphro, when I ask you what is the essence of holiness, to offer an attribute only, and not the essence — the attribute of being loved by all the gods. But you still refuse to explain to me the nature of holiness. And therefore, if you please, I will ask you not to hide your treasure, but to tell me once more what holiness or piety really is, whether dear to the gods or not (for that is a matter about which we will not quarrel) and what is impiety?

Eu: I really do not know, Socrates, how to express what I mean. For somehow or other our arguments, on whatever ground we rest them, seem to turn round and walk away from us.

Soc: Your words, Euthyphro, are like the handiwork of my ancestor Daedalus; and if I were the sayer or propounder of them, you might say that my arguments walk away and will not remain fixed where they are placed because I am a descendant of his. But now, since these notions are your own, you must find some other gibe, for they certainly, as you yourself allow, show an inclination to be on the move.

Eu: Nay, Socrates, I shall still say that you are the Daedalus who sets arguments in motion; not I, certainly, but you make them move or go round, for they would never have stirred, as far as I am concerned.

Soc: Then I must be a greater than Daedalus: for whereas he only made his own inventions to move, I move those of other people as well. And the beauty of it is, that I would rather not. For I would give the wisdom of Daedalus, and the wealth of Tantalus, to be able to detain them and keep them fixed. But enough of this. As I perceive that you are lazy, I will myself endeavor to show you how you might instruct me in the nature of piety; and I hope that you will not grudge your labor. Tell me, then — Is not that which is pious necessarily just?

Eu: Yes.

Soc: And is, then, all which is just pious? Or, is that which is pious all just, {12} but that which is just, only in part and not all, pious?

Eu: I do not understand you, Socrates.

Soc: And yet I know that you are as much wiser than I am, as you are younger. But, as I was saying, revered friend, the abundance of your wisdom makes you lazy. Please to exert yourself, for there is no real difficulty in understanding me. What I mean I may explain by an illustration of what I do not mean. The poet Stasinus sings — "Of Zeus, the author and creator of all these things, / You will not tell: for where there is fear there is also / reverence." Now I disagree with this poet. Shall I tell you in what respect?

Eu: By all means.

Soc: I should not say that where there is fear there is also reverence; for I am sure that many persons fear poverty and disease, and the like evils, but I do not perceive that they reverence the objects of their fear.

Eu: Very true.

Soc: But where reverence is, there is fear; for he who has a feeling of reverence and shame about the commission of any action, fears and is afraid of an ill reputation.

Eu: No doubt.

Soc: Then we are wrong in saying that where there is fear there is also reverence; and we should say, where there is reverence there is also fear. But there is not always reverence where there is fear; for fear is a more extended notion, and reverence is a part of fear, just as the odd is a part of number, and number is a more extended notion than the odd. I suppose that you follow me now?

Eu: Quite well.

Soc: That was the sort of question which I meant to raise when I asked whether the just is always the pious, or the pious always the just; and whether there may not be justice where there is not piety; for justice is the more extended notion of which piety is only a part. Do you dissent?

Eu: No, I think that you are quite right.

Soc: Then, if piety is a part of justice, I suppose that we should enquire what part? If you had pursued the enquiry in the previous cases; for instance, if you had asked me what is an even number, and what part of number the even is, I should have had no difficulty in replying, a number which represents a figure having two equal sides. Do you not agree?

Eu: Yes, I quite agree.

Soc: In like manner, I want you to tell me what part of justice is piety or holiness, that I may be able to tell Meletus not to do me injustice, or indict me for impiety, as I am now adequately instructed by you in the nature of piety or holiness, and their opposites.

Eu: Piety or holiness, Socrates, appears to me to be that part of justice which attends to the gods, as there is the other part of justice which attends to men.

{13}   *Soc:* That is good, Euthyphro; yet still there is a little point about which I should like to have further information, What is the meaning of "attention"? For attention can hardly be used in the same sense when applied to the gods as when applied to other things. For instance, horses are said to require attention, and not every person is able to attend to them, but only a person skilled in horsemanship. Is it not so?

Eu: Certainly.

Soc: I should suppose that the art of horsemanship is the art of attending to horses?

Eu: Yes.

Soc: Nor is every one qualified to attend to dogs, but only the huntsman?

Eu: True.

Soc: And I should also conceive that the art of the huntsman is the art of attending to dogs?

Eu: Yes.

Soc: As the art of the ox herd is the art of attending to oxen?

Eu: Very true.

Soc: In like manner holiness or piety is the art of attending to the gods? — That would be your meaning, Euthyphro?

Eu: Yes.

Soc: And is not attention always designed for the good or benefit of that to which the attention is given? As in the case of horses, you may observe that when attended to by the horseman's art they are benefited and improved, are they not?

Eu: True.

Soc: As the dogs are benefited by the huntsman's art, and the oxen by the art of the ox herd, and all other things are tended or attended for their good and not for their hurt?

Eu: Certainly, not for their hurt.

Soc: But for their good?

Eu: Of course.

Soc: And does piety or holiness, which has been defined to be the art of attending to the gods, benefit or improve them? Would you say that when you do a holy act you make any of the gods better?

Eu: No, no; that was certainly not what I meant.

Soc: And I, Euthyphro, never supposed that you did. I asked you the question about the nature of the attention, because I thought that you did not.

Eu: You do me justice, Socrates; that is not the sort of attention which I mean.

Soc: Good. But I must still ask what is this attention to the gods which is called piety?

Eu: It is such, Socrates, as servants show to their masters.

Soc: I understand — a sort of ministration to the gods.

Eu: Exactly.

Soc: Medicine is also a sort of ministration or service, having in view the attainment of some object — would you not say of health?

Eu: I should.

Soc: Again, there is an art which ministers to the shipbuilder with a view to the attainment of some result?

Eu: Yes, Socrates, with a view to the building of a ship.

Soc: As there is an art which ministers to the housebuilder with a view to the building of a house?

Eu: Yes.

Soc: And now tell me, my good friend, about the art which ministers to the gods: what work does that help to accomplish? For you must surely know if, as you say, you are of all men living the one who is best instructed in religion.

Eu: And I speak the truth, Socrates.

Soc: Tell me then, oh tell me — what is that fair work which the gods do by the help of our ministrations?

Eu: Many and fair, Socrates, are the works which they do.

{14}   *Soc:* Why, my friend, and so are those of a general. But the chief of them is easily told. Would you not say that victory in war is the chief of them?

Eu: Certainly.

Soc: Many and fair, too, are the works of the husbandman, if I am not mistaken; but his chief work is the production of food from the earth?

Eu: Exactly.

Soc: And of the many and fair things done by the gods, which is the chief or principal one?

Eu: I have told you already, Socrates, that to learn all these things accurately will be very tiresome. Let me simply say that piety or holiness is learning, how to please the gods in word and deed, by prayers and sacrifices. Such piety, is the salvation of families and states, just as the impious, which is unpleasing to the gods, is their ruin and destruction.

Soc: I think that you could have answered in much fewer words the chief question which I asked, Euthyphro, if you had chosen. But I see plainly that you are not disposed to instruct me — clearly not: else why, when we reached the point, did you turn, aside? Had you only answered me I should have truly learned of you by this time the nature of piety. Now, as the asker of a question is necessarily dependent on the answerer, where he leads — I must follow; and can only ask again, what is the pious, and what is piety? Do you mean that they are a sort of science of praying and sacrificing?

Eu: Yes, I do.

Soc: And sacrificing is giving to the gods, and prayer is asking of the gods?

Eu: Yes, Socrates.

Soc: Upon this view, then piety is a science of asking and giving?

Eu: You understand me capitally, Socrates.

Soc: Yes, my friend; the reason is that I am a votary of your science, and give my mind to it, and therefore nothing which you say will be thrown away upon me. Please then to tell me, what is the nature of this service to the gods? Do you mean that we prefer requests and give gifts to them?

Eu: Yes, I do.

Soc: Is not the right way of asking to ask of them what we want?

Eu: Certainly.

Soc: And the right way of giving is to give to them in return what they want of us. There would be no meaning in an art which gives to any one that which he does not want.

Eu: Very true, Socrates.

Soc: Then piety, Euthyphro, is an art which gods and men have of doing business with one another?

Eu: That is an expression which you may use, if you like.

Soc: But I have no particular liking for anything but the truth. I wish, however, that you would tell me what benefit accrues to the gods from our gifts. {15} There is no doubt about what they give to us; for there is no good thing which they do not give; but how we can give any good thing to them in return is far from being equally clear. If they give everything and we give nothing, that must be an affair of business in which we have very greatly the advantage of them.

Eu: And do you imagine, Socrates, that any benefit accrues to the gods from our gifts?

Soc: But if not, Euthyphro, what is the meaning of gifts which are conferred by us upon the gods?

Eu: What else, but tributes of honor; and, as I was just now saying, what pleases them?

Soc: Piety, then, is pleasing to the gods, but not beneficial or dear to them?

Eu: I should say that nothing could be dearer.

Soc: Then once more the assertion is repeated that piety is dear to the gods?

Eu: Certainly.

Soc: And when you say this, can you wonder at your words not standing firm, but walking away? Will you accuse me of being the Daedalus who makes them walk away, not perceiving that there is another and far greater artist than Daedalus who makes them go round in a circle, and he is yourself; for the argument, as you will perceive, comes round to the same point. Were we not saying that the holy or pious was not the same with that which is loved of the gods? Have you forgotten?

Eu: I quite remember.

Soc: And are you not saying that what is loved of the gods is holy; and is not this the same as what is dear to them — do you see?

Eu: True.

Soc: Then either we were wrong in former assertion; or, if we were right then, we are wrong now.

Eu: One of the two must be true.

Soc: Then we must begin again and ask, What is piety? That is an enquiry which I shall never be weary of pursuing as far as in me lies; and I entreat you not to scorn me, but to apply your mind to the utmost, and tell me the truth. For, if any man knows, you are he; and therefore I must detain you, like Proteus, until you tell. If you had not certainly known the nature of piety and impiety, I am confident that you would never, on behalf of a serf, have charged your aged father with murder. You would not have run such a risk of doing wrong in the sight of the gods, and you would have had too much respect for the opinions of men. I am sure, therefore, that you know the nature of piety and impiety. Speak out then, my dear Euthyphro, and do not hide your knowledge.

Eu: Another time, Socrates; for I am in a hurry, and must go now.

Soc: Alas! my companion, and will you leave me in despair? I was hoping that you would instruct me in the nature of piety and impiety; and then I might {16} have cleared myself of Meletus and his indictment. I would have told him that I had been enlightened by Euthyphro, and had given up rash innovations and speculations, in which I indulged only through ignorance, and that now I am about to lead a better life.

For American idealist philosopher Josiah Royce (1855-1916), spirituality and therefore genuine religious consciousness is ineluctably social, yet at the same time rooted in the character of the individual. Spirituality arises first, and becomes the basis of ethics, both personal and social. The following excerpt is from the final chapter of Royce's 1908 book, *The Philosophy of Loyalty*:

Loyalty, so we said at the outset, is the willing and thoroughgoing devotion of a person to a cause. We defined a cause as something that unifies many human lives in one. Our intent in making these definitions was mainly practical. Our philosophy of loyalty was and is intended to be a practical philosophy. We used our definition first to help us to find out the purpose of life, and the supreme good which human beings can seek for themselves. We found this good to be, indeed, of a paradoxical seeming. It was a good found only by an act of sacrifice. ...

Now, this mysterious speech of loyalty implies something which is not only moral, but also metaphysical. Purely practical considerations, then, a study of our human needs, an ideal of the business of life, — these inevitably lead us into a region which is more than merely a realm of moral activities. This region is either one of delusions or else one of spiritual realities of a level higher than is that of our present individual human experience. ...

Thus our ethical theory has transformed itself into a general philosophical doctrine; and loyalty now appears to us not only as a guide of life but as a revelation of our relation to a realm which we have been obliged to define as one of an eternal and all-embracing unity of spiritual life. ...

I now propose a new definition of loyalty ... *Loyalty is the will to manifest, so far as possible, the Eternal, that is, the conscious and superhuman unity of life, in the form of the acts of an individual Self.* Or, if you prefer to take the point of view of an individual human self, if you persist in looking at the world just as we find it in our ordinary experience, and if you regard [my] metaphysical doctrine ... merely as an ideal theory of life, and *not* as a demonstrable philosophy, I can still hold to my definition of loyalty by borrowing a famous phrase from [my] dear friend and colleague [William James] ... I can, then, simply state my new definition of loyalty in plainer and more directly obvious terms thus: *Loyalty is the Will to Believe in something eternal, and to express that belief in the practical life of a human being.*

This, I say, is my new definition of loyalty, and in its metaphysical form, it is my final definition. ...

We have now defined loyalty as the will to manifest the eternal in and through the deeds of individual selves. As for religion, — in its highest historical forms (which here alone concern us), — religion, as I think, may be defined as ... *the interpretation both of the eternal and of the spirit of loyalty through emotion, and through a fitting activity of the imagination.*

Religion, in any form, has always been an effort to interpret and to make use of some superhuman world. ... The superhuman has been conceived by men in terms that were often far enough from those which loyalty requires. ...

People often say that mere morality is something very remote from true religion. Sometimes people say this in the interests of religion, meaning to point out that mere morality can at best make you only a more or less tolerable citizen, while only religion can reconcile you, as such people say, to that superhuman world whose existence and whose support alone make human life worth living. But sometimes almost the same assertion is made in the interest of pure morality, viewed as something independent of religion. Some people tell you, namely, that since, as they say, religion is a collection of doubtful beliefs, of superstitions, and of more or less exalted emotions, morality is all the better for keeping aloof from religion. Suffering man needs your help; your friends need as much happiness as you can give them; conventional morality is, on the whole, a good thing. Learn righteousness, therefore, say they, and leave religion to the fantastic-minded who love to believe. The human is what we need. Let the superhuman alone.

Now, our philosophy of loyalty, aiming at something much larger and richer than the mere sum of human happiness in individual men, has taught us that there is no such sharp dividing line between the human and the superhuman as these attempts to sunder the provinces of religion and morality would imply. The loyal serve something more than individual lives. Even Nietzsche, individualist and ethical naturalist though he was, illustrates our present thesis. ...

If our philosophy of loyalty is right, Nietzsche was not wrong in ... appeal to the superhuman. The superhuman we indeed have always with us. Life has no sense without it. But the superhuman need not be the magical. It need not be the object of superstition. And if we are desirous of unifying the interests of morality and religion, it is well indeed to begin, as rugged old Amos began, by first appreciating what righteousness is, and then by interpreting righteousness, in a perfectly reasonable and non-superstitious way, in superhuman terms. Then we shall be ready to appreciate what religion, whose roots are indeed by no means wholly in our moral nature, nevertheless has to offer us as a supplement to our morality.

Loyalty is a service of causes. But, as we saw, we do not, we cannot, wait until somebody clearly shows us how good the causes are in themselves, before we set about serving them. We first practically learn of the goodness of our causes through the very act of serving them. ...

In so far, then, one can indeed be loyal without being consciously and explicitly religious. One's cause, in its first intention, appears to him human, concrete, practical. It is *also* an ideal. It is *also* a superhuman entity. It also really *means* the service of the eternal. ...

... such an imperfectly developed but loyal man may also accept, upon traditional grounds, a religion. This religion will then tell him about a superhuman world. But in so far the religion need not be, to his mind, an essential factor in his practical loyalty. He may be superstitious; or he may be a religious formalist; or he may accept his creed and his church simply because of their social respectability and usefulness; or, finally, he may even have a rich and genuine religious experience, which still may remain rather a mysticism than a morality, or an aesthetic comfort rather than a love of his cause.

In such cases, loyalty and religion may long keep apart. But the fact remains that loyalty, if sincere, involves at least a latent belief in the superhuman reality of the cause, and means at least an unconscious devotion to the one and eternal cause. But such a belief is also a latent union of morality and religion. Such a service is an unconscious piety. ...

Everybody ought to serve the universal cause in his own individual way. ... But whoever thus serves inevitably *loses* his cause in our poor world of human sense-experience, because his cause is too good for this present temporal world to express it. ... Our deepest loyalty lies in devoting ourselves to causes that are just now lost to our poor human nature. ... Loyalty means a transformation of our nature. ...

And now, finally, to sum up our whole doctrine of loyalty and religion. Two things belonging to the world-life we know — two at least, if my theory is true: *it is defined in terms of our own needs; and it includes and completes our experience*. Hence, in any case, it is precisely as live and elemental and concrete as we are; and there is not a need of ours which is not its own. If you ask why I call it good — well, the very arguments which recent pragmatism has used are ... here my warrant. A truth cannot be a merely theoretical truth. True is that which successfully fulfils an idea. Whoever ... is not succeeding, or is facing an evil, or is dissatisfied, is inevitably demanding and defining facts that are far beyond him, and that are not yet consciously his own. A knower of the totality of truth is therefore, of necessity, in possession of the fulfilment of all rational purposes. ... Our theory of evil is indeed no "shallow optimism," but is founded upon the deepest, the bitterest, and the dearest moral experience of the human race. The *loyal*, and they alone, know the one great good of suffering, of ignorance, of finitude, of loss, of defeat — *and that is just the good of loyalty*, so long as the cause itself can only be viewed as indeed a living whole. Spiritual peace is surely no easy thing. We win that peace only through stress and suffering and loss and labor. But when we find the preciousness of the idealized cause emphasized through grief, we see that, whatever evil is, it at least *may* have its place in an ideal order. What would be the universe without loyalty; and what would loyalty be without trial. ...

Religion, therefore, precisely in so far as it attempts to conceive the universe as a conscious and personal life of superhuman meaning, and as a life that is in close touch with our own meaning, is eternally true. But now it is just this *general view* of the universe as a rational order that is indeed open to our rational knowledge. No part of such a doctrine gives us, however, the present right as human beings to determine with any certainty the details of the world-life, except in so far as they come within the scope of our scientific and of our social inquiries. Hence, when religion, in the service of loyalty, interprets the world-life to us with symbolic detail, it gives us indeed merely symbols of the eternal truth. That this truth is indeed eternal, that our loyalty brings us into personal relations with a personal world-life, which values our every loyal deed, and needs that deed, all this is true and rational. And just this is what religion rightly illustrates.

13

How Does Religion Affect Personal Ethics?

Personal conduct has always been a concern of and an inspiration for religion. Religious codes of personal ethics typically take the form of "Thou shalt ..." and "Thou shalt not ..." commands, but their emphasis is more on building character and enhancing spirituality than on regulating behavior. In that respect they differ from secular legislation and even from some kinds of philosophical principles. The law just wants to be obeyed and does not care either whether people obey willingly or what people in other jurisdictions do, but religion wants every believer to obey willingly and wants everyone to be a believer. Obedience is not the same as reverence. Obedience is merely proper and often superficial; reverence is heartfelt.

The difference between ethics and morality is that the former is a set of principles while the latter is feelings or conduct according to such principles. Simply put, the law promotes obedience and wants to control behavior, philosophy promotes ethics and wants to awaken minds, and religion promotes morality and wants to develop feelings. Calvin expected believers to feel the righteousness of theocracy. Russian author and moralist Lev Tolstoi (1828-1910) preached in *The Law of Violence and the Law of Love* that world peace and human salvation alike depended upon each person's spiritual transformation toward non-violence. Austrian philosopher Ludwig Wittgenstein (1889-1951) lamented lack of reverence for life, asserting that if suicide is allowed, then everything is allowed.

In 1756 Hume prepared for the press "The Natural History of Religion," "Of the Passions," "Of Tragedy," "Of Suicide," and "Of the Immortality of the Soul" in a collection called *Five Dissertations*. Censors threatened to prosecute the publishers if the latter two essays were included, so Hume substituted "Of the Standard of Taste" and released the book in 1757 as *Four Dissertations*. The two suppressed anti-Christian essays first appeared almost "underground" one year posthumously in 1777 as *Two Essays* (nowadays a very scarce book) and definitively in 1783 as *Essays on Suicide, and the Immortality of the Soul*. Following is "On Suicide":

One considerable advantage that arises from Philosophy, consists in the sovereign antidote which it affords to superstition and false religion. All other remedies against that pestilent distemper are vain, or at least uncertain. Plain good sense and the practice of the world, which alone serve most purposes of life, are here found ineffectual: History, as well as daily experience, furnish instances of men endowed with the strongest capacity for business and affairs, who have all their lives crouched under slavery to the grossest superstition. Even gaiety and sweetness of temper, which infuse a balm into every other wound, afford no remedy to so virulent a poison; as we may particularly observe of the fair sex, who, tho' commonly possest of their rich presents of nature, feel many of their joys blasted by this importunate intruder. But when sound Philosophy has once gained possession of the mind, superstition is effectually excluded, and one may fairly affirm, that her triumph over this enemy is more complete than over most of the vices and imperfections incident to human nature. Love or anger, ambition or avarice, have their root in the temper and affections, which the soundest reason is scarce ever able fully to correct, but superstition being founded on false opinion, must immediately vanish when true philosophy has inspired juster sentiments of superior powers. The contest is here more equal between the distemper and the medicine; and nothing can hinder the latter from proving effectual, but its being false and sophisticated.

    It will here be superfluous to magnify the merits of Philosophy by displaying the pernicious tendency of that vice of which it cures the human mind. The superstitious man, says *Tully*, is miserable in every scene, in every incident in life; even sleep itself, which banishes all other cares of unhappy mortals, affords to him matter of new terror; while he examines his dreams, and finds in those visions of the night prognostications of future calamities. I may add, that tho' death alone can put a full period to his misery, he dares not fly to this refuge, but still prolongs a miserable existence, from a vain fear lest he offend his Maker, by using the power, with which that beneficent being has endowed him. The presents of God and Nature are ravished from us by this cruel enemy; and notwithstanding that one step would remove us from the regions of pain and sorrow, her menaces still chain us down to a hated being, which she herself chiefly contributes to render miserable.

    'Tis observed by such as have been reduced by the calamities of life to the necessity of employing this fatal remedy, that if the unseasonable care of their friends deprive them of that species of Death which they proposed to themselves, they seldom venture upon any other, or can summon up so much resolution a second time, as to execute their purpose. So great is our horror of death, that when it presents itself under any form, besides that to which a man has endeavoured to reconcile his imagination, it acquires new terrors, and overcomes his feeble courage: but when the menaces of superstition are joined to this natural timidity, no wonder it quite deprives men of all power over their lives, since even many pleasures and enjoyments, to which we are carried by a strong propensity, are torn from us by this inhuman tyrant. Let us here endeavour to restore men to their native liberty, by examining all the common arguments against Suicide, and shewing that that action may be free from every imputation of guilt or blame, according to the sentiments of all the antient philosophers.

If Suicide be criminal, it must be a transgression of our duty either to God, our neighbour, or ourselves. — To prove that Suicide is no transgression of our duty to God, the following considerations may perhaps suffice. In order to govern the material world, the almighty Creator has established general and immutable laws, by which all bodies, from the greatest planet to the smallest particle of matter, are maintained in their proper sphere and function. To govern the animal world, he has endowed all living creatures with bodily and mental powers; with senses, passions, appetites, memory, and judgement, by which they are impelled or regulated in that course of life to which they are destined. These two distinct principles of the material and animal world, continually encroach upon each other, and mutually retard or forward each other's operation. The powers of men and of all other animals are restrained and directed by the nature and qualities of the surrounding bodies; and the modifications and actions of these bodies are incessantly altered by the operation of all animals. Man is stopt by rivers in his passage over the surface of the earth; and rivers, when properly directed, lend their force to the motion of machines, which serve to the use of man. But tho' the provinces of the material and animal powers are not kept entirely separate, there results from thence no discord or disorder in the creation; on the contrary, from the mixture, union, and contrast of all the various powers of inanimate bodies and living creatures, arises that surprizing harmony, and proportion, which affords the surest argument of supreme wisdom.

The providence of the Deity appears not immediately in any operation, but governs every thing by those general and immutable laws, which have been established from the beginning of time. All events, in one sense, may be pronounced the action of the Almighty; they all proceed from those powers with which he has endowed his creatures. A house which falls by its own weight, is not brought to ruin by his providence, more than one destroyed by the hands of men; nor are the human faculties less his workmanship, than the laws of motion and gravitation. When the passions play, when the judgment dictates, when the limbs obey; this is all the operation of God, and upon these animate principles, as well as upon the inanimate, has he established the government of the universe.

Every event is alike important in the eyes of that infinite Being, who takes in at one glance the most distant regions of space, and remotest periods of time. There is no event, however important to us, which he has exempted from the general laws that govern the universe, or which he has peculiarly reserved for his own immediate action and operation. The revolution of states and empires depends upon the smallest caprice or passion of single men; and the lives of men are shortened or extended by the smallest accident of air or diet, sunshine or tempest. Nature still continues her progress and operation; and if general laws be ever broke by particular volitions of the Deity, 'tis after a manner which entirely escapes human observation. As, on the one hand, the elements and other inanimate parts of the creation carry on their action without regard to the particular interest and situation of men; so men are intrusted to their own judgment and discretion in the various shocks of matter, and may employ every faculty with which they are endowed, in order to provide for their ease, happiness, or preservation.

What is the meaning then of that principle, that a man, who, tired of life, and hunted by pain and misery, bravely overcomes all the natural terrors of death, and makes his escape from this cruel scene; that such a man, I say, has incurred the indignation of his Creator, by encroaching on the office of divine providence, and disturbing the order of the universe? Shall we assert, that the Almighty has reserved to himself, in any peculiar manner, the disposal of the lives of men, and has not submitted that event, in common with others, to the general laws by which the universe is governed? This is plainly false: the lives of men depend upon the same laws as the lives of all other animals; and these are subjected to the general laws of matter and motion. The fall of a tower, or the infusion of a poison, will destroy a man equally with the meanest creature; an inundation sweeps away every thing without distinction that comes within the reach of its fury. Since therefore the lives of men are for ever dependent on the general laws of matter and motion, is a man's disposing of his life criminal, because in every case it is criminal to encroach upon these laws, or disturb their operation? But this seems absurd: all animals are intrusted to their own prudence and skill for their conduct in the world; and have full authority as far as their power extends, to alter all the operations of nature. Without the excercise of this authority, they could not subsist a moment; every action, every motion of a man, innovates on the order of some parts of matter, and diverts from their ordinary course the general laws of motion. Putting together, therefore, these conclusions, we find *that* human life depends upon the general laws of matter and motion, and *that* it is no encroachment on the office of providence to disturb or alter these general laws: has not every one, of consequence, the free disposal of his own life? And may he not lawfully employ that power with which nature has endowed him?

In order to destroy the evidence of this conclusion, we must shew a reason why this particular case is excepted; is it because human life is of such great importance, that 'tis a presumption for human prudence to dispose of it? But the life of a man is of no greater importance to the universe than that of an oyster: and were it of ever so great importance, the order of human nature has actually submitted it to human prudence, and reduced us to a necessity, in every incident, of determining concerning it. — Were the disposal of human life so much reserved as the peculiar province of the Almighty, that it were an encroachment on his right, for men to dispose of their own lives; it would be equally criminal to act for the preservation of life as for its destruction. If I turn aside a stone which is falling upon my head, I disturb the course of nature, and I invade the peculiar province of the Almighty, by lengthening out my life beyond the period, which, by the general laws of matter and motion, he has assigned it.

A hair, a fly, an insect, is able to destroy this mighty being whose life is of such importance. Is it an absurdity to suppose that human prudence may lawfully dispose of what depends on such insignificant causes?

It would be no crime in me to divert the *Nile* or *Danube* from its course, were I able to effect such purposes. Where then is the crime of turning a few ounces of blood from their natural channels? — Do you imagine that I repine at Providence, or curse my creation, because I go out of life, and put a period to a being, which, were it to continue, would render me miserable? Far be such sentiments from me; I am only convinced of a matter of fact, which you yourself acknowledge possible, that human life may be unhappy; and that my existence, if further prolonged, would become ineligible: but I thank Providence, both for the good which I have already enjoyed, and for the power with which I am endowed of escaping the ill that threatens me. To you it belongs to repine at Providence, who foolishly imagine that you have no such power; and who must still prolong a hated life, tho' loaded with pain and sickness, with shame and poverty. — Do not you teach, that when any ill befalls me, tho' by the malice of my enemies, I ought to be resigned to Providence; and that the actions of men are the operations of the Almighty, as much as the actions of inanimate beings? When I fall upon my own sword, therefore, I receive my death equally from the hands of the Deity as if it had proceeded from a lion, a precipice, or a fever.

The submission which you require to Providence, in every calamity that befalls me, excludes not human skill and industry, if possibly by their means I can avoid or escape the calamity: And why may I not employ one remedy as well as another? — If my life be not my own, it were criminal for me to put it in danger, as well as to dispose of it; nor could one man deserve the appellation of *Hero*, whom glory or friendship transports into the greatest dangers, and another merit the reproach of *Wretch* or *Miscreant* who puts a period to his life, from the same or like motives.— There is no being, which possesses any power or faculty, that it receives not from its Creator; nor is there any one, which by ever so irregular an action, can encroach upon the plan of his Providence, or disorder the universe. Its operations are his works equally with that chain of events which it invades; and which ever principle prevails, we may for that very reason conclude it to be most favoured by him. Be it animate, or inanimate; rational, or irrational; 'tis all the same case: its power is still derived from the supreme Creator, and is alike comprehended in the order of his Providence. When the horror of pain prevails over the love of life; when a voluntary action anticipates the effects of blind causes; 'tis only in consequence of those powers and principles which he has implanted in his creatures. Divine Providence is still inviolate, and placed far beyond the reach of human injuries.

'Tis impious, says the old *Roman* superstition, to divert rivers from their course, or invade the prerogatives of nature. 'Tis impious, says the *French* superstition, to inoculate for the small-pox, or usurp the business of providence by voluntarily producing distempers and maladies. 'Tis impious, says the modern *European* superstition, to put a period to our own life, and thereby rebel against our Creator: and why not impious, say I, to build houses, cultivate the ground, or sail upon the ocean? In all these actions we employ our powers of mind and body, to produce some innovation in the course of nature; and in none of them do we any more. They are all of them therefore equally innocent, or equally criminal.

But you are placed by Providence, like a sentinel, in a particular station; and when you desert it without being recalled, you are equally guilty of rebellion against your Almighty Sovereign, and have incurred his displeasure. — I ask, Why do you conclude that Providence has placed me in this station? For my part, I find that I owe my birth to a long chain of causes, of which many depended upon voluntary actions of men. *But Providence guided all these causes, and nothing happens in the universe without its consent and coöperation.* If so, then neither does my death, however voluntary, happen without its consent; and whenever pain or sorrow so far overcome my patience, as to make me tired of life, I may conclude that I am recalled from my station in the clearest and most express terms.

'Tis Providence surely that has placed me at this present moment in this chamber: but may I not leave it when I think proper, without being liable to the imputation of having deserted my post or station? When I shall be dead, the principles of which I am composed will still perform their part in the universe, and will be equally useful in the grand fabrick, as when they composed this individual creature. The difference to the whole will be no greater than betwixt my being in a chamber and in the open air. The one change is of more importance to me than the other; but not more so to the universe.

'Tis a kind of blasphemy to imagine that any created being can disturb the order of the world, or invade the business of Providence! It supposes, that that being possesses powers and faculties, which it received not from its Creator, and which are not subordinate to his government and authority. A man may disturb society, no doubt, and thereby incur the displeasure of the Almighty: but the government of the world is placed far beyond his reach and violence. And how does it appear that the Almighty is displeased with those actions that disturb society? By the principles which he has implanted in human nature, and which inspire us with a sentiment of remorse if we ourselves have been guilty of such actions, and with that of blame and disapprobation, if we ever observe them in others: — Let us now examine, according to the method proposed, whether Suicide be of this kind of actions, and be a breach of our duty to our *neighbour* and to society.

A man who retires from life does no harm to society: he only ceases to do good; which, if it is an injury, is of the lowest kind. — All our obligations to do good to society seem to imply something reciprocal. I receive the benefits of society, and therefore ought to promote its interests; but when I withdraw myself altogether from society, can I be bound any longer?

But allowing that our obligations to do good were perpetual, they have certainly some bounds; I am not obliged to do a small good to society at the expense of a great harm to myself: why then should I prolong a miserable existence, because of some frivolous advantage which the public may perhaps receive from me? If upon account of age and infirmities, I may lawfully resign any office, and employ my time altogether in fencing against these calamities, and alleviating, as much as possible, the miseries of my future life; why may I not cut short these miseries at once by an action which is no more prejudicial to society? — But suppose that it is no longer in my power to promote the interest of the public; suppose that I am a burden to it; suppose that my life hinders some person from being much more useful to the public: in such cases, my resignation of life must not only be innocent, but laudable. And most people who lie under any temptation to abandon existence, are in some such situation; those who have health, or power, or authority, have commonly better reason to be in humour with the world.

A man is engaged in a conspiracy for the public interest; is seized upon suspicion; is threatened with the rack; and knows from his own weakness that the secret will be extorted from him: could such a one consult the public interest better than by putting a quick period to a miserable life? This was the case of the famous and brave [Filippo] *Strozzi* [1488-1538] of *Florence.* — Again, suppose a malefactor is justly condemned to a shameful death, can any reason be imagined, why he may not anticipate his punishment, and save himself all the anguish of thinking on its dreadful approaches? He invades the business of Providence no more than the magistrate did, who ordered his execution; and his voluntary death is equally advantageous to society, by ridding it of a pernicious member.

That Suicide may often be consistent with interest and with our duty to *ourselves*, no one can question, who allows that age, sickness, or misfortune, may render life a burthen, and make it worse even than annihilation. I believe that no man ever threw away life, while it was worth keeping. For such is our natural horror of death, that small motives will never be able to reconcile us to it; and though perhaps the situation of a man's health or fortune did not seem to require this remedy, we may at least be assured, that any one who, without apparent reason, has had recourse to it, was curst with such an incurable depravity or gloominess of temper as must poison all enjoyment, and render him equally miserable as if he had been loaded with the most grievous misfortunes. — If Suicide be supposed a crime, 'tis only cowardice can impel us to it. If it be no crime, both prudence and courage should engage us to rid ourselves at once of existence, when it becomes a burthen. 'Tis the only way that we can then be useful to society, by setting an example, which, if imitated, would preserve to every one his chance for happiness in life, and would effectually free him from all danger of misery.

Mill's *On Liberty* (1859), a classic in liberal political theory, has among its topics the degree of constraint which individuals may reasonably expect religion to put on them in their everyday lives, social encounters, or ethical decisions. This excerpt is from Chapter Four, "Of the Limits to the Authority of Society over the Individual":

What ... is the rightful limit to the sovereignty of the individual over himself? Where does the authority of society begin? How much of human life should be assigned to individuality, and how much to society?

 Each will receive its proper share, if each has that which more particularly concerns it. To individuality should belong the part of life in which it is chiefly the individual that is interested; to society, the part which chiefly interests society.

 Though society is not founded on a contract, and though no good purpose is answered by inventing a contract in order to deduce social obligations from it, every one who receives the protection of society owes a return for the benefit, and the fact of living in society renders it indispensable that each should be bound to observe a certain line of conduct towards the rest. This conduct consists first, in not injuring the interests of one another; or rather certain interests, which, either by express legal provision or by tacit understanding, ought to be considered as rights; and secondly, in each person's bearing his share (to be fixed on some equitable principle) of the labours and sacrifices incurred for defending the society or its members from injury and molestation. These conditions society is justified in enforcing at all costs to those who endeavour to withhold fulfilment. ... As soon as any part of a person's conduct affects prejudicially the interests of others, society has jurisdiction over it, and the question whether the general welfare will or will not be promoted by interfering with it, becomes open to discussion. But there is no room for entertaining any such question when a person's conduct affects the interests of no persons besides himself, or needs not affect them unless they like (all the persons concerned being of full age, and the ordinary amount of understanding). In all such cases there should be perfect freedom, legal and social, to do the action and stand the consequences.

It would be a great misunderstanding of this doctrine to suppose that it is one of selfish indifference, which pretends that human beings have no business with each other's conduct in life, and that they should not concern themselves about the well-doing or well-being of one another, unless their own interest is involved. Instead of any diminution, there is need of a great increase of disinterested exertion to promote the good of others. But disinterested benevolence can find other instruments to persuade people to their good, than whips and scourges, either of the literal or the metaphorical sort. ...

Whoever fails in the consideration generally due to the interests and feelings of others, not being compelled by some more imperative duty, or justified by allowable self-preference, is a subject of moral disapprobation for that failure, but not for the cause of it, nor for the errors, merely personal to himself, which may have remotely led to it. In like manner, when a person disables himself, by conduct purely self-regarding, from the performance of some definite duty incumbent on him to the public, he is guilty of a social offence. No person ought to be punished simply for being drunk; but a soldier or a policeman should be punished for being drunk on duty. Whenever, in short, there is a definite damage, or a definite risk of damage, either to an individual or to the public, the case is taken out of the province of liberty, and placed in that of morality or law. ...

Armed not only with all the powers of education, but with the ascendancy which the authority of a received opinion always exercises over the minds who are least fitted to judge for themselves; and aided by the *natural* penalties which cannot be prevented from falling on those who incur the distaste or the contempt of those who know them; let not society pretend that it needs, besides all this, the power to issue commands and enforce obedience in the personal concerns of individuals, in which, on all principles of justice and policy, the decision ought to rest with those who are to abide the consequences. Nor is there anything which tends more to discredit and frustrate the better means of influencing conduct, than a resort to the worse. If there be among those whom it is attempted to coerce into prudence or temperance, any of the material of which vigorous and independent characters are made, they will infallibly rebel against the yoke. No such person will ever feel that others have a right to control him in his concerns, such as they have to prevent him from injuring them in theirs; and it easily comes to be considered a mark of spirit and courage to fly in the face of such usurped authority, and do with ostentation the exact opposite of what it enjoins; as in the fashion of grossness which succeeded, in the time of Charles II, to the fanatical moral intolerance of the Puritans. With respect to what is said of the necessity of protecting society from the bad example set to others by the vicious or the self-indulgent; it is true that bad example may have a pernicious effect, especially the example of doing wrong to others with impunity to the wrong-doer. But we are now speaking of conduct which, while it does no wrong to others, is supposed to do great harm to the agent himself: and I do not see how those who believe this, can think otherwise than that the example, on the whole, must be more salutary than hurtful, since, if it displays the misconduct, it displays also the painful or degrading consequences which, if the conduct is justly censured, must be supposed to be in all or most cases attendant on it.

But the strongest of all the arguments against the interference of the public with purely personal conduct, is that when it does interfere, the odds are that it interferes wrongly, and in the wrong place. On questions of social morality, of duty to others, the opinion of the public, that is, of an overruling majority, though often wrong, is likely to be still oftener right; because on such questions they are only required to judge of their own interests; of the manner in which some mode of conduct, if allowed to be practised, would affect themselves. But the opinion of a similar majority, imposed as a law on the minority, on questions of self-regarding conduct, is quite as likely to be wrong as right; for in these cases public opinion means, at the best, some people's opinion of what is good or bad for other people; while very often it does not even mean that; the public, with the most perfect indifference, passing over the pleasure or convenience of those whose conduct they censure, and considering only their own preference. There are many who consider as an injury to themselves any conduct which they have a distaste for, and resent it as an outrage to their feelings; as a religious bigot, when charged with disregarding the religious feelings of others, has been known to retort that they disregard his feelings, by persisting in their abominable worship or creed. But there is no parity between the feeling of a person for his own opinion, and the feeling of another who is offended at his holding it; no more than between the desire of a thief to take a purse, and the desire of the right owner to keep it. And a person's taste is as much his own peculiar concern as his opinion or his purse. It is easy for any one to imagine an ideal public, which leaves the freedom and choice of individuals in all uncertain matters undisturbed, and only requires them to abstain from modes of conduct which universal experience has condemned. But where has there been seen a public which set any such limit to its censorship? or when does the public trouble itself about universal experience? In its interferences with personal conduct it is seldom thinking of anything but the enormity of acting or feeling differently from itself; and this standard of judgment, thinly disguised, is held up to mankind as the dictate of religion and philosophy, by nine-tenths of all moralists and speculative writers. These teach that things are right because they are right; because we feel them to be so. They tell us to search in our own minds and hearts for laws of conduct binding on ourselves and on all others. What can the poor public do but apply these instructions, and make their own personal feelings of good and evil, if they are tolerably unanimous in them, obligatory on all the world?

The evil here pointed out is not one which exists only in theory; and it

may perhaps be expected that I should specify the instances in which the public of this age and country improperly invests its own preferences with the character of moral laws. ... And it is not difficult to show, by abundant instances, that to extend the bounds of what may be called moral police, until it encroaches on the most unquestionably legitimate liberty of the individual, is one of the most universal of all human propensities.

As a first instance, consider the antipathies which men cherish on no better grounds than that persons whose religious opinions are different from theirs, do not practise their religious observances, especially their religious abstinences. To cite a rather trivial example, nothing in the creed or practice of Christians does more to envenom the hatred of Mahomedans against them, than the fact of their eating pork. There are few acts which Christians and Europeans regard with more unaffected disgust, than Mussulmans regard this particular mode of satisfying hunger. It is, in the first place, an offence against their religion; but this circumstance by no means explains either the degree or the kind of their repugnance; for wine also is forbidden by their religion, and to partake of it is by all Mussulmans accounted wrong, but not disgusting. Their aversion to the flesh of the "unclean beast" is, on the contrary, of that peculiar character, resembling an instinctive antipathy, which the idea of uncleanness, when once it thoroughly sinks into the feelings, seems always to excite even in those whose personal habits are anything but scrupulously cleanly, and of which the sentiment of religious impurity, so intense in the Hindoos, is a remarkable example. Suppose now that in a people, of whom the majority were Mussulmans, that majority should insist upon not permitting pork to be eaten within the limits of the country. This would be nothing new in Mahomedan countries. Would it be a legitimate exercise of the moral authority of public opinion? and if not, why not? The practice is really revolting to such a public. They also sincerely think that it is forbidden and abhorred by the Deity. Neither could the prohibition be censured as religious persecution. It might be religious in its origin, but it would not be persecution for religion, since nobody's religion makes it a duty to eat pork. The only tenable ground of condemnation would be, that with the personal tastes and self-regarding concerns of individuals the public has no business to interfere.

To come somewhat nearer home: the majority of Spaniards consider it a gross impiety, offensive in the highest degree to the Supreme Being, to worship him in any other manner than the Roman Catholic; and no other public worship is lawful on Spanish soil. The people of all Southern Europe look upon a married clergy as not only irreligious, but unchaste, indecent, gross, disgusting. What do Protestants think of these perfectly sincere feelings, and of the attempt to enforce them against non-Catholics? Yet, if mankind are justified in interfering with each other's liberty in things which do not concern the interests of others, on what principle is it possible consistently to exclude these cases? or who can blame people for desiring to suppress what they regard as a scandal in the sight of God and man? No stronger case can be shown for prohibiting anything which is regarded as a personal immorality, than is made out for suppressing these practices in the eyes of those who regard them as impieties; and unless we are willing to adopt the logic of persecutors, and to say that we may persecute others because we are right, and that they must not persecute us because they are wrong, we must beware of admitting a principle of which we should resent as a gross injustice the application to ourselves.

The preceding instances may be objected to, although unreasonably, as drawn from contingencies impossible among us: opinion, in this country, not being likely to enforce abstinence from meats, or to interfere with people for worshipping, and for either marrying or not marrying, according to their creed or inclination. The next example, however, shall be taken from an interference with liberty which we have by no means passed all danger of. Wherever the Puritans have been sufficiently powerful, as in New England, and in Great Britain at the time of the Commonwealth, they have endeavoured, with considerable success, to put down all public, and nearly all private, amusements: especially music, dancing, public games, or other assemblages for purposes of diversion, and the theatre. ... How will the remaining portion of the community like to have the amusements that shall be permitted to them regulated by the religious and moral sentiments of the stricter Calvinists and Methodists? Would they not, with considerable peremptoriness, desire these intrusively pious members of society to mind their own business? This is precisely what should be said to every government and every public, who have the pretension that no person shall enjoy any pleasure which they think wrong. But if the principle of the pretension be admitted, no one can reasonably object to its being acted on in the sense of the majority, or other preponderating power in the country; and all persons must be ready to conform to the idea of a Christian commonwealth, as understood by the early settlers in New England, if a religious profession similar to theirs should ever succeed in regaining its lost ground, as religions supposed to be declining have so often been known to do. ...

It remains to be proved that society or any of its officers holds a commission from on high to avenge any supposed offence to Omnipotence, which is not also a wrong to our fellow creatures. The notion that it is one man's duty that another should be religious, was the foundation of all the religious persecutions ever perpetrated, and if admitted, would fully justify them. Though the feeling which breaks out in the repeated attempts to stop railway travelling on Sunday ... and the like, has not the cruelty of the old persecutors, the state of mind indicated by it is fundamentally the same. It is a determination not to tolerate others in doing what is permitted by their religion, because it is not permitted by the persecutor's religion. It is a belief that God not only abominates the act of the misbeliever, but will not hold us guiltless if we leave him unmolested. ...

14

How Does Religion Affect Social Ethics?

Believers may interpret each respective religion however they please, or however their God, priests, or theologians tell them to interpret it. If this were as far as religious belief went, there would be nothing objectionable in it. On the other hand, religion is not only belief and devotion, but also practice. Belief and devotion are private or internal dimensions of religion, and can safely be unbounded; but practice is a public or external dimension, and any believer's right or justification to practice religion ends wherever it conflicts with another believer's practice or with more nearly universal values of ethics, morality, comportment, decency, or culture as encoded in law, philosophy, or common human consensus.

For example, consider the mass murder of September 11, 2001 as a religious event. The perpetrators of this gigantic crime apparently believed sincerely that their interpretation of Islam was correct. They apparently regarded their attacks as ultimate expressions of religious devotion and sacrifice. If their version of Islam were correct, then Islam would be a barbaric, despicable religion, because all religions must be subject to the universal command that killing innocent human beings is always wrong. Several passages in the Koran assert precisely and unequivocally this very command. Thus Osama bin Laden and all the planners of surprise attacks on civilians in the name of Islam should have re-examined their interpretation of Islam before acting disastrously on its behalf, because their final decision was clearly wrong, evil, and un-Islamic.

In the scriptures of many religions are passages where the command of God comes into conflict with human moral laws or ethical principles. These passages most often concern killing, and typically provide divine excuses for believers to kill in certain circumstances, or to prove their devotion by killing. In the *Bhagavad Gita*, the warrior Arjuna learned that fulfilling his duty, or being true to his karma as a warrior, entailed not only killing, but killing abundantly and efficiently, without regard for the humanity of the enemy, in order to win the battle, even though killing is a sin for non-warriors. Yahweh punished Saul for showing mercy and allowing looting rather than obeying the divine command to annihilate the Amalekites (1 Sam. 15:2-23). Agamemnon murdered his daughter Iphigenia to win the favor of the gods as he launched his fleet toward Troy. Abraham, no different in intent from Agamemnon, resolved to murder his son Isaac for God's sake — but at the last moment God stayed his hand (Gen. 22:2-12). For all major religions, some kinds of killing are permitted, and some wars are just.

Following Aristotle and Thomas Aquinas, G. Scott Davis in *Warcraft and the Fragility of Virtue* (1992) lists five criteria for launching a just war, that is, criteria for determining whether the war in question is just or unjust:

1. Legitimate authority — The side that starts the war must comprise a duly constituted government.

2. Just cause — The side that starts the war must have a clear and specific objective that meets the standard of general principles of ethics.

3. Just intent — The side that starts the war must desire that the worldwide or regional situation show a net improvement because of the war.

4. Last resort — The side that starts the war must have exhausted all other possibilities for resolving the dispute.

5. Reasonable chance of success — The side that starts the war must not be suicidal, or willing to inflict undue suffering on its own people.

To these a sixth can be added, namely, that any side which finds itself the victim of an injust invasion or war of aggression has the right to defend itself by going to war in retaliation.

By these six criteria, few sides ever had better justification for war than the North in the American Civil War, America in World War II, or the United Nations coalition in the Persian Gulf War of 1990-1991. By the same criteria — a violation of only one of the six being sufficient to render a war unjust — America in the Vietnam War, in which it tried to prop up an illegitimate foreign government without reasonable chance of success, was an unjust combatant.

The "God-is-on-our-side" mentality that is so often felt in times of war fails to consider the humanity of the enemy. This is acceptable if the enemy truly lacks humanity, as did Hitler; but usually it is wrong because its insularity gives a false picture of the world. Similar arguments could be made for theocracy, henotheism, and any nationalistic fanaticism that exploits religion.

Social ethics must avoid being grounded in the particular, but should strive toward consonance with the universal. To regard the smaller, narrower, more particular groups in which we find ourselves as more important or more worthy of allegiance than the larger, broader, more nearly universal groups to which we also belong is ethically problematic. For example, to put the interests of one's country above those of humanity in general is wrong. If something seems good for one's country, but is bad for humanity, then it is bad for the country. If something seems good for one's religion, but is bad for humanity, then it is bad for the religion. Countries and religions are non-natural institutions to which individuals can choose to belong or not. Our membership in all categories except the biological ones and especially the full category of humanity is voluntary. That is an important point. We are humans first, and in every other earthly category second. If any religion seems to point toward behavior, such as murder, that denies our essential humanity, then either it is not a good religion or the believer's reasoning is faulty.

One's conscience should not only be clear, but oriented as nearly toward the universal as possible. Even such natural opponents in ethical theory as Kant, with his categorical imperative to be obeyed heedless of social consequences, and Hegel, with his socially grounded ethics (*Sittlichkeit*) ultimately dependent upon the gradual discovery of absolute law in history, can agree on this point. For both Kant and Hegel, true religion, i.e., the religion which is most nearly in accord with philosophy, will always preach against singling out some groups for special favors and others for contempt. As Coleridge wrote in *The Rime of the Ancient Mariner*, lines 614-617: "He prayeth best, who loveth best / All things both great and small; / For the dear God who loveth us, / He made and loveth all."

Families are a special case. Although to know whether to owe primary allegience to one's nuclear family or to one's religion, country, or race is often difficult, the best interests of humanity should in general trump all other best interests, even those of the family. Yet attempts to destroy the family, from either within or without, should usually be resisted. Missionary religions, which seek to convert those who may already be perfectly comfortable in their own religion and have no spiritual need to be converted, may encourage new believers to abandon or repudiate their nuclear families in order to follow the religion. This practice is probably always unethical. Fortunately the best interests of the family more often coincide with those of humanity than with those of religion or the state.

Any socially responsible religion must enter some kind of constructive encounter with natural science, not necessarily agreeing with all its findings, but still allowing it to flourish unhindered by dogma. Reciprocally, natural science must not try to dictate religious truth, must acknowledge that spirituality lies beyond empirical study, and must mediate through philosophy any rapprochement between religion and itself. When science and religion interact without the benefit of philosophy to keep them each in check, the result is often disastrous for humanity. A case in point is the venture into religion of German biologist Ernst Heinrich Philipp August Haeckel (1834-1919), who used evolutionary theory not only for science, but also as a sort of religion to bolster his own racism and thus to lay the ideological foundations of what would later become Nazism.

Kant's ineffable triad in metaphysics of God, freedom, and immortality is mirrored by another ineffable triad in social ethics: peace, love, and understanding. Each of the two triads shows the minimal conditions or axioms under which, respectively, metaphysics and social ethics may thrive. They cannot be explained exhaustively or even defined adequately, but nor can they be denied. What is good for humanity must be the final determinant of human ethical action. To act so is not necessarily a utilitarian serving of the greatest good for the greatest number. It could just as well be seen as either a Kantian deontological adherence to absolute moral duty as written in the divine law or an Aristotelian upholding of classical human virtue. In other words, we act for the sake of the greater good of humanity because it is right, by either religious or secular criteria, not because of any anticipated consequences.

For Mill and many subsequent secular thinkers, a demythologized, deritualized, or desanctified religion would reduce to a code of ethics. In the following excerpt from "Fraternity," Chapter Six of *Liberty, Equality, Fraternity*, Fitzjames Stephen compares religion based on morality, as he interprets Mill, with his own position of morality based on religion:

I cannot but think that many persons must share the feeling of disgust with which I for one have often read and listened to expressions of general philanthropy. Such love is frequently an insulting intrusion. ... I know hardly anything in literature so nauseous as Rousseau's expressions of love for mankind when read in the light of his confessions. "Keep your love to yourself, and do not daub me or mine with it," is the criticism which his books always suggest to me. ... It is not love that one wants from the great mass of mankind, but respect and justice. ...

This worship and service of humanity in the abstract are taught in many shapes. The one which I propose to examine is to be found in Mr. Mill's essay on Utilitarianism. It shares the merit which is characteristic of all his writings of being the gravest, the clearest, and the most measured statement with which I, at all events, am acquainted of the dogmatic form of the popular sentiment. ...

He thinks otherwise than I of men and of human life in general. He appears to believe that if men are all freed from restraints and put, as far as possible, on an equal footing, they will naturally treat each other as brothers, and work together harmoniously for their common good. I believe that many men are bad, a vast majority of men indifferent, and many good, and that the great mass of indifferent people sway this way or that according to circumstances, one of the most important of which circumstances is the predominance for the time being of the bad or good. I further believe that between all classes of men there are and always will be real occasions of enmity and strife, and that even good men may be and often are compelled to treat each other as enemies either by the existence of conflicting interests which bring them into collision, or by their different ways of conceiving goodness. ...

To say to a man who is grossly sensual, false all through, coldly cruel and ungrateful, and absolutely incapable of caring for anyone but himself, We, for reasons which satisfy us, will in various ways discourage and stigmatize your way of life, and in some cases punish you for living according to your nature, is to speak in an intelligible, straightforward way. To say to him, We act thus because we love you, and with a view to your own happiness, appears to me to be a double untruth. In the first place, I for one do not love such people, but hate them. In the second place, if I wanted to make them happy, which I do not, I should do so by pampering their vices, which I will not. ...

The point at which Mr. Mill and I should part company is his belief that this natural feeling for oneself and one's friends, gradually changing its character, is sublimated into a general love for the human race; and in that shape is capable of forming a new religion, of which we need only fear that it may be too strong for human liberty and individuality. ...

In general terms I think that morality depends upon religion — that is to say, upon the opinions which men entertain as to matters of fact, and particularly as to God and a future state of existence — and that it is incapable of being in itself a religion binding on mankind at large. I think that if we entirely dismiss from our minds not only the belief that there are, but a doubt whether there may not be, a God and a future state, the morality of people in general, and in particular the view which people in general will take of their relation to others, will have to be changed. I admit that in the case of a few peculiarly constituted persons it may be otherwise, but I think that minds so constituted as to be capable of converting morality pure and simple into a religion by no means deserve unqualified admiration. I think that the disposition and power to do so is in many instances a case not of strength but of weakness, and that it almost always involves a considerable amount of self-deception. ...

Mr. Mill's theory is ... that the progress of civilization will lead people to feel a general love for mankind so strong that it will in process of time assume the character of a religion, and have an influence greater than that of all existing religions. Mr. Mill admits that the feeling is at present an exceptional one. ...

The believer in the religion of fraternity ... is bound to love all mankind. If he wants me to do so too, he must show me a reason why. Not only does he show me none, as a rule, but he generally denies either the truth or the relevancy of that which, if true, is a reason — the doctrine that God made all men and ordered them to love each other. Whether this is true is one question; how it is proposed to get people to love each other without such a belief I do not understand. It would want the clearest of all imaginable revelations to make me to try to love a considerable number of people whom it is unnecessary to mention, or affect to care about masses of men with whom I have nothing to do. ...

The general result of all this is, that fraternity, mere love for the human race, is not fitted in itself to be a religion. That is to say, it is not fitted to take command of the human faculties, to give them their direction, and to assign to one faculty a rank in comparison with others which but for such interference it would not have.

I might have ... pointed out that the most elementary notions of religion imply that no one human faculty or passion can ever in itself be a religion. It can but be one among many competitors. If human beings are left to themselves, their faculties, their wishes, and their passions will find a level of some sort or other. They will produce some common course of life and some social arrangement. Alter the relative strength of particular passions, and you will alter the social result, but religion means a great deal more than this. It means the establishment and general recognition of some theory about human life in general, about the relation of men to each other and to the world, by which their conduct may be determined. Every religion must contain an element of fact, real or supposed, as well as an element of feeling, and the element of fact is the one which in the long run will determine the nature and importance of the element of feeling. The following are specimens of religions, stated as generally as possible, but still with sufficient exactness to show my meaning.

I. The statements made in the Apostles' Creed are true. Believe them, and govern yourselves accordingly.

2. There is one God, and Mahomet is the prophet of God. Do as

Mahomet tells you.

3. All existence is an evil, from which, if you knew your own mind, you would wish to be delivered. Such and such a course of life will deliver you most speedily from the misery of existence.

4. An infinitely powerful supreme God arranged all of you whom I address in castes, each with its own rule of life. You will be fearfully punished in all sorts of ways if you do not live according to your caste rules. Also all nature is full of invisible powers more or less connected with natural objects, which must be worshipped and propitiated.

All these are religions in the proper sense of the word. Each of the four theories expressed in these few words is complete in itself. It states propositions which are either true or false, but which, if true, furnish a complete practical guide for life. No such statement of what Mr. Mill calls the ultimate sanction of the morals of utility is possible. You cannot get more than this out of it: "Love all mankind." "Influences are at work which at some remote time will make men love each other." These are respectively a piece of advice and a prophecy, but they are not religions. If a man does not take the advice or believe in the prophecy, they pass by him idly. ...

It is not very easy to insist upon the connection between morals and religion without running the risk of falling into very obvious commonplace; but the extent to which the habit prevails of maintaining that morals are independent of religion makes it necessary to point out that it is impossible to solve anyone of the great questions which the word "fraternity" suggests without distinct reference to the fundamental questions of religion.

First, fraternity implies love for some one — a desire to promote some one's happiness. But what is happiness? In particular, is anything which can properly be called virtue essential to it? — if so, what is virtue — the way of life which becomes a man? Every answer which can be given to these questions depends upon the further question, What are men? Is this life all, or is it only a stage in something wider and larger? The great disproportion which exists between the stronger and more abiding human feelings and the objects to which they relate has often been used as an argument in favour of immortality. Whether it is entitled to weight in that capacity I need not enquire, but the fact on which the inference is based is, I think, certain. We do care far more about all sorts of things and people than is at all rational if this life is all; and I think that if we dismiss from our minds every thought of life after death, if we determine to regard the grave as the end of all things, it will be not merely natural and proper to contract our sympathies and interests, and to revise the popular estimate of the comparative value of many things — health, for instance, and honesty — but not to do so will be simply impossible. ...

If ... there is a Providence, then morality ceases to be a mere fact and becomes a law. The very meaning of a belief in a Providence is that the physical and the moral world alike are the sphere of conscious arrangement and design; that men, the members of the moral world, transcend the material world in which they are placed, and that the law imposed on them is this — Virtue, that is to say, the habit of acting upon principles fitted to promote the happiness of men in general, and especially those forms of happiness which have reference to the permanent element in men, is connected with, and will, in the long run, contribute to the individual happiness of those who practise it, and especially to that part of their happiness which is connected with the permanent elements of their nature. The converse is true of vice.

This law is unwritten and unspoken, and its sanctions (except for those who believe in a definite literal heaven and hell) are indefinite. These circumstances constitute the moral trial of life, and no doubt immensely diminish the force of the law in question, and enable anyone who is disposed to do so to deny its very existence. If, however, a man is led to accept this interpretation of life, it affords a real sanction for morals. I cannot understand how a person who believed that a Being capable of arranging the physical and moral world as we know it, had by so arranging it tacitly commanded him thus to act, could hesitate about the wisdom of obeying that command.

Utilitarianism appears to me to rest on its own foundations. It is a consequence from the ultimate fact that men have powers and wishes. Add a future state, and you give to happiness a special meaning, and establish a scale among different kinds of happiness. Add a belief in God, and virtue ceases to be a mere fact, and becomes the law of a society, the members of which may by a strong metaphor be called brothers if and in so far as they obey that law. Virtue as a law implies social relations, and the law "Be virtuous" can hardly be obeyed except by a person who wishes good men to be happy, and who also wishes to some extent to make men good. Take away the belief in a future state, and belief in God ceases to be of any practical importance. Happiness means whatever each man likes. Morality becomes a mere statement as to facts — this is what you can get if you want it, and this is the way to get it. Love for mankind becomes a matter of taste, sanctioned by the fear of being called a fool or a brute, as the case may be, by people who do not agree with you.

These two ways of looking at the world and at morais are both complete, consistent, intelligible, and based upon facts. The practical distinction between them is that the first does and the second does not give a rational account of the feeling that it is a duty to be virtuous. If virtue is God's law, to be virtuous is man's duty. Where there is no lawgiver there can be no law; where there is no law there can be no duty, though of course there may be a taste for doing what, if there were a law, would be a duty. This taste may, for what I know, be inherited. I think it a mere question of curiosity whether it is or not, for when a man learns that his sense of duty is a mere fact which, however convenient to others, is apt to be very inconvenient to him, and rests upon nothing, he will easily get rid of it. ... Duty is so very often inconvenient that it requires a present justification as well as an historical explanation, and no such justification can be given to a man who wants one except that God is a legislator and virtue a law in the proper sense of the word.

It would be a matter of equal difficulty and interest to trace out systematically the relation of religious belief to a sense of duty. The relation, of course, depends upon the nature of the religion. Some forms of religion are distinctly unfavourable to a sense of social duty. ...

Though the sense of duty which is justified by this form of religion has become instinctive with many of those who feel it, I think that if the belief should ever fail, the sense of duty which grows out of it would die by degrees. I do not believe that any instinct will long retain its hold upon the conduct of a rational and enterprising man when he has discovered that it is a mere instinct which he need not yield to unless he chooses. People who think otherwise would do well to remember that, though custom makes some duties so easy to some people that they are discharged as a matter of course, there are others which it is extremely difficult to discharge at all; and that obvious immediate self-interest, in its narrowest shape, is constantly eating away the edges of morality, and would destroy it if it had not something deeper for its support than an historical or physiological explanation. We cannot judge of the effects of Atheism from the conduct of persons who have been educated as believers in God and in the midst of a nation which believes in God. If we should ever see a generation of men, especially a generation of Englishmen, to whom the word God had ho meaning at all, we should get a light upon the subject which might be lurid enough. Great force of character, restrained and directed by a deep sense of duty, is the noblest of noble things. Take off the restraint which a sense of duty imposes, and the strong man is apt to become a mere tyrant and oppressor. ...

God, himself, some people seem to feel, must recognize human equality, the equal right of human creatures to happiness, and if men are not equal in fact, it is because they are the product not of will, but of blind chance. Rather than acknowledge a God who does not acknowledge the equality of men, let us, they say, acknowledge no God at all, and establish human equality as far as we can, in despite of the blind fate to which we owe our origin, and which we do not and will not reverence. Man in the future, Man as we would have him, is the object of our reverence and love; not any thing or anyone who is outside of Man, least of all anyone who is in any way responsible for what we see around us. ...

If the order which we observe in the physical universe and in the moral world suggests to us the existence of God, we must not shrink from the inference that the character of God, in so far as we have anything to do with it, is to be inferred from that order. To say that the Author of such a world is a purely benevolent being is, to my mind, to say something which is not true, or, at the very least, something which is highly improbable in itself, impossible to be proved, and inconsistent with many notorious facts, except upon hypotheses which it is hardly possible to state or to understand, and of which there is absolutely no evidence whatever. Therefore, to the question, "Admitting the existence of God, do you believe him to be good?" I should reply, If by "good" you mean "disposed to promote the happiness of mankind absolutely," I answer No. If by "good" you mean virtuous, I reply, The question has no meaning. A virtuous man is a being of whom we can form an idea more or less distinct, but the ideas of virtue and vice can hardly be attached to a Being who transcends all or most of the conditions out of which virtue and vice arise. If the further question is asked, Then what moral attributes do you ascribe to this Being, if you ascribe to him any at all? I should reply, I think of him as conscious and having will, as infinitely powerful, and as one who, whatever he may be in his own nature, has so arranged the world or worlds in which I live as to let me know that virtue is the law which he has prescribed to me and to others. If still further asked, Can you love such a Being? I should answer, Love is not the word which I should choose, but awe. The law under which we live is stern, and, as far as we can judge, inflexible, but it is noble and excites a feeling of awful respect for its Author and for the constitution established in the world which it governs, and a sincere wish to act up to and carry it out as far as possible. If we believe in God at all, this, I think, is the rational and manly way of thinking of him.

This leads to the further question how belief in such a Being would affect a man's view of this present life. Would not such a belief, it may be said, justify and sanctify much of the injustice and many of the wrongs of life? To this I answer thus. The general constitution of things, by which some people are better off than others, and some very badly off in all respects, is neither just nor unjust, right nor wrong. It simply is. It affects the question of the benevolence, not the question of the justice, of its author. The idea of justice and right is subsequent to the idea of law. ... As against God or fate, whichever you please, men have no rights at all, not even the right of existence. Right, wrong, and obligation begin after laws, properly so called, have been established, and the first laws, properly so called, which we have any reason to believe to exist are moral laws imposed upon beings, of whom some are far more favourably situated for keeping them than others. All moral codes and customs are so many different versions, more or less correct and more or less fully expressed, of these laws. ...

The answer, then, to the question, How does a belief in God thus explained affect our view of human life? is this: Every man born into the world finds himself placed in a position in which he has a variety of wants, passions, faculties, and powers of various kinds, and in which some objects better or worse are attainable by him. The religious theory of life may be thrown into the shape of the following command or advice: Do the best you can for yourselves, but do it in a definitely prescribed manner and not otherwise, or it will be the worse for you. Some of you are happy; it is the better for them. Some are miserable; by all means let them help themselves in the appointed manner; let others help them on the appointed terms, but when all is done much will remain to bear. Bear it as you can, and whether in happiness or in misery, take with you the thought that the strange world in which you live seems not to be all, and that you yourselves who are in it are not altogether of it. ...

This does not show or tend to show that there is a God, but only that the belief in God is not immoral. That belief is immoral only if the unreserved acceptance of the terms on which life is offered to us, and an honest endeavour to live upon those terms are immoral. If some theory about human happiness and equality and fraternity makes it our duty to kick against the pricks, to live as rebels against that, whatever it is, in which we find ourselves, a belief in God is immoral but not otherwise. To my mind the immoral and unmanly thing is revolt, impatience of inevitable evils, gratuitous indiscriminate affection for all sorts of people, whether they deserve it or not, and in particular, a weak, ill-regulated sympathy for those whose sufferings are their own fault. These are sufferings which I, for one, should not wish either to relieve or to avert. I would leave the law to take its course. Why there should be wicked people in the world is like the question, Why there should be poisonous snakes in the world? Though no men are absolutely good or absolutely bad, yet if and in so far as men are good and bad they are not brothers but enemies, or, if the expression is preferred, they are brothers at enmity whose enmity must continue till its cause is removed. ...

It must also be borne in mind that, though Christianity expresses the tender and charitable sentiments with passionate ardour, it has also a terrible side. Christian love is only for a time and on condition. It stops short at the gates of hell, and hell is an essential part of the whole Christian scheme. Whether we look at the formal doctrines or at the substance of that scheme, the tenderness and the terrors mutually imply each other. There would be something excessive in such an outpouring of sympathy and sorrow about mere transitory sufferings, which do not appear after all to have been specially acute or specially unrelieved with happiness in Judaea in the first century. The horrors of the doctrine of hell would have been too great for human endurance if the immediate manifestations of the religion had not been tender and compassionate. ...

Many professions besides just the ministry are integrally connected to religion. Chief among them is medicine. Patients and their loved ones facing serious illness, injury, or end-of-life issues often have recourse to the comfort of religion, and physicians must be ready for this common but highly varied phenomenon and supportive of it in all its manifestations. The best physician is not only a superb clinical technician, but also one who can minister gently, wisely, and respectfully to frightened and troubled people in absolute confidence and with much the same degree of emotional intimacy that is typical of consultations with clergy. Such a physician must be sensitive and impartial to each patient's most deeply held religious convictions, should write in each patient's chart a clear description of these convictions, and, prior to crisis, should discuss with the patient all possible medical conflicts with them.

Some religions prohibit certain medical or surgical procedures, such as blood transfusion, that they admit may save physical lives but believe will destroy spiritual lives. Some religions insist on using only their own methods of medical treatment, even though these methods may be at odds with mainstream medical science. Patients, as believers in such doctrines, must each be helped to choose serenely their own most appropriate treatments, with all relevant information available and, optimally, with the full support of their loved ones. Each competent patient is free to refuse any prescribed treatment, and physicians must be ready for that too. The physician's own religious belief, or lack of it, should never become an issue in medical practice. The physician's first duty is to the patient, which means attending to each patient with the greatest possible respect, beneficence, and skill, and above all with no condescension toward what the physician may privately see as the patient's silly religion.

The physician's work is not just to create medical or surgical conditions by which the body may heal itself, but also to promote the spiritual processes by which patients either recover their health or grow to accept death, and by which their loved ones either energize the recovery or complete the whole course of grieving as placidly as possible. Canadian physician William Osler (1849-1919), one of the finest clinicians of his age and an outstanding philosopher of medicine, offered sound spiritual as well as medical advice in an address to Albany Medical College students in 1899: "... I would urge upon you in your practice ... to care more particularly for the individual patient than for the special features of the disease."

The ethical relation between the physician's mode of practice and the spiritual needs and expectations of patients and their loved ones is a philosophical question, not only because medical ethics is a branch of philosophy, but also because these spiritual and emotional issues are vital to the well-being of patients, central to the best practice of medicine, and inherently so delicate that practical philosophical wisdom must be brought to bear upon them.

15

What is a Religious Life?

Weber suggested four possible ways, i.e., two pairs of opposites, in which humans might seek the good life: (1) ascetism, actively pressing for enlightenment or control, opposed to (2) mysticism, passively awaiting enlightenment and relinquishing control; and (3) a thisworldly or "innerworldly" approach, seeking salvation on earth, opposed to (4) an otherworldly or "outerworldly" approach, seeking salvation in heaven. Thus all human attitudes resolve into four categories: (1) thisworldly asceticism, (2) thisworldly mysticism, (3) otherworldly asceticism, and (4) otherworldly mysticism. Philosophical anthropology shows a tenuous correlation between Weber's categories and the Hutchison-Geoghegan schema: thisworldly asceticism with reason primary excluding faith, because unspiritual people oriented toward this world want to control and manipulate it; thisworldly mysticism with reason primary including faith, because spiritual people oriented toward this world are generally content to enjoy nature and let it be as it is; otherworldly asceticism with faith primary including reason, because some spiritual people still want to control conditions and analyze propositions; and otherworldly mysticism with faith primary excluding reason; because fideists prefer just to accept the word and works of God and all the attendant mysteries.

One might be tempted to conclude that thisworldly asceticism is irreligious, that the other three are all by degrees religious, and that otherworldly mysticism is the most religious. But things are not quite that simple. The question must be asked, what kind of person does the best service to God? True spirituality involves developing integrity, honesty, serenity, morality, self-assurance without self-righteousness, and unity with the divine — and such wholeness is not entirely the province of either otherworldly mystics or those faithful who exclude reason. For example, since believing with ulterior motives is inferior to believing purely and straightforwardly and with good reason, accepting Pascal's wager may entail losing one's self-respect, to the extent that believing in God because of the wager is tantamount to groveling before a phantom in order to get into heaven. True belief in God does not require the wager. In the same vein as Pascal, Kierkegaard proposed that the religious man take a "leap of faith" beyond both reason and the church in order to devote himself to God. Kierkegaard was an otherworldly man with both ascetic and mystic aspects, but his own moral life was a shambles. He was a pathologically selfish and self-destructive liar, cheat, backstabber, seducer, whiner, and pest, not at all a shining example of the absurd but sincere religious man that he extolled in his writings. By contrast, two apostles of non-violence, Tolstoi, a thisworldly mystic, and Indian spiritual and political leader Mohandas Karamchand Gandhi (1869-1948), called "Mahatma" or "Great Soul," an ascetic with both thisworldly and otherworldly tendencies, were each more saintly than Kierkegaard. Moreover, even confirmed thisworldly ascetics can have genuine religious sensibilities without being hypocritical, as this excerpt from Chapter Two of Mill's *Autobiography* illustrates:

I was brought up from the first without any religious belief, in the ordinary acceptation of the term. My father [James Mill], educated in the creed of Scotch presbyterianism, had by his own studies and reflections been early led to reject not only the belief in revelation, but the foundations of what is commonly called Natural Religion. I have heard him say, that the turning point of his mind on the subject was reading [Joseph] Butler's *Analogy* [*of Religion, Natural and Revealed, to the Constitution and Course of Nature*]. That work, of which he always continued to speak with respect, kept him, as he said, for some considerable time, a believer in the divine authority of Christianity; by proving to him, that whatever are the difficulties in believing that the Old and New Testaments proceed from, or record the acts of, a perfectly wise and good being, the same and still greater difficulties stand in the way of the belief, that a being of such a character can have been the Maker of the universe. He considered Butler's argument as conclusive against the only opponents for whom it was intended. Those who admit an omnipotent as well as perfectly just and benevolent maker and ruler of such a world as this, can say little against Christianity but what can, with at least equal force, be retorted against themselves. Finding, therefore, no halting place in Deism, he remained in a state of perplexity, until, doubtless after many struggles, he yielded to the conviction, that, concerning the origin of things nothing whatever can be known. This is the only correct statement of his opinion; for dogmatic atheism he looked upon as absurd; as most of those, whom the world has considered Atheists, have always done. These particulars are important, because they show that my father's rejection of all that is called religious belief, was not, as many might suppose, primarily a matter of logic and evidence: the grounds of it were moral, still more than intellectual. He found it impossible to believe that a world so full of evil was the work of an Author combining infinite power with perfect goodness and righteousness. His intellect spurned the subtleties by which men attempt to blind themselves to this open contradiction. The Sabaean, or Manichaean theory of a Good and Evil Principle, struggling against each other for the government of the universe, he would not have equally condemned; and I have heard him express surprise, that no one revived it in our time. He would have regarded it as a mere hypothesis; but he would have ascribed to it no depraving influence. As it was, his aversion to religion, in the sense usually attached to the term, was of the same kind with that of Lucretius: he regarded it with the feelings due not to a mere mental delusion, but to a great moral evil. He looked upon it as the greatest enemy of morality: first, by setting up factitious excellencies, — belief in creeds, devotional feelings, and ceremonies, not connected with the good of human kind, — and causing these to be accepted as substitutes for genuine virtues: but above all, by radically vitiating the standard of morals; making it consist in doing the will of a being, on whom it lavishes indeed all the phrases of adulation, but whom in sober truth it depicts as eminently hateful. I have a hundred times heard him say, that all ages and nations have represented their gods as wicked, in a constantly increasing progression, that mankind have gone on adding trait after trait till they reached the most perfect conception of wickedness which the human mind can devise, and have called this God, and prostrated themselves before it. This *ne plus ultra* of wickedness he considered to be embodied in what is commonly presented to mankind as the creed of Christianity. Think (he used to say) of a being who would make a Hell — who would create the human race with the infallible foreknowledge, and therefore with the intention, that the great majority of them were to be consigned to horrible and everlasting torment. The time, I believe, is drawing near when this dreadful conception of an object of worship will be no longer identified with Christianity; and when all persons, with any sense of moral good and evil, will look upon it with the same indignation with which my father regarded it. My father was as well aware as anyone that Christians do not, in general, undergo the demoralizing consequences which seem inherent in such a creed, in the manner or to the extent which might have been expected from it. The same slovenliness of thought, and subjection of the reason to fears, wishes, and affections, which enable them to accept a theory involving a contradiction in terms, prevents them from perceiving the logical consequences of the theory. Such is the facility with which mankind believe at one and the same time things inconsistent with one another, and so few are those who draw from what they receive as truths, any consequences but those recommended to them by their feelings, that multitudes have held the undoubting belief in an Omnipotent Author of Hell, and have nevertheless identified that being with the best conception they were able to form of perfect goodness. Their worship was not paid to the demon which such a being as they imagined would really be, but to their own idea of excellence. The evil is, that such a belief keeps the ideal wretchedly low; and opposes the most obstinate resistance to all thought which has a tendency to raise it higher. Believers shrink from every train of ideas which would lead the mind to a clear conception and an elevated standard of excellence, because they feel (even when they do not distinctly see) that such a standard would conflict with many of the dispensations of nature, and with much of what they are accustomed to consider as the Christian creed. And thus morality continues a matter of blind tradition, with no consistent principle, nor even any consistent feeling, to guide it.

It would have been wholly inconsistent with my father's ideas of duty, to allow me to acquire impressions contrary to his convictions and feelings respecting religion: and he impressed upon me from the first, that the manner in which the world came into existence was a subject on which nothing was known: that the question, "Who made me?" cannot be answered, because we have no experience or authentic information from which to answer it; and that any answer only throws the difficulty a step further back, since the question immediately presents itself, Who made God? He, at the same time, took care that I should be acquainted with what had been thought by mankind on these impenetrable problems. I have mentioned at how early an age he made me a reader of ecclesiastical history; and he taught me to take the strongest interest in the Reformation, as the great and decisive contest against priestly tyranny for liberty of thought.

I am thus one of the very few examples, in this country, of one who has, not thrown off religious belief, but never had it: I grew up in a negative state with regard to it. I looked upon the modern exactly as I did upon the ancient religion, as something which in no way concerned me. It did not seem to me more strange that English people should believe what I did not, than that the men I read of in Herodotus should have done so. History had made the variety of opinions among mankind a fact familiar to me, and this was but a prolongation of that fact. This point in my early education had, however, incidentally one bad consequence deserving notice. In giving me an opinion contrary to that of the world, my father thought it necessary to give it as one which could not prudently be avowed to the world. This lesson of keeping my thoughts to myself, at that early age, was attended with some moral disadvantages; though my limited intercourse with strangers, especially such as were likely to speak to me on religion, prevented me from being placed in the alternative of avowal or hypocrisy. I remember two occasions in my boyhood, on which I felt myself in this alternative, and in both cases I avowed my disbelief and defended it. My opponents were boys, considerably older than myself: one of them I certainly staggered at the time, but the subject was never renewed between us: the other who was surprised, and somewhat shocked, did his best to convince me for some time, without effect.

The great advance in liberty of discussion, which is one of the most important differences between the present time and that of my childhood, has greatly altered the moralities of this question; and I think that few men of my father's intellect and public spirit, holding with such intensity of moral conviction as he did, unpopular opinions on religion, or on any other of the great subjects of thought, would now either practise or inculcate the withholding of them from the world, unless in the cases, becoming fewer every day, in which frankness on these subjects would either risk the loss of means of subsistence, or would amount to exclusion from some sphere of usefulness peculiarly suitable to the capacities of the individual. On religion in particular the time appears to me to have come, when it is the duty of all who being qualified in point of knowledge, have on mature consideration satisfied themselves that the current opinions are not only false but hurtful, to make their dissent known; at least, if they are among those whose station or reputation, gives their opinion a chance of being attended to. Such an avowal would put an end, at once and for ever, to the vulgar prejudice, that what is called, very improperly, unbelief, is connected with any bad qualities either of mind or heart. The world would be astonished if it knew how great a proportion of its brightest ornaments — of those most distinguished even in popular estimation for wisdom and virtue — are complete sceptics in religion; many of them refraining from avowal, less from personal considerations, than from a conscientious, though now in my opinion a most mistaken apprehension, lest by speaking out what would tend to weaken existing beliefs, and by consequence (as they suppose) existing restraints, they should do harm instead of good.

Of unbelievers (so called) as well as of believers, there are many species, including almost every variety of moral type. But the best among them, as no one who has had opportunities of really knowing them will hesitate to affirm (believers rarely have that opportunity), are more genuinely religious, in the best sense of the word religion, than those who exclusively arrogate to themselves the title. The liberality of the age, or in other words the weakening of the obstinate prejudice which makes men unable to see what is before their eyes because it is contrary to their expectations, has caused it to be very commonly admitted that a Deist may be truly religious: but if religion stands for any graces of character and not for mere dogma, the assertion may equally be made of many whose belief is far short of Deism. Though they may think the proof incomplete that the universe is a work of design, and though they assuredly disbelieve that it can have an Author and Governor who is absolute in power as well as perfect in goodness, they have that which constitutes the principal worth of all religions whatever, an ideal conception of a Perfect Being, to which they habitually refer as the guide of their conscience; and this ideal of Good is usually far nearer to perfection than the objective Deity of those, who think themselves obliged to find absolute goodness in the author of a world so crowded with suffering and so deformed by injustice as ours.

My father's moral convictions, wholly dissevered from religion, were very much of the character of those of the Greek philosophers; and were delivered with the force and decision which characterized all that came from him. Even at the very early age at which I read with him the Memorabilia of Xenophon, I imbibed from that work and from his comments a deep respect for the character of Socrates; who stood in my mind as a model of ideal excellence: and I well remember how my father at that time impressed upon me the lesson of the "Choice of Hercules." At a somewhat later period the lofty moral standard exhibited in the writings of Plato operated upon me with great force. My father's moral inculcations were at all times mainly those of the "Socratici viri;" justice, temperance (to which he gave a very extended application), veracity, perseverance, readiness to encounter pain and especially labour; regard for the public good; estimation of persons according to their merits, and of things according to their intrinsic usefulness; a life of exertion in contradiction to one of self-indulgent sloth. These and other moralities he conveyed in brief sentences, uttered as occasion arose, of grave exhortation, or stern reprobation and contempt.

But though direct moral teaching does much, indirect does more; and the effect my father produced on my character, did not depend solely on what he said or did with that direct object, but also, and still more, on what manner of man he was.

In his views of life he partook of the character of the Stoic, the Epicurean, and the Cynic, not in the modern but the ancient sense of the word. In his personal qualities the Stoic predominated. His standard of morals was Epicurean, inasmuch as it was utilitarian, taking as the exclusive test of right and wrong, the tendency of actions to produce pleasure or pain. But he had (and this was the Cynic element) scarcely any belief in pleasure; at least in his later years, of which alone, on this point, I can speak confidently. He was not insensible to pleasures; but he deemed very few of them worth the price which, at least in the present state of society, must be paid for them. The greater number of miscarriages in life, he considered to be attributable to the overvaluing of pleasures. Accordingly, temperance, in the large sense intended by the Greek philosophers — stopping short at the point of moderation in all indulgences — was with him, as with them, almost the central point of educational precept. His inculcations of this virtue fill a large place in my childish remembrances. He thought human life a poor thing at best, after the freshness of youth and of unsatisfied curiosity had gone by. This was a topic on which he did not often speak, especially, it may be supposed, in the presence of young persons: but when he did, it was with an air of settled and profound conviction. He would sometimes say, that if life were made what it might be, by good government and good education, it would be worth having: but he never spoke with anything like enthusiasm even of that possibility. He never varied in rating intellectual enjoyments above all others, even in value as pleasures, independently of their ulterior benefits. The pleasures of the benevolent affections he placed high in the scale; and used to say, that he had never known a happy old man, except those who were able to live over again in the pleasures of the young. For passionate emotions of all sorts, and for everything which has been said or written in exaltation of them, he professed the greatest contempt. He regarded them as a form of madness. "The intense" was with him a bye-word of scornful disapprobation. He regarded as an aberration of the moral standard of modern times, compared with that of the ancients, the great stress laid upon feeling. Feelings, as such, he considered to be no proper subjects of praise or blame. Right and wrong, good and bad, he regarded as qualities solely of conduct — of acts and omissions; there being no feeling which may not lead, and does not frequently lead, either to good or to bad actions: conscience itself, the very desire to act right, often leading people to act wrong. Consistently carrying out the doctrine, that the object of praise and blame should be the discouragement of wrong conduct and the encouragement of right, he refused to let his praise or blame be influenced by the motive of the agent. He blamed as severely what he thought a bad action, when the motive was a feeling of duty, as if the agents had been consciously evil doers. He would not have accepted as a plea in mitigation for inquisitors, that they sincerely believed burning heretics to be an obligation of conscience. But though he did not allow honesty of purpose to soften his disapprobation of actions, it had its full effect on his estimation of characters. No one prized conscientiousness and rectitude of intention more highly, or was more incapable of valuing any person in whom he did not feel assurance of it. But he disliked people quite as much for any other deficiency, provided he thought it equally likely to make them act ill. He disliked, for instance, a fanatic in any bad cause, as much or more than one who adopted the same cause from self-interest, because he thought him even more likely to be practically mischievous. And thus, his aversion to many intellectual errors, or what he regarded as such, partook, in a certain sense, of the character of a moral feeling. All this is merely saying that he, in a degree once common, but now very unusual, threw his feelings into his opinions; which truly it is difficult to understand how any one who possesses much of both, can fail to do. None but those who do not care about opinions, will confound it with intolerance. Those, who having opinions which they hold to be immensely important, and their contraries to be prodigiously hurtful, have any deep regard for the general good, will necessarily dislike, as a class and in the abstract, those who think wrong what they think right, and right what they think wrong: though they need not therefore be, nor was my father, insensible to good qualities in an opponent, nor governed in their estimation of individuals by one general presumption, instead of by the whole of their character. I grant that an earnest person, being no more infallible than other men, is liable to dislike people on account of opinions which do not merit dislike; but if he neither himself does them any ill office, nor connives at its being done by others, he is not intolerant: and the forbearance which flows from a conscientious sense of the importance to mankind of the equal freedom of all opinions, is the only tolerance which is commendable, or, to the highest moral order of minds, possible.

John Stuart Mill was in all respects his father's son. Yet for all that he can be called a religious man. He never understood the ontological concept of the Godhead or the ground of being, but conceived of God ontically as a particular being, which always makes rejecting theism easier — but personal moral principles and a theory of social ethics, inherited from his father, gave him a clear "system of thought, feeling, and action," that provided "a frame of orientation, a meaning of life, and an object of devotion ... regarded as a matter of ultimate concern." Thus, though the group with whom he shared this system was only a loose confederation of social and political reformers, Mill's life fits the Fromm-Tillich definition of religion.

By the same token, Nietzsche's life fits this definition. His thisworldly ascetic proclamation, "God is dead!" means that the world has lost sight of the transcendent, i.e., that which is definitely real but beyond any possible experience. For Nietzsche, the death of God and the loss of transcendence was a worthy development in history, but others bewailed their lost ability to see the one in the many and to derive spiritual unity from material multiplicity. Nietzsche held that being true to the earth and to one's own nature was the highest virtue, and that this virtue was achieved by refusing to countenance anything supernatural, by not looking toward anything outside this world for salvation, and by fostering the high cultural creativity of the world-historical future. A Nietzschean life requires courage, resoluteness, self-sacrifice, and an undying love of one's fate, but has no room for guilt, fear, humility, prayer, or obedience, all of which serve devotional and therefore decadent rather than psychologically emboldening, ameliorative, and therefore artistically productive and culturally creative purposes.

What does prayer accomplish? It turns one's focus away from this world and leaves deeds which ought to be done in this world undone. Yet the power of prayer depends much upon what the praying person wants prayer to accomplish. The most effective prayers may be those for which the praying person holds the fewest expectations. The least we can each expect is tolerance.

For Further Reading

Adams, Robert Merrihew. *Finite and Infinite Goods: A Framework for Ethics*. New York: Oxford University Press, 1999.

Alston, William P. *Perceiving God: The Epistemology of Religious Experience*. Ithaca, N.Y.: Cornell University Press, 1991.

Anselm. Basic Writings: *Proslogium, Monologium, Gaunilon's On Behalf of the Fool, Cur Deus Homo*, translated by Sidney Norton Deane. LaSalle, Illinois: Open Court, 1968.

Anselm. *Proslogion*, translated by M.J. Charlesworth. Oxford: Oxford University Press, 1965.

Aristotle. *De Anima; Metaphysics; Nicomachean Ethics; Physics; Politics* (many editions).

Armstrong, Karen. *A History of God: The 4000-Year Quest of Judaism, Christianity, and Islam*. New York: Alfred A. Knopf, 1993.

Augustine. *On the Free Choice of the Will*, translated by Anna S. Benjamin and L.H. Hackstaff. Indianapolis: Bobbs-Merrill, 1964.

Bataille, Georges. *Theory of Religion*, translated by Robert Hurley. New York: Zone, 1992.

Beach, Edward Allen. *The Potencies of God(s): Schelling's Philosophy of Mythology*. Albany: SUNY Press, 1994.

Bernstein, Richard J. *Radical Evil: A Philosophical Interrogation*. Cambridge: Polity, 2002.

Bertocci, Peter Anthony. *Introduction to the Philosophy of Religion*. New York: Prentice-Hall, 1951.

Boethius. *The Consolation of Philosophy*, translated by Richard Green. Indianapolis: Bobbs-Merrill, 1962.

Bonaventura. *The Mind's Road to God*, translated by George Boas. Indianapolis: Bobbs-Merrill, 1953.

Brightman, Edgar Sheffield. *Person and Reality: An Introduction to Metaphysics*. New York: Ronald Press, 1958.

Brightman, Edgar Sheffield. *A Philosophy of Religion*. New York: Prentice-Hall, 1940.

Broad, Charlie Dunbar. *Religion, Philosophy, and Psychical Research*. London: Routledge and Kegan Paul, 1930.

Buber, Martin. *I and Thou* — 2nd edition — translated by Ronald Gregor Smith. New York: Charles Scribner's Sons, 1958.

Caputo, John D. *On Religion*. London: Routledge, 2001.

Carabine, Deirdre. *John Scottus Eriugena*. New York: Oxford University Press, 2000.

Clifford, William Kingdon. *The Ethics of Belief and Other Essays*. Amherst, New York: Prometheus Books, 1999.

A Companion to Philosophy of Religion, edited by Philip L. Quinn and Charles Taliaferro. Cambridge, Massachusetts: Blackwell, 1997.

Craig, William Lane. *Divine Foreknowledge and Human Freedom: The Coherence of Theism: Omniscience*. Leiden: E.J. Brill, 1990.

Davis, Grady Scott. *Warcraft and the Fragility of Virtue: An Essay in Aristotelian Ethics*. Moscow, Idaho: University of Idaho Press, 1992.

Davis, Stephen T. *God, Reason, and Theistic Proofs*. Grand Rapids, Michigan: Eerdmans, 1997.

Descartes, René. *The Philosophical Works of Descartes*, translated by Elizabeth S. Haldane and G.R.T. Ross. Cambridge: Cambridge University Press, 1931.

Dougherty, Jude P. *The Logic of Religion*. Washington, D.C.: Catholic University of America Press, 2003.

Early Responses to Hume's Writings on Religion, edited and introduced by James Fieser. Bristol, England: Thoemmes, 2001.

Eckhart, Meister Johannes. *Meister Eckhart: A Modern Translation*, by Raymond B. Blakney. New York: Harper, 1941.

Eliade, Mircea. *The Sacred and the Profane: The Nature of Religion*, translated by Willard R. Trask. New York: Harper, 1961.

Existence of God, edited by John R. Jacobson and Robert Lloyd Mitchell. Lewiston, New York: Edwin Mellen, 1988.

The Existence of God, edited by Richard M. Gale and Alexander R. Pruss. Aldershot, England: Ashgate / Dartmouth, 2003.

Ferré, Frederick. *Basic Modern Philosophy of Religion*. New York: Charles Scribner's Sons, 1967.

Feuerbach, Ludwig Andreas. *Principles of the Philosophy of the Future*, translated by Manfred Vogel. Indianapolis: Hackett, 1986.

Frank, Erich. *Philosophical Understanding and Religious Truth*. New York: Oxford University Press, 1966.

Haeckel, Ernst Heinrich Philipp August. *The Evolution of Man: A Popular Exposition of the Principal Points of Human Ontogeny and Phylogeny*. New York: D. Appleton, 1876. Translation of *Anthropogenie, oder, Entwickelungsgeschichte des Menschen* (1874).

Hartshorne, Charles. *The Logic of Perfection, and Other Essays in Neoclassical Metaphysics*. LaSalle, Illinois: Open Court, 1962.

Hartshorne, Charles. *Omnipotence and Other Theological Mistakes*. Albany: SUNY Press, 1984.

Harvey, Van. *Feuerbach and the Interpretation of Religion.*
Cambridge: Cambridge University Press, 1995.

Harvey, Van. *The Historian and the Believer: The Morality of
Historical Knowledge and Christian Belief.* Urbana: University of
Illinois Press, 1996.

Hauerwas, Stanley. *The Hauerwas Reader*, edited by John Berkman
and Michael Cartwright. Durham: Duke University Press, 2001.

Hegel, Georg Wilhelm Friedrich. *Lectures on the Philosophy of
Religion: One-Volume Edition: The Lectures of 1827*, edited by
Peter C. Hodgson. Berkeley: University of California Press, 1988.

Hegel, Georg Wilhelm Friedrich. *Theologian of the Spirit*, edited
by Peter C. Hodgson. Minneapolis: Fortress, 1997.

Helm, Paul. *Faith with Reason.* Oxford: Clarendon, 2000.

Hick, John. *Disputed Questions in Theology and the Philosophy of
Religion.* New Haven: Yale University Press, 1993.

Hodgson, Peter C. *God in History: Shapes of Freedom.* Nashville:
Abingdon, 1989.

Hume, David. *Enquiries Concerning Human Understanding and
Concerning the Principles of Morals*, edited be L.A. Selby-Bigge.
Oxford: Clarendon, 1975.

Hume, David. *Writings on Religion*, introduction by Antony Flew.
LaSalle, Illinois: Open Court, 1992.

Hutchison, John A. *Faith, Reason, and Existence: An Introduction
to Contemporary Philosophy of Religion.* New York: Oxford
University Press, 1956.

James, William. *Human Immortality: Two Supposed Objections to
the Doctrine.* New York: Dover, 1956.

James, William. *The Varieties of Religious Experience: A Study in
Human Nature: Being the Gifford Lectures on Natural Religion
Delivered at Edinburgh in 1901-1902.* London: Longmans,
Green, 1904.

James, William. *The Will to Believe and Other Essays in Popular
Philosophy.* New York: Dover, 1956.

John Scotus Erigena ("John the Scot"). *Periphyseon / On the
Division of Nature*, edited and translated by Myra Uhlfelder,
summaries by Jean A. Potter. Indianapolis: Bobbs-Merrill, 1976.

Kant, Immanuel. *Religion Within the Limits of Reason Alone*,
translated by Theodore M. Greene and Hoyt H. Hudson. New
York: Harper, 1960.

Kenny, Anthony. *The Five Ways: St. Thomas Aquinas' Proofs of
God's Existence.* Notre Dame, Indiana: University of Notre Dame

Press, 1969.

Kenny, Anthony. *The God of the Philosophers*. Oxford: Oxford University Press, 1979.

Kierkegaard, Søren. *Philosophical Fragments; Johannes Climacus*, translated by Howard V. Hong and Edna H. Hong. Princeton: Princeton University Press, 1985.

Leibniz, Gottfried Wilhelm Freiherr von. *The Philosophical Works of Leibnitz*, translated by George Martin Duncan. New Haven: Tuttle, Morehouse & Taylor, 1890 — 2nd edition — 1908.

Leibniz, Gottfried Wilhelm Freiherr von. *Theodicy: Essays on the Goodness of God, the Freedom of Man, and the Origin of Evil*, edited by Austin Farrer, translated by E.M. Huggard. LaSalle, Illinois: Open Court, 1985.

MacGregor, Geddes. *Introduction to Religious Philosophy*. Boston: Houghton Mifflin, 1959.

MacQuarrie, John. *God-Talk: An Examination of the Language and Logic of Theology*. New York: Harper & Row, 1967.

Malebranche, Nicolas. *Dialogues on Metaphysics and on Religion*, edited by Nicholas Jolley, translated by David Scott. Cambridge: Cambridge University Press, 1997.

Merklinger, Philip M. *Philosophy, Theology, and Hegel's Berlin Philosophy of Religion, 1821-1827*. Albany: SUNY Press, 1993.

Mill, John Stuart. *Autobiography*. Indianapolis: Bobbs-Merrill, 1957.

Mill, John Stuart. *Nature and Utility of Religion*. Indianapolis: Bobbs-Merrill, 1958.

Mill, John Stuart. *Theism*. Indianapolis: Bobbs-Merrill, 1957.

Neiman, Susan. *Evil in Modern Thought: An Alternative History of Philosophy*. Princeton University Press, 2002.

Oppenheim, Frank M. *Royce's Mature Philosophy of Religion*. Notre Dame, Indiana: University of Notre Dame Press, 1987.

Otto, Rudolf. *The Idea of the Holy*, translated by John W. Harvey. London: Oxford University Press, 1958.

Our Knowledge of God: Essays on Natural and Philosophical Theology, edited by Kelly James Clark. Dordrecht: Kluwer, 1992.

Paley, William. *Natural Theology: Selections*, edited by Frederick Ferré. Indianapolis: Bobbs-Merrill, 1963.

Pascal, Blaise. *Pensées and Other Writings*, translated by Honor Levi (Sellier numbering). Oxford: Oxford University Press, 1999.

Pascal, Blaise. *Pensées*, translated by A.J. Krailsheimer (Lafuma numbering). Harmondsworth: Penguin, 1966.

Pascal, Blaise. *Pensées*, translated by William Finlayson Trotter

(Brunschvicg numbering). Mineola, New York: Dover, 2003.

Pascal, Blaise. *Pensées: Notes on Religion and Other Subjects*, translated by John Warrington (Lafuma numbering). London: Dent, 1973.

Philosophy of Religion: An Anthology, edited by Charles Taliaferro and Paul J. Griffiths. Malden, Massachusetts: Blackwell, 2003.

Philosophy of Religion: An Anthology, edited by Louis P. Pojman — 3rd edition — Belmont, California: Wadsworth, 1998.

Plantinga, Alvin. *The Ontological Argument from St. Anselm to Contemporary Philosophers*. London: Macmillan, 1968.

Plato. *The Collected Dialogues*, edited by Edith Hamilton and Huntington Cairns. Princeton: Princeton University Press, 1963.

The Problem of Evil, edited by Marilyn McCord Adams and Robert Merrihew Adams. New York: Oxford University Press, 1990.

Problems and Perspectives in the Philosophy of Religion, edited by George I. Mavrodes and Stuart C. Hackett. Boston: Allyn and Bacon, 1967.

Proudfoot, Wayne. *Religious Experience*. Berkeley: University of California Press, 1985.

Pseudo-Dionysius the Areopagite. *The Complete Works*, translated by Colm Luibheid. New York: Paulist Press, 1987.

Pseudo-Dionysius the Areopagite. *The Divine Names and the Mystical Theology*, translated by Clarence Edwin Rolt. Berwick, Maine: Ibis, 2004.

Purtill, Richard L. *Thinking About Religion: A Philosophical Introduction to Religion*. Englewood Cliffs, New Jersey: Prentice-Hall, 1978.

Ramsey, Paul. *Basic Christian Ethics*. Louisville: Westminster / John Knox, 1993.

Ramsey, Paul. *The Just War: Force and Political Responsibility*. Lanham, Maryland: University Press of America, 1983.

Ramsey, Paul. *Nine Modern Moralists: Paul Tillich, Karl Marx, H. Richard Niebuhr, Fyodor Dostoevski, Reinhold Niebuhr, Jacques Maritain, Jean-Paul Sartre, Emil Brunner, Edmond Cahn*. Lanham, Maryland: University Press of America, 1983.

Religious Imagination, edited by James P. Mackey. Edinburgh: Edinburgh University Press, 1986.

Rescher, Nicholas. *Pascal's Wager: A Study of Practical Reasoning in Philosophical Theology*. Notre Dame, Indiana: University of Notre Dame Press, 1985.

Rice, Hugh. *God and Goodness*. Oxford: Oxford University Press,

2000.

Royce, Josiah. *The Conception of God*. New York: Macmillan, 1898.

Royce, Josiah. *The Philosophy of Loyalty*. New York: Macmillan, 1908.

Royce, Josiah. *The Problem of Christianity*. New York: Macmillan, 1913.

Royce, Josiah. *The Religious Aspect of Philosophy*. Boston: Houghton Mifflin, 1885.

Royce, Josiah. *The Sources of Religious Insight*. New York: Charles Scribner's Sons, 1912.

Russell, Bertrand. *Why I Am Not a Christian, and Other Essays on Religion and Related Subjects*. New York: Simon and Schuster, 1957.

Stephen, James Fitzjames. *Liberty, Equality, Fraternity*. London: Cambridge University Press, 1967.

Swinburne, Richard. *The Coherence of Theism*. Oxford: Clarendon, 1993.

Swinburne, Richard. *The Existence of God*. Oxford: Clarendon, 1991.

Thomas Aquinas. *Introduction to St. Thomas Aquinas*, edited by Anton C. Pegis. New York: Modern Library, 1948.

Thomas Aquinas. *Philosophical Texts*, translated by Thomas Gilby. London: Oxford University Press, 1960.

Thomas, George Finger. *Religious Philosophies of the West: A Critical Analysis of the Major Figures from Plato to Tillich*. New York: Charles Scribner's Sons, 1965.

Tillich, Paul. *The Courage to Be*. New Haven: Yale, 1952.

Tillich, Paul. *My Search for Absolutes*. New York: Simon and Schuster, 1969.

Van Inwagen, Peter. *God, Knowledge, and Mystery: Essays in Philosophical Theology*. Ithaca: Cornell University Press, 1995.

Viney, Donald Wayne. *Charles Hartshorne and the Existence of God*. Albany: SUNY Press, 1985.

Weinberg, Julius R. *A Short History of Medieval Philosophy*. Princeton: Princeton University Press, 1967.

Wernham, James C.S. *James's Will-to-Believe Doctrine: A Heretical View*. Kingston: McGill-Queen's University Press, 1987.

Westphal, Merold. *God, Guilt, and Death*. Bloomington: Indiana University Press, 1987.

Whitehead, Alfred North. *Religion in the Making*. New York: World, 1960.

Yandell, Keith E. *Philosophy of Religion: A Contemporary Introduction*. London: Routledge, 1999.

Index

About the Author

Eric v.d. Luft received his A.B. *magna cum laude* in philosophy and religion from Bowdoin College in 1974, his M.A. and Ph.D. in philosophy from Bryn Mawr College in 1977 and 1985, and his M.L.S. from Syracuse University in 1993. Both his master's thesis and his doctoral dissertation were on Hegel's philosophy of religion. He taught at the Humanistic Studies Center in the University College of Syracuse University from 1986 until 2004, and since 1987 he has been Curator of Historical Collections in the Health Sciences Library of SUNY Upstate Medical University. He formerly taught philosophy at Villanova University and was Historical Collections Assistant at the College of Physicians of Philadelphia. He has held Surdna, Whiting, Wood, and U.S. Department of Education Fellowships and is listed in *Who's Who in America* and *Who's Who in the World*. Most of his approximately 485 publications are encyclopedia articles, but also include about thirty peer-reviewed articles in professional journals and anthologies. Besides philosophy, among the topics of his writing are librarianship, clinical medicine, history of medicine, history of science, military history, cultural history, intellectual history, popular culture, medieval Iceland, and contract bridge.